James Ker-Lindsay is Eurobank Senior Research Fellow on the Politics of South East Europe at the European Institute, London School of Economics and Political Science. His previous books include *An Island in Europe: The EU and the Transformation of Cyprus* (I.B.Tauris, co-edited with Hubert Faustmann and Fiona Mullen), *Crisis and Conciliation: A Year of Rapprochement between Greece and Turkey* (I.B.Tauris), *The Government and Politics of Cyprus* (co-edited with Hubert Faustmann) and *The Cyprus Problem: What Everyone Needs to Know*.

RESOLVING CYPRUS

New Approaches to Conflict Resolution

Edited by
JAMES KER-LINDSAY

I.B. TAURIS
LONDON · NEW YORK

Published in 2015 by I.B.Tauris & Co Ltd
6 Salem Road, London W2 4BU
175 Fifth Avenue, New York NY 10010
www.ibtauris.com

Distributed in the United States and Canada Exclusively by Palgrave Macmillan
175 Fifth Avenue, New York NY 10010

References to websites were accurate at the time of writing.

International Library of Twentieth Century History 76

ISBN: 978 1 78453 000 6
eISBN: 978 0 85773 601 7

A full CIP record for this book is available from the British Library
A full CIP record is available from the Library of Congress

Library of Congress Catalog Card Number: available

Printed and bound by CPI Group (UK) Ltd, Croydon, CRO 4YY
from camera-ready copy edited and supplied by the author

MIX
Paper from
responsible sources
FSC
www.fsc.org   FSC® C013604

Contents

List of Abbreviations

AKEL	Progressive Party for the Working People
AKP	Justice and Development Party
BBF	bizonal, bicommunal federation
CBMs	confidence-building measures
CIA	Central Intelligence Agency
CMP	Committee for Missing Persons
CSDP	Common Security and Defence Policy
CSO	Civil Society Organisations
CTP	Turkish Republican Party
DIKO	Democratic Party
DISY	Democratic Rally
DMZ	demilitarised zone
ECB	European Central Bank
EDEK	Movement of Social Democrats
EDON	United Democratic Youth Organisation
EEZ	exclusive economic zone
EOKA	National Organisation of Cypriot Fighters
EU	European Union
EUFOR	European Union Force
EVROKO	European Party
GAT	Gender Advisory Team
GDP	gross domestic product
HAD	Hands Across the Divide
IMF	International Monetary Fund
LNG	liquefied natural gas
NATO	North Atlantic Treaty Organisation
NGO	non-governmental organisation

PASOK	Pan-Hellenic Socialist Movement
PEO	Pancyprian Federation of Labour
RoC	Republic of Cyprus
SAFE	Synchronised Armed Forces Europe
SBA	Sovereign Base Area
TBF	trizonal, bicommunal federation
TMT	Turkish Resistance Organisation
TRC	Truth and Reconciliation Commission
TRNC	Turkish Republic of Northern Cyprus
UDI	unilateral declaration of independence
UN	United Nations
UNDP	United Nations Development Programme
UNFICYP	United Nations Peacekeeping Force in Cyprus
USAID	US Agency for International Development

Editor and Contributors

Editor

James Ker-Lindsay is Eurobank Senior Research Fellow on the Politics of South East Europe at the European Institute, London School of Economics and Political Science. His research focuses on conflict, peace and security in the Eastern Mediterranean and the Western Balkans and on issues relating to secession and recognition in international politics. His books include *The Cyprus Problem: What Everyone Needs to Know* (2011), *An Island in Europe: The EU and the Transformation of Cyprus* (2011, co-edited with Hubert Faustmann and Fiona Mullen), *The Government and Politics of Cyprus* (2009, co-edited with Hubert Faustmann), *Crisis and Conciliation: A Year of Rapprochement between Greece and Turkey* (2007), *EU Accession and UN Peacemaking in Cyprus* (2005), *Britain and the Cyprus Crisis, 1963–1964* (2004) and *The Work of the UN in Cyprus: Promoting Peace and Development* (2001, co-edited with Oliver Richmond).

Contributors

Constantinos Adamides is a lecturer of European Studies and International Relations, and Finance and Economics at the University of Nicosia and a research fellow at the Research and Innovation Office. His research interests are securitisation, ethnic conflicts, regional security complexes and energy security.

Emel Akçali is an assistant professor at the International Relations and European Studies Department of Central European University in Budapest. She is the author of *Chypre: Un enjeu géopolitique actuel* (l'Harmattan, Paris, 2009) and has published articles in Security Dialogue, Eurasian Geography and Economics and Geopolitics.

Ahmet An was born in 1950 in Nicosia. A paediatrician by profession, he has published 22 books about Turkish Cypriots and the Cyprus Problem. As the Turkish Cypriot Coordinator of the Movement for an Independent and Federal Cyprus, he won his case against Turkey at the European Court of Human Rights in 2003, which resulted in the opening of the gates two months later.

Jan Asmussen is a political scientist and historian at the Institute of Social Sciences, Christian-Albrechts-University, Kiel and Visiting Research Fellow at the School of Politics, International Studies and Philosophy, Queens University, Belfast. He was previously Head of the conflict and security cluster at the European Centre for Minority Studies, Flensburg and has taught at several universities in Cyprus.

Tozun Bahcheli is Professor of Political Science at King's University College at Western University, London, Canada. He has written widely on ethnic conflict in Cyprus, secessionist conflicts in divided societies, and Turkish foreign policy. He is the author of *Greek-Turkish Relations Since 1955* (Westview Press, 1990) and co-editor of *De Facto States: The Quest for Sovereignty* (Routledge, 2004).

Giorgos Charalambous is Adjunct Lecturer in Politics at the University of Cyprus. His research centres on political parties, the domestic politics of European integration and South European politics. He is the author of *European Integration and the Communist Dilemma: Communist Party Responses to Europe in Greece, Cyprus and Italy* (Ashgate, 2013).

Odysseas Christou is a lecturer with the Department of European Studies and International Relations and a postdoctoral research fellow with the Center for European and International Affairs, University of Nicosia. His research focuses on international relations, comparative politics and political violence.

Costas M. Constantinou is Professor of International Relations at the University of Cyprus. He is the author of *On the Way to Diplomacy* (University of Minnesota Press, 1996) and *States of Political Discourse*

(Routledge, 2004) and co-editor of *Cultures and Politics of Global Communication* (Cambridge University Press, 2008) and *Sustainable Diplomacies* (Palgrave Macmillan, 2010).

Hubert Faustmann is Associate Professor for History and Political Science at the University of Nicosia. He is also the director of the office of the German Friedrich Ebert Foundation in Cyprus. He has published extensively on modern Cypriot politics, history and society. He is also the editor-in-chief of the refereed journal *The Cyprus Review*.

Ayla Gürel was originally an academic engineer. She is now a senior research consultant at the Peace Research Institute Oslo (PRIO) Cyprus Centre in Nicosia. She has worked on a range of projects concerning the Cyprus Problem, including the property rights dispute and the political issues of offshore hydrocarbons exploration.

Maria Hadjipavlou is an associate professor in the Department of Social and Political Sciences, University of Cyprus where she teaches conflict resolution and gender studies. She is a founding member of the Gender Advisory Team (GAT) and President of Hands across the Divide (HAD). She is the author of *Women and Change in Cyprus: Feminisms, Gender in Conflict* (I.B.Tauris, 2010).

Yeshim Harris is a conflict management professional with special interest in experience-sharing between countries/regions. She is the Co-founder and Director of Engi and a member of the UK All Party Parliamentary Group on Conflict Issues Secretariat. In this capacity, she regularly works with UK government departments on a number of conflict-related matters. She has initiated several Cyprus projects.

Alexis Heraclides is Professor of International Relations, Panteion University of Social and Political Sciences (Athens). His books include, *The Self-Determination of Minorities in International Politics* (1991), *Security and Co-operation in Europe: The Human Dimension* (1993), *The Greek-Turkish Conflict in the Aegean: Imagined Enemies* (2010) as well as two books in Greek on the Cyprus Problem.

Robert Holland is Visiting Professor at the Centre for Hellenic Studies in King's College London. He has written widely on British colonial history in the era of decolonisation and on Cyprus. His most recent book is *Blue-Water Empire: The British in the Mediterranean since 1800* (Allen Lane, 2012). He is currently working on the Mediterranean and Victorian culture.

Erol Kaymak is Associate Professor of International Relations at the Eastern Mediterranean University in Famagusta, Cyprus, and co-research director for the Cyprus 2015 project (www.cyprus2015.org). He has been serving as an adviser to the Turkish Cypriot negotiation team in the current round of settlement talks and is a member of the Greek–Turkish Forum.

Paschalis Kitromilides is Professor of Political Science at the Department of Political Science and Public Administration of the University of Athens and Secretary General of the Governing Board, Centre for Asia Minor Studies. His books include *The Enlightenment as Social Criticism* (Princeton University Press, 1992) and *Eleftherios Venizelos: The Trials of Statesmanship* (Edinburgh University Press, 2006).

Klearchos A. Kyriakides is a senior lecturer in the School of Law of the University of Hertfordshire. He is also a non-practising solicitor. He holds an LLB Hons (Law and Politics) Degree from the University of Birmingham, MPhil (International Relations) and PhD (History) Degrees from the University of Cambridge and a Postgraduate Diploma in Legal Practice from the University of Westminster.

George Kyris completed his doctoral research in European Politics at the University of Manchester. He has been a Research Fellow at the LSE Hellenic Observatory and has taught at the Universities of Manchester and Warwick. He has published on EU, Cyprus, Greece and Turkey in journals such as the *Journal of Common Market Studies* and *Comparative European Politics* and media, including the *Guardian*.

Neophytos Loizides is Senior Lecturer in International Conflict Analysis at the University of Kent. He is the author of *Designing Peace Processes: Institutional Innovation in Cyprus and Divided Societies* (University of Pennsylvania Press, 2014) and associate editor of the journal *Nationalism and Ethnic Politics*.

Robert McDonald is a freelance writer and broadcaster who has specialised in Greek, Cypriot and Turkish affairs since the 1960s. He is the author of the monograph, *The Problem of Cyprus* (Adelphi Paper 234, International Institute of Strategic Studies, 1988/89) and several volumes on the Greek economy. He is a regular contributor to the Economist Intelligence Unit and Oxford Analytica.

Husam Mohamad is a professor in the Department of Political Science, University of Central Oklahoma and a visiting professor of International Affairs, Qatar University. Previously he taught at the Eastern Mediterranean University in Cyprus. His research focuses on US policy towards the Muslim world, democratisation in Arab politics and social movements across the Middle East.

Michael Moran is a philosopher who has worked at the universities of Keele, Sussex, Oxford, Paris, Aix-en-Provence, Geneva and the Eastern Mediterranean University, Cyprus. He has produced several books on the international politics of Cyprus and is currently completing a book on modern European thought and sensibility.

Sid Noel is Emeritus Professor of Political Science at Western University and Senior Fellow in Nationalism and Ethnic Conflict Studies at King's University College, Canada. He has written widely on federalism, consociationalism and democracy in multinational societies, including articles and chapters on the Cyprus question.

Mustafa Ergün Olgun is the Former Undersecretary of the TRNC Presidency and Coordinator of the Turkish Cypriot Technical Committees which negotiated the 2004 UN Comprehensive Settlement Plan for Cyprus. He is currently the Coordinator of the Presidential Consultative Council for the Negotiating Process and External Relations Coordinator of the Besparmak Think Tank Group.

Yiannis Papadakis is Associate Professor of Social Anthropology at the Department of Social and Political Sciences, University of Cyprus. He is the author of *Echoes from the Dead Zone: Across the Cyprus Divide* (I.B.Tauris, 2005), translated into Greek and Turkish, co-edited *Divided Cyprus: Modernity, History and an Island in Conflict* (Indiana

University Press, 2006), and edited a special issue of *Postcolonial Studies* on Cyprus.

Oliver Richmond is Research Professor in International Relations, Peace and Conflict Studies at the University of Manchester, UK. He is also International Professor, School of International Studies, Kyung Hee University, Korea. His publications include *A Post Liberal Peace* (Routledge, 2011), *Peace in IR* (Routledge, 2008) and *The Transformation of Peace* (Palgrave Macmillan, 2005 and 2007).

Nikos Skoutaris is Lecturer in Law at the University of East Anglia. Prior to this, he was A.N. Hadjiyiannis Senior Research Fellow at the European Institute, LSE. He is the author of *The Cyprus Issue: The Four Freedoms in a Member State under Siege* (Hart Publishing, 2011) and of *Territorial Pluralism in Europe: Vertical Separation of Powers in the EU and its Member States* (Hart Publishing, 2014).

Mary Southcott is Coordinator of Friends of Cyprus, a role she performed from 1987 to 1991 and from 1997 and has been editor of the Friends of Cyprus Reports since 2002. Since standing for parliament in the UK in 1987, she has taken a particular interest in democracy and democratic reform and is the co-author of *Making Votes Count* (Profile, 1998).

Ahmet Sözen is Professor and Chair of the Department of International Relations at Eastern Mediterranean University. He was founding Co-Director of Cyprus 2015 Initiative. He has published extensively on the Cyprus conflict and Turkish foreign policy. He has also been very active on the policy and advocacy fronts and has participated in first- and second-track peace negotiations in Cyprus.

Zenon Stavrinides is a tutor in the School of Philosophy in the University of Leeds. He is General Secretary of the Association for Cypriot, Greek and Turkish Affairs, and Secretary of the Political Thought Specialist Group of the Political Studies Association in the UK. He is the author of *The Cyprus Conflict: National Identity and Statehood* (2nd edn 1999) as well as many papers on the Cyprus Problem.

Harry Tzimitras is Director of the Peace Research Institute Oslo (PRIO) Cyprus Centre. In this capacity, he coordinates research and dialogue activities on the search for a political settlement to the island's division. He is also an associate professor of International Law and International Relations, specialising in the law of the sea, foreign policy and Greek–Turkish relations.

Birte Vogel is a PhD candidate at the Humanitarian and Conflict Response Institute at the University of Manchester, UK. Her PhD is funded by an EU FP7 project entitled 'The role of governance in the resolution of socioeconomic and political conflict in India and Europe', where she focuses on the role of (political) space in conflict resolution. Her case studies are Cyprus and Kashmir.

Introduction

JAMES KER-LINDSAY

This book is based on a single, deceptively simple, question: can Cyprus be solved? Over the past 50 years, the Cyprus Problem has come to be seen as the archetype of an intractable ethnic conflict. Since 1964, when the United Nations Security Council first authorised the start of peacekeeping operations on the island and directed the Secretary-General to take the lead on peacemaking, considerable efforts have been made to find a political solution to the dispute between the island's Greek and Turkish communities. These have continued despite many upheavals, such as the 1974 Turkish invasion, the 1983 unilateral declaration of independence by the Turkish Cypriot community and the accession of Cyprus to the European Union, in 2004. However, despite the active involvement of six UN Secretaries-General – U Thant, Kurt Waldheim, Javier Perez de Cuellar, Boutros Boutros Ghali, Kofi Annan and Ban Ki-moon – every attempt to reach a mutually acceptable solution has failed.

The closest the international community came to reaching a settlement was in 2004, when the UN presented the two sides with a comprehensive reunification plan (the Annan Plan). While this was accepted by two thirds of Turkish Cypriots, it was rejected by almost three quarters of Greek Cypriot voters. Since then, yet another negotiation process has been started. But, like so many attempts made in the past, this initiative has failed to overcome the impasse between the two sides. As the conflict now enters its sixth decade, and the island has now been divided for 40 years, many have started to question whether the Cyprus Problem, as the issue has come to be widely known, can in fact be resolved

The origins of the book

At a personal level, and having followed events in Cyprus very closely for over 20 years, I certainly have come to have my doubts about whether the Cyprus Problem can actually be resolved. Speaking with others, I know that the vast majority of people, both on the island and internationally, now share the same view. Few seem to believe that the decades-long deadlock can be broken.

It was this overwhelming sense of hopelessness that drove me to ask what it was about the Cyprus Problem that makes it so difficult to resolve. Is there something wrong in the way that the process is being conducted? Or is it about the end goals that are being pursued? I was keen to find out what others thought. With this in mind, I approached the editors of the *Peace Review* about the possibility of publishing a special section of the journal that looked at these questions. The reason I approached them was because of the format of their articles. Unlike other academic journals – which publish long, heavily footnoted articles that shy away from taking strong normative positions – the *Peace Review* focuses on short discursive essays that are lightly referenced but nevertheless very well informed. This was an ideal format for this project. I did not want lengthy, very dry accounts of the Cyprus Problem that simply rehashed history. What I wanted were short, highly focused opinion pieces. Fortunately, the editors were very keen on the idea. They liked the idea of asking people a seemingly simple question about such a longstanding issue and seeing what responses would arrive.

Admittedly, there was mixed response to the initial call for papers. Some people were sceptical about the value of the project. They wondered whether all the papers would basically take the same approach or say the same things. As they saw it, the essays would be highly partisan, blaming one side or another. Others could not quite comprehend the question. It just seemed too straightforward. They wanted to know what exactly was wanted. I explained that it was entirely up to them how they interpreted the questions. Anything and everything was possible. In trying to explain the concept to them, I suggested that they think of it terms of an 'elevator pitch'. What would they say if they entered a lift one morning at the UN headquarters and in stepped the Secretary-General. With just a few minutes to make a difference, what would they try to change in terms of the way the Cyprus Problem is understood or tackled?

In the end, the response to the call for papers was excellent. Far from receiving a small number of pieces essentially saying the same thing, there were a large number of submissions covering a very diverse range of views and ideas. Another particularly gratifying outcome was that the submissions came from contributors from a disparate range of backgrounds. In addition to pieces from academics, they included contributions from leading practitioners and policy makers as well as civil society activists.

In fact, many more contributions were received than had been expected, or could be published in the journal. Given the high quality of the vast majority of the pieces, I approached I.B.Tauris about the possibility of publishing a selection of the pieces. Fortunately, they too were very keen on the idea. I therefore encouraged still more people to contribute. Once again, the response was excellent. As a result, this volume contains 30 contributions from many of the leading observers of the Cyprus Problem.

Scope of the contributions

As already noted, the 30 contributions included in this volume take the form of essays. The aim of the contributions is not to provide a comprehensive history of the Cyprus Problem, nor list the full range of issues that need to be addressed. Instead, each author has focused on one or two particular aspects of the problem that they have identified as being of particular importance, as they see it, in terms of explaining the intractability of the Cyprus Problem.

As a result, there is a wide range of perspectives. For some contributors, history is especially significant (An, Asmussen, Mohamad). For others, the failure to reach a settlement is about tackling specific issues, such as security (MacDonald). Some look at political factors, such as attitudes or internal political dynamics within the communities (Adamides, Christou, Charalambous, Kitromilides), or examine the wider legal dimensions of the Cyprus issue (Kyriakides, Skoutaris). A number of pieces place the emphasis on the settlement process, such as by examining the role of specific internal actors (Harris, Hadjipavlou, Vogel and Richmond), the way in which it is conducted (Kaymak), or by analysing the role of external parties (Kyris). Some make the case for reexamining the longstanding end goal of a bizonal, bicommunal federation

(Bahcheli and Noel, Ker-Lindsay). Others argue that it is essentially time to look towards separation (Akçali, Olgun). Importantly, there are a couple of chapters that focus on the discovery of natural gas; the latest dimension of the Cyprus Problem (Faustmann, Gürel and Tzimitras).

Despite the range of topics, as one might expect there is also a lot of cross over between the papers. For example, in the case of the two papers that focus on history, one looks at how this has shaped identity and the other tries to explain how this has undermined trust. For this reason, no attempt has been made to try to structure the book thematically. Rather, the essays are simply presented in the alphabetical order of the names of the contributors.

Acknowledgements

I am extremely grateful to the editorial team at the *Peace Review* – Robert Elias, Erika Myszinski and Kerry Donoghue – for their initial support for the idea. However, my greatest thanks go to everyone at I.B.Tauris, in particular Tomasz Hoskins and Joanna Godfrey, for agreeing to expand the project and for their help and assistance in bringing the volume to print. I would also like to thank Pat FitzGerald for all her hard work preparing the manuscript for publication.

References and recommended reading

Diez, Thomas and Nathalie Tocci (eds), *Cyprus: A Conflict at the Crossroads* (Manchester: Manchester University Press, 2009).
Ker-Lindsay, James, *The Cyprus Problem: What Everyone Needs to Know* (New York: Oxford University Press, 2011).
—— (ed.), 'Symposium: can Cyprus be solved?', *Peace Review: A Journal of Social Justice* 24/4 (2012), pp. 398–405.
Varnavas, Andrekos and Hubert Faustmann (eds), *Reunifying Cyprus: The Annan Plan and Beyond* (London: I.B.Tauris, 2009).

1

A Comfortable and Routine Conflict

Constantinos Adamides

The intractability of the Cyprus conflict has developed into an academic challenge for analysts. Many have strived for decades to present a comprehensive explanation as to why the 'Problem' remains unresolved. Few would argue in favour of a single, unique explanation for the so-called Cyprus imbroglio. Analyses are diverse and frequently depend on the analysts' ethnic affiliation as well as their academic and theoretical inclination. Some take for granted the presence of political and public determination for settlement, but question whether the failure to reach a deal can be explained by reasons ranging from the intransigent positions of the 'other', weak civil society actors or the involvement of external third parties. Others question the determination of one or both sides, emphasising the lack of sufficient incentives to reach a settlement; the focus being, inter alia, on the non-hurting stalemate.

More sociological approaches focus on factors that lead to, or contribute towards, the development and perpetuation of perceptions that maintain incompatible and 'unbridgeable' views. The Problem is thus understood as an identity conflict characterised by the deep mistrust of the 'other', significant communication problems and internalised and rigid positions through which all historical and current issues are viewed in such a way that there is only 'our truth' and 'their propaganda'. Attempts to explain the conflict in these terms frequently explore how historical events may be used to 'construct' threats for the future. Once formed, these views in turn perpetuate the status quo by highlighting mutually exclusive positions. Subsequently, according to these analyses, the unwillingness to arrive at a settlement is perceived as the outcome of socially constructed threats and the established perceptions that the two sides' positions are irreconcilable. Unwillingness is thus not treated as a 'stand alone factor' for the perpetuation of the conflict. Rather, it is derived from other factors.

Elite behaviour supports the above-stated view. They constantly attempt to highlight how agreeable and flexible they are, while simultaneously shifting all blame to the other side. Indeed, in their routine discourses, political elites constantly emphasise their willingness for resolution and the unwillingness of their counterparts across the divide. This is often necessary in order to demonstrate to their domestic constituents that they remain committed to the 'national cause'. However, it is also proves to outsiders their commitment to a settlement. This behaviour is supported by the public's conditioned demands for a solution as long as it is just and viable, often without any consideration that each community conceptualises the justice and viability of a settlement in diametrically opposite ways.

This chapter focuses on one particular factor that has exacerbated the complexity of this situation; namely the inability of elite, media and public to challenge the existing discourses and stop the 'automatic' recycling of threats and negative perceptions of the 'other'. This inability to stop such conflict-perpetuating behaviour is the outcome of two factors: the structure of the conflict, which, as argued below, is a comfortable one; and the internalised conflict-maintaining routines that cannot be interrupted without significant cost to those who attempt to disrupt them. Subsequently, the high cost of interruption leads to 'involuntary' behaviour where decision makers and public alike are left without real options other than those that maintain the conflict. It is also argued that a change in the first factor, whereby the conflict becomes less comfortable, may not suffice to change the second factor, namely the routines that perpetuate the conflict. This idea is tested by the severe financial crisis that could theoretically lead to a change in the incentive structure of the conflict.

The implications of a comfortable conflict

The Cyprus Problem is an interesting case, not only because it is one of the most prolonged conflicts on the international stage but also because it does not have many of the characteristics found in other ethnic conflict environments. The lack of violence since 1974 (with some minor exceptions), coupled with the partial lifting of the restrictions on freedom of movement in 2003 makes it difficult for an outsider – if not informed of the conflict – to figure out if a conflict exists, what form it takes and what the impact is on the two societies. The lack of violence coupled with the relatively high prosperity level of Cypriots makes it difficult even for Cypriots to identify the impact of the conflict on their everyday routines.

The conflict, in other words, has become rather comfortable and the stalemate is not particularly painful for either side. This structure has at least two main implications for potential settlement. The first is that there are no strong incentives for either side to take 'bold measures' towards a resolution. Political and other elites are unlikely to make daring proposals that could potentially lead to a breakthrough as such actions require sacrifices that are inevitably linked to high political cost. The second implication, which is closely linked to the first, is that significant parts of the population are also unwilling to take risks associated with the settlement. They therefore endorse the status quo as a desirable and comfortable option.

The risks linked to a potential settlement that would jeopardise the status quo can be examined on three levels: political, economic and societal. On the political level the risks revolve around issues of governance and the associated sense of security deriving from the current monoethnic administration of internal and external affairs. On the societal level, it is identity that is under threat. Specifically, both sides fear that settlement brings with it a risk that their identity would be diluted. The double minority environment, where both Greek and Turkish Cypriots could perceive themselves as a minority – the Turkish Cypriots on the island and the Greek Cypriots in a regional context vis-à-vis Turkey – exacerbates this fear. Lastly, the economic level focuses on risks associated to the economic prosperity of the community. The predominant Greek Cypriot position has been that in the event of settlement they will suffer the cost of reunification and their economy will be 'dragged down' by the weaker Turkish Cypriot one. Turkish Cypriots fear that the more prosperous Greek Cypriot side will 'overtake' them financially if there is no clear geographical, economic and political division. (However, as an aside, it is worth noting that these traditional views on the economic consequences of a settlement are likely to be challenged as a result of the financial crisis on the Greek Cypriot side.)

The conflict as part of Cypriots' routines

The perpetuation of the status quo complicates the prospects for a settlement in another way, namely through the incorporation of the conflict into people's daily routines. The lack of resolution has become a part of Cypriots' lives to the degree that it is no longer a variable that influences their daily routines or long-term plans; that is, Cypriots do not believe there will be a resolution in the near and medium term and thus accept the presence of the (comfortable) conflict as a given in the society in which they operate. At the same time there is essentially no fear about the escalation of the conflict; the vast majority considers a shift from a non-violent status quo to a violent one to be improbable. Thus proximity to the 'enemy' is no longer a security issue. Indicatively, the old city of Nicosia, which for decades after 1974 remained underdeveloped due to its proximity to the Green Line, is now one of the most rapidly growing areas in Cyprus. The partial freedom of movement helped alleviate fears further as it led to the deconstruction of several myths regarding the 'enemy other'. The 'other' has also become a source of income for the locals. Thus, the direct presence of the 'other' has over time become a 'natural' part of the two societies.

Despite the high level of comfort, the peace on the island remains an illiberal one; based on forced division and legal exceptionalities. The division allows the conflict to remain very central in Cyprus and so it is perhaps not surprising that we observe the same rhetoric about the enemies today as in the 1960s and 1970s. While Cypriots have incorporated the conflict into their lives and to a large extent ignore it during their daily routine activities, they still expect that their political elite and media will treat the conflict as a top priority and include it in their discourses. The public, especially Greek Cypriots, diminishes the importance of the lack of settlement in their everyday practices without, however, changing their expectations about how the problem should be handled. While opinion polls clearly indicate that the primary motivations for settlement for Greek Cypriots revolve around issues of security (armed conflict, departure of foreign troops and the termination of guarantees), their actions do not reflect these fears. There is no sense of urgency regarding a resolution, which would theoretically diminish such threats. Evidently the status quo provides Greek Cypriots with a sufficient sense of security; perhaps more than any proposed settlement.

With this in mind it seems that Cypriots – and especially Greek Cypriots – maintain two contradictory kinds of conflict-related routines: the first form ignores the presence of the conflict, while the second maintains it as part of the people's identities. The relatively good economic and social conditions contribute towards the 'ignoring' of the conflict. However, the psychological needs and related fears deriving from the conflict require that it remains central in people's routines, primarily through the acknowledgement by elites and media that the threat still exists. The reasons why people may choose to 'ignore' a comfortable conflict are understandable; it does not hurt enough to warrant too much attention on a daily basis. Why they choose to support conflict-perpetuating routines and essentially voluntarily perpetuate the status quo is less obvious and thus deserves some more attention.

The lack of credible commitment is an important factor that could make the perpetuation of conflict a preferred option. Lake and Rothchild (1996) explain that concerns that the 'other' side will not uphold mutually agreed positions leads to fears of exploitation. The fear of exploitation in turn creates anxiety as a failed agreement and exploitation means, for the 'losing' side, higher costs compared to the status quo (i.e. stalemate). Provided that people tend to overweigh losses relative to comparable gains they are more likely to engage in risk-averse behaviour (Levy 1992), meaning that in cases where there is fear of exploitation the less risky decision may be the perpetuation of the status quo (i.e. the conflict) rather than a mutually agreed settlement that is nevertheless based on distrust. The problem of credible commitments and the associated risks is very present on the island because of the turbulent history of the two communities. There is an inevitable lack of trust. This environment, as discussed below, contributes to development of conflict-perpetuating routines.

Routine-interruption and involuntary behaviour

Risks in protracted conflict environments could and should not only be considered in terms of the potential political, economic or military cost. They should also be considered in a looser manner, namely in terms of levels of anxiety. Deviation from a long-term status quo could lead to increased levels of anxiety as it disrupts routines that are useful in maintaining each side's ontological security (i.e. security of the 'self'). As Mitzen (2006) reminds us, people need ontological security as much as they need physical security.

The perpetuation of the conflict therefore may be a mechanism through which Greek and Turkish Cypriots maintain their sense of identity and any disruption of routines that are based on the conflict could be perceived, consciously or subconsciously, as a risk to their identities. Subsequently, Cypriots may be willing to maintain conflict-perpetuating routines because that is the option that is perceived to carry the least risk, but also because it contributes to the perpetuation of the existing identities.

Conflict routines have an ever-greater role to play as they become more internalised within society. The more internalised they are, the more difficult it is to disrupt them as there are increasing costs associated with their disruption. The degree of internalisation in turn depends on the conflict's duration and on how 'central' (important) it is for a society. The conflict in Cyprus is deeply internalised given that (1) it is one of the most protracted conflicts in the world and (2) it occupies a central position in the society, despite the fact that it is non-violent. The cost of disruption therefore is particularly high. The fact that the conflict is comfortable actually increases the potential cost and inevitably decreases the willingness to engage in status quo-changing activities. This leads to a vicious cycle where the unchanging routines help keep the conflict's 'centrality' and in turn the centrality of the problem highlights the need to maintain such routines.

Such routines become self-sustainable because they create an environment that supports elite and public 'involuntary' behaviour vis-à-vis issues related to the conflict. The centrality of the Problem in the society means that the public 'demands' that it receives particular and constant attention by elite and media. It is not surprising therefore that newspapers and television channels routinely dedicate several pages and airtime to covering developments and the elite's positions. Similarly, the political elite engage in routinised behaviour by constantly reiterating their positions, frequently reminding the public why they are more suitable than their opponents to handle the 'national cause'. More importantly, media and the elite to a large extend live off the perpetuation of the conflict. Journalists, politicians and political parties have identified themselves with specific positions regarding the 'sources' of the conflict as well as with the 'most appropriate' approaches for settlement. Thus, the elite routinely use their established positions on the conflict to differentiate themselves from their opponents and highlight their opponents' past actions that, in their opinion, jeopardised the community's future or even the status quo. An indicative example is the speech made by President Papadopoulos prior to the Annan Plan referenda in which he argued that he had 'received a state and will not deliver a community'. In this statement, he explicitly demonstrated how the status quo might be more preferable to the alternative settlement on offer.

The perpetuation of the conflict is therefore particularly important for the survival of many within the political elite. It is also important for the survival of many within the media, which routinely needs to remind audiences of the threats deriving from the 'other side'. The presence of threats makes their existence meaningful as 'guardians'. They are the most suitable agents to handle the Problem. Without the conflict the elite's importance diminishes, while the media may incur financial loses and potentially lose political influence. The fact that the conflict has become more comfortable and less 'visible' makes it even more important for these agents to maintain routines that perpetuate the image of the enemy and the perceptions of specific threats, as they are no longer 'naturally present' in the society. Thus the main actors dealing with the conflict have no real incentive to disrupt the routines that maintain such an environment. The problem with such behaviour, however, is that it sustains the conflict as part of people's identities, thereby inevitably reducing the possibility of finding a mutually acceptable plan for a solution.

As mentioned, such routines become self-sustainable. This means that they do not solely depend on the agents' willingness to maintain them. Some issues may remain central in the discourses, even if elite do not wish to keep them as such. The routinised discourses and the subsequent public internalisation have rendered specific threats and positions 'untouchable'. It has become inconceivable that the elite will challenge 'realities' that exist and are perpetuated for decades, such as the threat of Turkish guarantees; the presence of settlers; the need for complete freedom of movement, etc. For any elites, the risk of challenging these deeply established threats is now just too high. Indeed, the risk does not exist only if one actively challenges those discourses. It also exists if one does not reiterate them as expected. Holding a neutral position could be just as costly as holding a view that challenges the established perceptions. One runs the risk of being perceived as 'soft', indifferent (and thus disrespectful) and even incapable of protecting the community. As a result, the political elite and the media are 'forced' to reiterate the same positions so as to avoid the potential 'cost of indifference'. In other words, they could potentially contribute to the perpetuation of the conflict 'involuntarily' by maintaining discourses they may not necessarily fully agree with, but that are still perceived as necessary to repeat given the high associated costs of alternative actions.

Interestingly, such 'involuntary' behaviour is not limited to an elite level. It also extends to the public as well. Specifically, the deeply embedded beliefs regarding specific threats generate significant social pressure on the entire population to acknowledge their presence and the associated dangers. Thus, as is the case with the elite, significant parts of the population 'involuntarily' contribute to the conflict-perpetuating routines by: (1) not actively challenging the existing discourses; (2) unquestioningly accepting the reiteration of these positions; and (3) by occasionally even demanding that such discourses are repeated. Attempts to challenge the established positions could lead to severe social pressure from peers and family, ranging from characterisations of softness, through to 'character assassinations' and even occasionally to 'ostracisation' – as has been the case with high school students who 'dared' to engage in bicommunal activities. Interestingly, the same risks apply to those who overemphasise the potential threats. They are often perceived as nationalists and fascists. The safest path, therefore, is the one of perpetuating the established positions.

Nevertheless, it is worth noting that there are individuals who have managed to challenge existing discourses. However, they still remain the minority and they have not yet managed to influence the wider public. The environment does not yet 'allow' for effective challenges. The fact that these groups have yet to receive any major support from the elite and the media is also evident of the pressure for the perpetuation of the existing discourses.

Could the financial crisis provide an opportunity for resolution?

Several studies have argued that reunification would lead to better economic performance for the two communities, significant GDP growth and subsequently more prosperity for Cypriots. However, the potential economic benefits of reunification have tended to be ignored. The deeply securitised environment in the political sector has been too powerful to overcome. Meanwhile, the potential economic benefits have been too weak to change the established perceptions. Simply put, the prospect of increased prosperity was insufficient to lessen the aforementioned anxieties about a potential settlement. The question now is whether a less comfortable economic environment for Greek Cypriots – due to the financial crisis – changes the parameters hindering a settlement. As discussed below, it cannot; even though it has influenced the *frequency* of the discourse to some extent.

While there is a change in the frequency of the political discourse, the content remains unchanged. For sure, the economic crisis ensured that the political discourses on the conflict were downgraded for the first time since 1974, taking second place to the economic developments. This, however, does not mean that Greek Cypriots are willing to make political concessions for the sake of an improved economy. Rather, it means that their attention is temporarily focused elsewhere. Indeed, the crisis provides an opportunity to demonstrate how resilient the aforementioned routines are and the impact they have on the perpetuation of the conflict. Neither the elite nor the public is willing to link the crisis to a settlement, despite the potential economic benefits the latter could have. Perhaps the most indicative example is the unwillingness of Greek Cypriot elite and public to seriously consider the idea of gas pipelines passing through Turkey; even though this is widely regarded as the most sensible financial option. Politically, however, the risk is too great for Greek Cypriots to allow Turkey to have control of the flow of their natural gas. Thus it is obvious that political fears and entrenched perceptions of threats cannot be overcome through the carrot of improved economic conditions and financial benefits. This in turn means that the view held by several scholars that the lack of economic incentives is the sole reason for the absence of a solution is erroneous, or at least incomplete.

If not positive, then what is the impact of the crisis on the settlement? It seems that instead of generating incentives it further complicates the situation and reduces the chances of a settlement. Specifically, the growing financial problems of the Greek Cypriots have 'forced' more people to sell their property to the Turkish Cypriot authorities, despite the political and media warnings of the political consequences of such actions. This essentially means that there is now an 'à la carte' cross-ethnic settlement of the property issue taking place without the involvement of political elite. This automatically reduces further the desire for a settlement amongst those individuals whose primary incentive for resolution was to return, or have access, to their properties.

Conclusion

The established conflict-perpetuating routines, coupled with the relatively non-hurting stalemate, will continue to support behaviour – involuntary or otherwise – that does not allow for much optimism for resolution to the Problem. Small groups that manage to deviate from the 'expected behaviour' will most likely continue their efforts but, unless there is an adjustment in the overall mentality of the populations at large, it is unlikely that they will have an impact. Mentalities, however, cannot change if there is no change in the local political discourses that perpetuate threats and internalise beliefs of enemy-others. Provocative remarks from elites, especially from the elites in Ankara, only help support the internalised fears of Greek Cypriots and provide justification for the need to maintain a defensive stance that is essentially manifested through a preference for the status quo.

While there may be renewed efforts for settlement in the future the voices that will likely prevail will not be the pro-reunification ones given that the threats from any settlement will be highlighted much more than any potential benefits. It will thus be particularly difficult for any elite to seek an acceptable solution or even to engage in discussions that could potentially break the deadlock. Meanwhile, as the problem is being resolved step by step, with one individual at a time, the chances of resolution will decrease even further. The status quo will remain, in principle, the preferred outcome even though both sides will continue to voice, loud and clear, their conditional willingness to reach a settlement to one of the most protracted conflicts in the world.

References and recommended reading

Adamides, Constantinos, *Enhancing Civil Society's Role in Conflict Prevention and Peace-Building in Cyprus* (European Commission/ Cyprus Center for European and International Affairs, 2011). Available at http://unic.academia.edu/ ConstantinosAdamides.

—— and Costas Constantinou, 'Comfortable conflict and (il)liberal peace in Cyprus', in Oliver P. Richmond and Audra Mitchell (eds), *Hybrid Forms of Peace: From the 'Everyday' to Post-liberalism* (Basingstoke: Palgrave Macmillan, 2012).

Constantinou, M.C., 'Cypriot's Problem, or how not to deal with existential anxiety', *Naked Punch* (2010). Available at http://www.nakedpunch.com/articles/72.

Cyprus 2015, 'Next steps in the peace talks: an island-wide study of public opinion in Cyprus' (December 2010). Available at www.cyprus2015.org.

Heraclides, Alexis, 'The Cyprus Gordian knot: an intractable ethnic conflict', *Nationalism and Ethnic Politics* 17/2 (2011), pp. 117–39.

Ker-Lindsay, James, *The Cyprus Problem: What Everyone Needs to Know* (Oxford: Oxford University Press, 2011).

Lake, David A. and Donald Rothchild, 'Containing fear: the origins and management of ethnic conflict', *International Security* 21/2 (1996), pp. 41–75.

Levy, Jack S., 'Prospect theory and international relations: theoretical applications and analytical problems', *Political Psychology* 13/2 (1992), pp. 283–310.

Mitzen, Jennifer, 'Ontological security in world politics: state identity and the security dilemma', *European Journal of International Relations* 12/3 (2006), pp. 341–70.

2

A New Vision of Good Neighbourliness

Emel Akçalı

As a half Cypriot scholar who wrote a PhD thesis on the political geography of the partition of Cyprus, and having published on various dimensions of the 'Cyprus Problem', I must admit that I have struggled enormously while writing this short piece as to whether Cyprus can be solved. There are several reasons for my unease in this endeavour. First, what is identified as the 'Cyprus Problem' has over the years tilted in so many directions and produced so many diverse results, including some good ones, that it is counterproductive in my view to classify the current situation in Cyprus as being solely a problem. From being a 'conflict-ridden Eastern Mediterranean island', Cyprus has become a quasi-EUropean territory and this new status has even (trans)formed Turkish Cypriots and some Turks into EUropeans granting them the very same rights as the 'authentic' Europeans; such as a respectable passport, the dignity of freedom of mobility and work and residence permits in EUropean lands. This new situation is a *sui generis* one in Europe today and, as a political geographer by training, rather than viewing it as a mere problem, I prefer to qualify it as a pioneering approach in dealing with *de-facto* territories and citizenships that exist elsewhere in the EU's periphery.

I am not quite convinced about some other conditions that render the current situation in Cyprus a mere problem, either. The modified demographical structure of the island by the Turkish settlers is argued to be one of the main sources of the continuing 'Cyprus Problem'. However, it would perhaps not be too much of an exaggeration to suggest that the 1974 Turkish settlers may now be outnumbered by a combination of Turkmen, Sri Lankan, Filipino, Kurdish, Arabic, Moldavian, Russian and Pontian immigrants who were until very recently invited to the island by Cypriots themselves. Migration, emigration and immigration are realities of the world today. Movement of peoples in the Mediterranean has in fact rendered Cyprus a multicultural island. I thus do not understand why Turkish settlers who have lived and worked on the island since 1974 should not be considered by now as a part of that multicultural setting. Finally and most importantly, what really problematises the notion of the 'Cyprus Problem' for me is the fact that there has been no armed conflict on the island since 1974. People remember it, talk about it and even render it a part of their daily communication, but are not tangibly affected by it. 'The Cyprus Problem' hence does not equate to a 'Cyprus conflict' and is accordingly physically harmless and only at times psychologically disturbing. Due to such qualifications, I am thus unable to give a direct answer to the question 'Can the Cyprus Problem be solved?' Instead, I offer my humble suggestions about the ways in which Cypriots can overcome the current impasse.

Partition: the bitter reality of Cypriots

Every time I find myself in Cyprus, I observe that the territorial, administrative, economical and even cultural partitioning of the island is the bitter reality of Cypriots despite the opened borders and ongoing peace negotiations. One needs thus to be ultra-apathetic, in my view, in order not to recognise this *fait accompli*. To my eyes, then, Cyprus looks willingly divided and most Cypriots seem to want it that way, especially in the sense that they do not want to make concessions to reach a peaceful settlement. As all other Mediterranean islands, Cyprus suffers from environmental degradation and water scarcity. However, even the environment is divided along territorial lines, 'so that *our* environment matters more than *theirs*' (Akçali and Antonsich 2009: 946, author's emphasis). Very sadly, the recent Cypriot obsession with private swimming pools constructed in the backyards of villas (on an island that suffers from water shortages) seems to be one of the few remaining bonds between Greek and Turkish Cypriots. Hence, as suggested by Vincent Morelli, in a report prepared for the US Congress in 2009, 'if the apparent suspension of the talks is really the beginning of the end of the negotiations, the permanent division of the island would no longer be seen as the simple musings of a small group of separatists' (21). The biggest problem resulting from this potential path, according to Morelli, would certainly fall on the European Union, which would then have to determine how to deal with a separate Turkish Cypriot entity and what to do with Turkish Cypriots who hold EU passports (ibid.: 22). Such an outcome would also of course create some uncertainties for Cyprus–Turkey, Greece–Turkey, EU–Turkey and NATO–EU relations as well (ibid.).

Furthermore, Cypriots nowadays seem to be concerned with more 'serious' matters than the 'Cyprus Problem', such as the economic crisis and threat of state bankruptcy on both sides. Certainly, there is a section of Cypriots, especially on the Turkish side, that links the solution of the island's economic crises to the solution of the Cyprus Problem through reunification under the umbrella of the European Union. I fear, however, that this group of people (I cannot decide whether they do this willingly or unconsciously) overlooks the economic burden of such a reunification and the economic shock therapy that the Turkish Cypriot side, especially, needs to undergo in order to harmonise with EU standards. The aggravation of the economic hardships, coupled with the financial burden of the reunification, may lead to deeper divides and grievances between the Cypriot communities, as the reunification example in Germany has demonstrated. Turkish Cypriot experts and opinion leaders understandably shy away from explaining this dimension of the reunification to their community so as not to lose support in a future referendum. However, Cypriots on both sides need transparent information about the economic consequences of a possible reunification and harmonisation. During the 2004 Annan Referendum period, for example, the Republican Turkish Party (CTP), which was then in power on the Turkish Cypriot side, published advertisements making false promises to the Turkish Cypriots that they would own brand new villas if they voted yes to the Annan Plan. Such campaigning is comprehensible in a national election context, where most Cypriots are known to take political decisions driven by material and economic interests, but is utterly unethical when campaigning for a peace agreement, inasmuch as it creates a type of wonderland for an already fragile people.

Finally, it would not been entirely wrong to advance – as has been observed in Cyprus and within the European Union, and has also been already acknowledged by Newman – that 'the opening of borders does not, automatically, result in the hybridisation of ethnic and national identities' (2006: 147). Newman further argues that although we have become more mobile and easily cross the boundaries that previously hindered our movement, this has not radically transformed our strong ethnic or national affiliations and loyalties, be they territorially-focused or group affiliations (ibid. and Sigurdson 2000). Language, for example, is 'the one significant boundary' which, 'for so many of us, remains difficult to cross in the absence of a single, global, borderless form of communication' (ibid.: 147–8). Additionally, as long as political passions remain coupled with economic rationality, they tend to undermine inter-ethnic commonalities and harmony. One should thus not underestimate the notion of 'affective borders' (Paasi 1996); those invisible, but nevertheless existent, social, emotional and mental lines that are harder to eradicate than the 'effective' ones.

A progressive understanding of borders

Drawing upon this last suggestion, it is then perhaps time to start thinking more seriously about the role, and the necessity, of borders and boundaries in our lives and then contemplate the ways in which such borders can progressively be transformed into more creative, inclusive and productive delineations. Hence, rather than putting all efforts into establishing full reconciliation, or creating a common identity and/or history to start with, Cypriots perhaps first need to search for ways to construct and maintain some good fences between each other; epitomised in the proverb 'Good fences make good neighbours'. As clichéd as it may sound, especially in the context of territorial conflicts, this proverb nevertheless contains a degree of wisdom. In his poem *Mending Wall*, written in 1914, Robert Frost problematises such wisdom by being irritated by the old-fashioned insistence of his neighbour that a fence is necessary to keep good relations with neighbours. However, in some other lines of the poem, he also seems to suggest that perhaps the act of repairing the wall is what brings neighbours together and keeps the relationship functioning on a healthier basis. This is because working on keeping the 'good fences' may represent for all sides maintaining the fundamental rights and independence of neighbours.

Hence, rather than being viewed as outlandish, conflictual or antagonistic, fences or borders can be conceptualised as demarcations that honour the affective ties, history, values, goals and concerns that distinctly belong to Greek or Turkish Cypriots; at least until the time protagonists are able to create or consolidate common inter-ethnic bonds. Such borders do not need just to live on difference. They can also 'thrive on difference' (Cadaval 1993) and can, as such, be perceived as an environment of opportunity. One should also always keep in mind that 'borders are artifacts of history' and may transform over time (ibid.). 'Good fences' thus may be conceptualised as dynamic constructions that are open to new and multiple meaning and societal changes. This would further require a redefinition of good neighbourly relations, as well. As emerged in peace park studies (Ali 2007), to cooperate, neighbouring countries do not have to share common interests but a common aversion to mischief. The parties need also to perceive early in the process clear evidence of benefit, a win-win solution and a respectful and transparent setting open to cooperation. However, it should also be acknowledged that good neighbours need first to start talking and listening to one another before attempting to construct any fences.

If Cypriots are able to achieve all this, it can then easily be argued that they should as well live together in one common state or in a federation acquiring a common citizenship. However, the main point that I am trying to stress in this piece is that perhaps it is time to acknowledge that investing all efforts towards the possibility of reunification may just be the root cause of why we view every development since 1974 in Cyprus, especially in the Turkish Cypriot part, as a problem. It is thus perhaps wiser for Cypriots to emphasise the productive sides of this *de-facto* situation and find ways of dealing with 'the Cyprus Problem' from within this situation and create interdependencies with each other as neighbours first, before moving on to any reunified solution.

Contemplating on good neighbourliness

One caveat to such a suggestion comes from *Solving the Cyprus Problem: Hopes and Fears* which was prepared by the Cyprus 2015 Initiative by drawing upon island-wide public opinion poll results. According to this report, Greek Cypriots in general strongly prefer a unitary state over federation (and the continuation of the Republic of Cyprus) whereas the Turkish Cypriots prefer a two-state solution entailing the international recognition of the unrecognised Turkish Republic of Northern Cyprus (2011: 18). These results are really not that different from the findings I obtained when I was conducting my PhD fieldwork back in 2004–6. During March–August 2005, and

December 2005–January 2006, I asked 100 respondents – recruited through snowballing or self-selected sampling techniques: 50 in the cities of North Nicosia, Kyrenia, Famagusta, Morphou and in the villages of Akdogan and Yalya in the Turkish Republic of Northern Cyprus (TRNC), and 50 in the cities of South Nicosia, Paphos, Limassol and Larnaca in the Republic of Cyprus (RoC) – to sketch two maps. The first one was of the country in which they live and the second one of the country in which they would like to live. The question was asked in order to stimulate the individuals to think in terms of lived territories, rather than only in terms of lived neighbourhoods, cities, towns or regions (see Akçali 2010). The results obtained on each side of the island varied, even though the idea of territory as emphasised by statesmen, school or media has emerged as the most important mental representation of 'the country' for most of the respondents and this trend seems to continue in Cyprus as also revealed in the Cyprus 2015 Initiative public opinion poll results. Thus, the majority of Greek Cypriots sketched maps of territorially and administratively unitary Cyprus whereas the Turkish Cypriots stressed bizonality on their maps.

However, the ways in which Cypriots represented their mental territory were quite diverse, not only inter-ethnically, but intra-ethnically, and most of the time they did not reflect the ethnic belonging of the respondents only. This diversity thus can be a departing point when contemplating new and progressive borders and good neighbourliness in Cyprus. The identities revealed by the sketched maps were plural and multidimensional and Cypriots attributed diverse meanings and symbols to Cyprus. These mental maps also showed that Cypriots' emotions, perceptions and representations stem, at times, more from personal hopes, goals and desires rather than ethnic or cultural belonging and this can help us to learn about an important dimension about the 'Cyprus Problem', namely that although territorial representations are influenced by existing societal and 'national' discourses, personal aspirations and worries do not connect with a national or ethnic identity and objective only (Akçali 2010: 56–7). Thus, any solution envisaged for Cyprus that includes fences, borders or some other innovative delineations can also expect to be based on such multiple characteristics of Cypriots, and they may also show variations in time.

Conclusion

In this piece, I have tried to suggest that, as things stand, Cypriots do not seem to be ready for a reunification and/or reconciliation over the 'Cyprus Problem' at the moment, as they are voluntarily divided and are neighbours only *perforce*. The trick of solving the 'Cyprus Problem' would therefore seem to lie in transforming this awkward neighbourliness into a genuine and a good one. This may require the construction and maintenance of some stable but enterprising fences at the beginning. However, the progressive and innovative character of such fences may then give Cypriots incentives to cooperate, communicate, respect, help, give, receive and learn. This in turn may allow them to develop good neighbourly relations. The reunification of the island can still be achieved one day by relying on such good neighbourliness. Unfortunately such an enterprise is absent in Cyprus today. Cypriots who are committed to a peaceful agreement should perhaps take steps to initiate it.

References and recommended reading

Akçali, Emel, 'Reading the Cyprus conflict through mental maps: An interdisciplinary approach to ethno-nationalism', in Adrian Guelke (ed.), *The Challenges of Ethno-Nationalism: Case Studies in Identity Politics* (Basingstoke and New York: Palgrave Macmillan, 2010).

—— and Marco Antonsich, '"Nature knows no boundaries" – a critical reading of UNDP environmental peacemaking in Cyprus', *The Annals of the Association of American Geographers* 99/5 (2009), pp. 940–7.

Ali, Saleem H. (ed.), *Peace Parks* (Cambridge, MA: MIT Press, 2007).

Cadaval, Olivia, 'United States-Mexico Borderlands/Frontera' (1993) Available at http://smithsonianeducation.org/migrations/bord/intro.html (accessed May 2013).

Cyprus 2015 Initiative, *Solving the Cyprus Problem: Hopes and Fears* (Nicosia: Interpeace and Cyprus, 2015 Initiative, 2011).

Morelli, Vincent, 'Cyprus: reunification proving elusive', Congressional Research Service Report for Congress, 25 June 2013. Available at http://www.fas.org/sgp/crs/row/R41136.pdf (accessed May 2013).

Newman, David, 'The lines that continue to separate us: borders in our "borderless" world', *Progress of Human Geography* 30/2 (2006), pp. 143–61.

Paasi, Anssi, *Territories, Boundaries, and Consciousness: The Changing Geographies of the Finnish-Russian Border* (Chichester: John Wiley & Sons, 1996).

Sigurdson, Richard, 'Crossing borders: immigration, citizenship and the challenge to nationality', in Martin Pratt and Janet Brown (eds), *Borderlands under Stress* (London: Kluwer, 2000).

3

'Cypriotism' and the Path to Reunification

Ahmet An

History deals with the sum of the events that happened in the past. It should be studied in order to understand the present. Today's reality in Cyprus is influenced by history. It directs our attitudes and preferences. In this context, an awareness of history, the way the history is written and the teaching of history are crucial. As Cypriots, how much do we know about the history of our country and the history of the inter-communal relations?

The emergence of Greek and Turkish nationalisms in Cyprus

When the British occupied the island of Cyprus in 1878, ending a 300-year period of Ottoman rule that had began in 1571, they preferred to keep the existing structures of education in Cyprus. Christian and Moslem schools were kept separate from one another. There were two Boards of Education, one Christian and the other Moslem. They ensured that the curriculums of the two communities mirrored those in Greece and Turkey respectively. The Greek Orthodox community was educated by teachers who had mainly graduated from Greek educational institutions and the educational system was under the control of the Greek Orthodox Church of Cyprus. At the request of the Cyprus government, the headmaster of the only lyceum in Nicosia was always sent from Istanbul. They were all Turkish nationalists. The Boards also prescribed the books to be used in the schools, insisting that the history textbooks were written in the so-called motherlands. As a result, the books emphasised the conflicts between Greece and Turkey, who had fought against each other in 1821, resulting in Greece's independence from the Ottoman Empire, and again in 1921, when the Turkish Army defeated the Greek troops that had invaded Western Anatolia, leading to the formation of the Republic of Turkey in 1923. Both events therefore influenced the Moslem Turkish and the Christian Greek community in Cyprus. This was particularly the case with Turkish nationalism, which had developed during the national struggle to liberate the Ottoman Empire from occupation by imperial powers. Though it developed almost a century after Greek nationalism, this Turkish nationalism became influential among the Moslem Turkish population in Cyprus after the military defeat of the Greek occupation of Western Anatolia.

As well as through the schools, Turkish nationalism was disseminated in Cyprus by the Turkish Cypriot press, which followed the example of the mainland Turkish press, as well as through the activities of the Turkish Consulate on the island, which opened after the foundation of the Turkish Republic. Meanwhile, the Greek Cypriots also pursued their own nationalism. They aimed to bring about the union of the island with Greece; a demand often put before the Legislative Council, which had been established by the British in 1879. The Turkish Cypriot Members of Parliament used to resist these demands by saying that the island should be returned to its original owner, Turkey. However, following the annexation of Cyprus by the British Empire in 1914, Turkey gave up all of her rights to Cyprus when it signed the Treaty of Lausanne Agreement, in 1923. This was confirmed in 1925, when Britain declared Cyprus to be a Crown Colony – a status it retained until 1960.

The nationalism of both Greek and Turkish Cypriots did not originate from local historical circumstances, but was imported to the island through the teachers, books and newspapers that came from mainland Greece and Turkey. This nationalism was encouraged by the British colonial administration and the British tried to disseminate it among the unaware masses of people in accordance with their traditional policy of 'divide and rule'.

The consolidation of nationalisms

When the Greek Cypriots started a terror campaign in 1955 to end British colonial administration, the Turkish Cypriot leadership collaborated with the British and provoked the Greek Cypriots by recommending that Turkish Cypriot youth become auxiliary police and commandoes in order to oppose the Greek Cypriot rebels, thereby defending the colonialists. Thereafter, as the Greek Cypriot EOKA (National Organisation of Cypriot Fighters) underground organisation killed Turkish Cypriot security forces, the Turkish Cypriot TMT underground organisation began to kill Greek Cypriots in retaliation. As both organisations were anti-communist, they also killed progressive Cypriots who were against the partitionist policies of the British and their local collaborators. The growing demand of the Greek Cypriots for the union of the island with Greece (*enosis*) was countered by the demand of the Turkish Cypriots for the partition (*taksim*) of the island between Turkey and Greece.

Finally, neither the Greek Cypriots' objective of union nor the Turkish Cypriots' of partition materialised. Instead, a limited independence was given to a new partnership, the Republic of Cyprus, which was established in 1960. The British maintained their sovereignty over the two military bases and the island was declared an independent state, banning both *enosis* and *taksim* in its constitution. The Turkish Cypriots, with 18 per cent of the island's population, were given a 30 per cent say in the administration of the new Republic of Cyprus. This was strongly opposed by the Greek Cypriots. In December 1963, the President of the Republic, Archbishop Makarios, tried to change the 13 points of the constitution by abolishing the veto power of the Turkish Cypriot Vice-President Dr Fazil Kuchuk. Inter-communal clashes began and, at the beginning of 1964, the Turkish Cypriots withdrew from the state apparatus. This conflict of nationalisms between the pro-union Greek Cypriot leadership and the pro-partition Turkish Cypriot leadership complicated the solution of the ethnic-national question in Cyprus. The unity of action and aim of the Cypriots could not be developed under a common shared aim and this caused new bitterness.

Meanwhile, those who sought to promote coexistence were silenced. In 1958, Turkish Cypriot trade unionists started to come under attack. In 1962, two prominent lawyers, Ahmet Muzaffer Gurkan and Ayhan Hikmet, founders of the *Cumhuriyet* weekly newspaper, which advocated cooperation between the two main communities of new Cyprus state, were murdered. In 1965, Dervis Ali Kavazoglu, a Turkish Cypriot communist trade unionist, was murdered by the Turkish Cypriot underground organisation TMT

(Turkish Resistance Organisation). These actions of intimidation silenced the democratic opposition within the Turkish Cypriot community, which was fighting against the partitionist policy of the Turkish Cypriot leadership. As a result, the separatist policy that the Turkish Cypriot leadership had pursued since 1958 was one of the reasons that Turkish Cypriots and Greek Cypriots did not have a common political aim during the inter-communal negotiations that began in 1968.

From 1968 until 1974, various rounds of inter-communal negotiations were carried out, ending with a coup d'état by mainland Greek Army officers against Makarios, on 15 July 1974. This was followed by the invasion of the island by the mainland Turkish Army, on 20 July 1974. Together with Great Britain, Greece and Turkey were supposed to be the guarantor powers of the independence, sovereignty and the territorial integrity of the Republic of Cyprus. The Turkish Cypriot leadership unilaterally declared independence in 1983, forming the Turkish Republic of Northern Cyprus on the Turkish occupied territory of the island; a move that was immediately condemned by the UN Security Council. Nevertheless, in Turkish Cypriot history textbooks, the Turkish invasion in 1974 was described as an act of salvation. In contrast, Greek Cypriot students were taught nothing about the events between 1963 and 1974. The struggle for the union of the island with Greece during 1955–9 was portrayed as a struggle for the independence of the island. The Turkish Cypriots were ignored and excluded.

As imperialist foreign powers were against the independent development of the Republic of Cyprus, which followed an independent non-aligned foreign policy, they continuously incited nationalistic and anti-communist feelings among the island's population. Yet again, a Cypriot awareness could not be developed to a sufficient degree. The guarantors of the independence, sovereignty and territorial integrity of Cyprus were members of NATO (North Atlantic Treaty Organisation) and did not want to see a Cypriot state free from their influence. That is why they still do whatever they can to prevent the development of independent internal political and cultural structures.

Challenging nationalist histories

In order to draw useful lessons for the future, we have to have a good knowledge of our history and a multi-perspective approach to our past, without any prejudice. For this purpose, it is necessary to have well-educated historians; rich archives open for all; multi-communal platforms, where everything can be discussed freely; and a democratic environment free from all taboos. Without all these, it would be very difficult to bring historical realities to light. Even then, it cannot be said that the Cypriot communities are likely to be at ease discussing these subjects.

History has to play a unifying rather than a discriminatory role between nations and communities. In the nationalist way of history writing, the writer chooses 'we' at every stage of history and sees 'the others' as enemy. Seeing those from their own nationality as different from and superior to others is the minimum characteristic of nationalist history writers. Some writers state this in a hard form. Others take a softer approach. But what is seen in all nationalist history writers is seeing their own nation state as superior and defending, if necessary, the interests of their own nation at the expense of the others. This way of looking at history and commentating on the past is a dominant characteristic in various stages of writing official history and in the development of a nation state.

The review of textbooks and history teaching with multilateral and international efforts is a very long and tiring process. Efforts to produce new models for textbooks in European countries as well as in Turkey, Greece and the Balkans are being conducted by non-governmental bodies, historians and social scientists. In this respect, it would be very valuable to form a common committee of Turkish Cypriot and Greek Cypriot historians which could try to achieve an interpretation of the common history of the communities living in Cyprus. I can name some subjects to be discussed and researched by such a Committee: the common rebellions during the Ottoman Occupation against the local governor's arbitrary taxations; the common struggles in the Legislative Council during the British colonial rule related to the economic policy; the common struggles of the trade-union movement, which was united until 1958; the common struggle of the Cypriots against fascism during World War II on the side of the Allied Forces.

Since 1974, the influx of mainland Turkish settlers in the occupied areas of Cyprus, which is contrary to the Geneva Convention, has been a threat to the existence of the Turkish Cypriots. This has led many of them to reassess their communal identity. Turkish Cypriot intellectuals, in particular, have started to ask themselves the question

'Who are we?' and 'How can we preserve our own identity?' as they have looked into the history of their cultural heritage. Cultural, scientific and literary heritage are three important components of the national consciousness. Here we see the responsibility of historical researchers for the development of a common Cypriot consciousness. They have to research the common cultural heritage of the island and use these common elements for a common political aim. The various examples of cooperation between the two communities in commercial and social life and in the trade-union movement in the past are good examples of the coexistence of the two main communities in Cyprus. This highlights the degree to which the class character of the state has a large role to play in the formation of the Cypriot consciousness. There has to be a clearly designed state policy for the support of a Cypriot identity. The organs of the mass media should also play a constructive role in this respect since they can easily reach the homes of almost all citizens.

Conclusion

Over the past century and a half two different identities have emerged in Cyprus. Since 1974, these have been consolidated. Today, one is North of the divide. This holds the separatist TRNC as an expression of the nationalist identity of the Turkish Cypriots. The other is on the South of the divide. This views itself as the sole owner of the Cypriot state, which has a distinctively Orthodox Greek Cypriot character. To combat this, there needs to be an effort to challenge the separate histories told by the two communities. However, it needs to go further than this. There also need to be common political parties of Turkish Cypriots and the Greek Cypriots, seeking common political aims. The New Cyprus Association, which was formed in March 1975, aimed to preserve the existence of the state of Cyprus and avert the danger of permanent partition by encouraging people to behave first as Cypriots and then as a member of their respective community. Unfortunately, during the past 37 years, this movement of intellectuals has been unable to become a political movement that could organise Turkish Cypriots and Greek Cypriots under a common Cypriot identity. Nevertheless, the full equality of all the communities living on the island in the fields of politics, economy and culture can only be achieved through common political parties that will fight for a democratic federal state and against all kinds of separatism and discrimination. As the Turkish Cypriot Coordinator

of the Bicommunal Movement for an Independent and Federal
Cyprus, which was formed in 1989, I fought for 11 years to win
a case against Turkey in the European Court of Human Rights, in
February 2003 (Djavit An v. Turkey, 20652/92) for depriving me
of my freedom of assembly due to my efforts to promote greater
contacts between the two communities in Cyprus. My experiences
since then have showed me that all Cypriots who want to see a
reunited island should organise themselves and fight for the same
goal: ending the occupation and the colonisation of the Northern
part of our island by Turkey and forming a democratic federal state
through power sharing. Policies are needed to solve the problem of
nationalities. Rather, a single Cypriot nationality is needed. This can
only be done by challenging the historical presentation of the past
and promoting political cooperation in the present.

References and recommended reading

An, Ahmet, 'An overview of the research studies on the identity of
the Turkish Cypriots', in *Articles on Turkish Cypriot Culture*
(Nicosia: Kıvılcım Publications No. 5, 1999), pp. 222–30 (in
Turkish).

——, *The Political History of the Turkish Cypriots (1930–1960): The
Forgotten Political History of the Turkish Cypriots and the Struggles
for the Leadership in the Mirror of the Press* (Nicosia: 2006) (in
Turkish).

Attalides, Michael, *Cyprus, Nationalism and International Politics*
(Basingstoke: Macmillan, 1979).

European Court of Human Rights, Djavit An v. Turkey (application
no. 20652/92).

Worsley, Peter and Paschalis Kitromilides (eds), *Small States in the
Modern World* (Nicosia: The New Cyprus Association, 1979).

4

Escaping the Tyranny of History

Jan Asmussen

When considering the current state of the Cyprus Problem, the question appears not to be whether, if and how the Cyprus question can be solved, but rather if there is even any detectable drive towards actually solving it. It is worth looking at some quotations regarding the prospects for a solution:

> The [Greek Cypriot leader] confirmed that the Turks had offered far-reaching concessions. The talks had, on the whole, gone very well. There were still differences on a number of matters, such as the terms for Turkish participation in the Executive, but these did not seem to be important differences of principle... The Turkish side had, however, been asked to give examples of how their proposals would apply in practice. The [Greek Cypriot leader] said that, when these examples were produced, it should be possible to settle the matter. He concluded, 'I think we will be able to reach a constitutional settlement.'

A second quote seems to echo the first:

> Since my... meeting with the leaders, both sides have worked on the difficult task of breaking down the complex Cyprus problem into its core issues. Through

this approach, the sides... have made some additional progress in resolving them.

Taking a more pessimistic view, we could point to the following two quotes:

> The... talks between the Greek and Turkish Cypriots continue, but the two sides are still very far apart on the crucial question of... government. Neither of the two parties (nor the Greek and Turkish Governments) at present see any alternative to the talks.

> The current window of opportunity is not limitless and there is little to suggest that the future will bring more propitious circumstances for a settlement. The United Nations remains convinced that if the necessary political will could be mustered on both sides, a durable settlement could be achieved in the interest of all Cypriots.

On balance, these statements do not carry any real surprises. Everyone engaged with the Cyprus Problem has encountered these sentiments from time-to-time. What is disturbing is that while the first and third quotations are from 1968/69 (TNA PREM 13/118 Costar to Edmonds Cyprus-Clerides/Denktash Talks, 14 August 1968/ PREM 13/119 FCO to Prime Minister United Nations Force in Cyprus – Memorandum by the Foreign and Commonwealth Office, 24 November 1969), the two others are from 2012 (S/2012/149 Assessment report of the Secretary-General on the status of the negotiations in Cyprus, 12 March 2012, paragraphs 16/23). They are, however, completely interchangeable. These text blocks can be used for all talks since 1968. Unfortunately, they are also likely to be equally useful to describe the situation at any point in the remote future of Cyprus negotiations. They always tend to contain optimistic features about a possible breakthrough, as well as pessimism tied to the claims about the insincerity of the adversaries.

The good news is that both sides insist that they want a solution. The bad news is that their views on how such a solution should be designed remain as far apart from each other as their presentations on the origins of the conflict. To the Greek Cypriots, the Cyprus Problem essentially started in 1974 when Turkey divided the island in the wake of a Greek coup d'état. Turkish Cypriots, on the other hand, emphasise the events starting in Christmas 1963, which resulted in the enclavement of their community for the next ten years. I do not wish to dive into the dispute as to who has a stronger claim on the issue of guilt. Instead I would like to examine two issues that result from the different perceptions of history. First, I should like to elaborate on the origins of the conflict in a wider regional perspective. Secondly, I shall demonstrate why the different perceptions of history contribute to the prevention of a durable solution.

Past legacies of harmony and strife

Before one can evaluate the causes of the troubles it is worthwhile examining the character of pre-conflict interethnic relations in Cyprus. Prior to 1571 Cyprus had long been an almost mono-ethnic island with a Greek-speaking Orthodox Christian population. This changed after 1571 as the Ottoman conquerors settled peasants and craftsmen from Anatolia on the Island. These were Turkish-speaking Sunni Muslims, the ancestors of today's Turkish Cypriots. Thereafter, the ethnic composition of the island remained roughly on a scale of 80 per cent Greek Cypriots to 20 per cent Turkish Cypriots; leaving the latter with the status of a local minority in what was a Muslim-dominated empire.

Interethnic relations during much of the Ottoman period remained peaceful, if not amicable. Many accounts report widespread cooperation between the two communities. The existence at one time of 346 mixed villages is perhaps proof of the intensity of this collaboration. Each culture influenced the other, as can be seen in the unique folk culture, cuisine and poetry of Cyprus. This high degree of cooperation can almost certainly be attributed in part to the difficult living conditions that existed on an island that suffered from a hot, dry climate and lacked permanent water resources. Daily life in mixed villages could be qualified as a recurring fight for survival. Village societies therefore collaborated across ethnic boundaries. These boundaries were crossed during celebrations and feasts as well. A brilliant example of this legacy was recorded by the German ethnologist Magda Ohnefalsch-Richter, who, in 1910, visited the Panayiri of the Aphrodite in Larnaca. This feast, which had ancient roots, was celebrated by both communities. Richter described a truly mixed event that was not only celebrated by ordinary Greeks and Turks, but also by the Christian priests and Muslim Hodjas. Turks and Greeks would play music and dance together. Religious feasts in Cyprus were not divisive, but enriched the life of all denominations. The fact that the Christian festival of St Mary, which emerged from the ancient pagan rite of Aphrodite, became a festival celebrated by Muslims speaks volumes about the nature of mixed Cypriot culture.

Cyprus, however, is not a special case of interethnic collaboration. Similar patterns of interethnic relations have been recounted across Anatolia and much of the Balkans. The striking difference is that the scene Ohnefalsch-Richter described would have been unthinkable in the Balkans in the same period. Interethnic relations had deteriorated in the territories surrounding the island. When Britain took over the administration of Cyprus, in 1878, it had an unintended side effect. While the struggles in Crete, the Balkan Wars, World War I and the Turkish War of Independence put an end to multi-ethnic harmony elsewhere in Southeast Europe, major ethnic strife did not occur in Cyprus for much of the British period. The British initially did not change the traditional Ottoman system of administration that devolved a considerable amount of control over everyday matters to the respective religious communities. One upshot of this was that schools remained under the influence of the Church and the Muslim religious foundations respectively. Nationalism could thereby find its way via schoolbooks and teachers exported from, and influenced by, the Greek and Turkish motherlands. Nevertheless, the unrest of 1931 remained confined to Greco-British clashes and did not result in confrontation between the two communities. Even the outbreak of the EOKA campaign to end British rule over the island was not coupled with immediate interethnic violence. It was only when the killings of security personal of Turkish Cypriot origin took place that the conflict took on an interethnic character. Subsequently, major violence broke out in 1958, resulting in the first Turkish and Greek Cypriots being forced to leave their homes and become refugees in their own country.

Two years later saw the birth of the Cyprus Republic. By that time trust between the two communities was damaged, albeit not broken. The new Republic was unwanted. Greek Cypriots hoped to unite Cyprus with Greece (*enosis*). For their part, the Turkish Cypriots would rather have had the British stay than find themselves as a small minority in a huge Greek state. *Taksim* (partition) – the official demand of the Turkish Cypriot leadership – did not really appeal to most Turkish Cypriots as it would have forced many of them to migrate to the North of the island and lose their ancestral homes. Therefore, they largely regarded the call for *taksim* rather as a propaganda slogan to counter Greek Cypriot demands for *enosis*. Meanwhile, the two communities were tasked with the implementation of a complicated constitution whose success depended on the good will of all sides involved. The failure of this endeavour was inevitable. Almost from the beginning, a petty-minded tug of war occurred on almost every constitutional issue. The two leaderships refused to cooperate with one another. Instead, deep distrust about each other's true motivations dominated the scene. This distrust came to affect the daily interaction between the communities on the ground. The Turkish Cypriots, in particular, started to feel discriminated against in workspaces and government offices.

In late 1963 the Greek Cypriot leadership decided to break the constitutional blockade by implementing a plan that amounted to a constitutional coup d'état. Christmas that year saw the outbreak of island-wide violence between the communities. This resulted in three major developments: the total Greek Cypriot take-over of the organs of the Republic of Cyprus; the retreat of Turkish Cypriots into fortified enclaves; and the deployments of United Nations troops and begin of the UN peacekeeping and peacemaking mission in Cyprus that continues to this day.

The following ten years saw a widening economic gap between the two communities. While Greek Cypriots experienced a small economic miracle, with gains in tourism and finance, Turkish Cypriots suffered from unemployment and growing poverty. Moreover, constant harassment by Greek Cypriot nationalist officials at control points, airports and government offices made the majority of Turkish Cypriots lose what was left of their trust in their Greek Cypriot compatriots, which in turn affected the first intercommunal talks (1968–74). Nevertheless, the talks might have succeeded as the economic and political disparity had softened maximalist demands of the Turkish Cypriot leadership. However, Makarios was not bold enough to seize this opportunity. Instead, the next chapter of the Cyprus drama unfolded. In 1974 Cyprus was divided following a Greek military coup against Makarios and a subsequent Turkish military landing. Most Greek Cypriots residing in the North of the island fled or were expelled; most Turkish Cypriots moved to the North. This event and the subsequent denial of refugee return destroyed the remaining trust Greek Cypriots had in Turkish Cypriot sincerity.

Now, devoid of any trust on both sides, negotiations started anew in order to find a lasting peaceful solution to the Cyprus Problem. Various rounds and formats of talks took place from 1974 until 2012. Little has been achieved so far. The 1977 and 1979 High-Level Agreements have determined that the shape of a new Cyprus should be one of 'an independent non-aligned bicommunal federal Republic' in which both communities would have their own administrative territories. No substantial progress has been achieved apart from these agreements.

Blame games and conspiracy theories

In order to evaluate the causes of these meagre results, it is perhaps useful to take a closer look at the common features of all negotiation rounds and the surrounding rhetoric. The common features include: blame games in which both sides emphasise historical guilt of the other, with Turkish Cypriots focusing on 1963 and the Greek Cypriots on 1974; openly expressed distrust regarding the true intentions of the other side; conspiracy theories about evil foreign powers that meddle with the process. These blame games usually result in long lectures on the origins of the conflict that highlight the actions of the other side and emphasise the victimhood of their own community. Very often these games also focus on the conduct of the other side in the peace talks. Negotiators frequently blame each other for being insincere or leaking details of confidential information to the press. In the case of the latter, such allegations are often well-founded. Both sides seemingly enjoy leaking for whatever purposes. As for the conspiracy theories surrounding the talks, these often tie in to the predominant narratives of Cypriot history. 'Perfidious Albion', the CIA, Henry Kissinger, Günter Verheugen, Alvaro de Soto, or – more recently – Alexander Downer, have all been blamed for negatively interfering with the fate of the island, either directly or in the negotiations. These allegations come to the fore whenever the international community appears losing faith in the chances of a settlement.

Why are these features so dominant? Why is it so important to all parties to identify culprits? Why does conflict history play such an important role? The answer lies deep in the abovementioned lack of trust that could not been mitigated in all the negotiations since 1968. The different and incompatible narratives on the history of the conflict serve to enforce this distrust. They are, therefore, instrumental to the lack of real progress.

Taking all this into consideration, how can the two Cypriot communities regain trust? Surely, it cannot be by engaging in disputes about the history of the island. As important as the questions relating to the origins of the conflict may seem, in the present circumstances a common reading of past conflict cannot be achieved. At least, this cannot be done at the negotiating table. It should instead be left to academic and societal discussions. Trust can only develop through mutual cooperation. Despite the overall negative outcome, recent negotiations have provided a glimmer of hope in that direction. While the discussions at the leadership level have produced conflicting histories, blame and political havoc, the work of the technical committees has brought some notable progress. Members of those committees have managed to create an atmosphere of professional collaboration that has long been absent from the talks.

But what would a solution that is acceptable to most Greek and Turkish Cypriots alike look like? Having observed many years of negotiation rounds and listened to the leaders and the public, it is hard to say. The true wishes and preferences of both sides appear to be further apart from each other than the 1977 and 1979 agreements seem to suggest. Do they really wish to live together in a common bicommunal, federal republic? Opinion polls on both sides suggest that both communities appear to be ready to accept this solution as the second best option. Greek Cypriots would still prefer a Greek Cypriot-dominated unitary political system that would see the return of all Greek Cypriot refugees to their homes. Turkish Cypriots would opt for their own internationally recognised state, preferably within the European Union. Apart from a very active and very committed group of Cypriots from both sides engaged in intercommunal activities, the majority on both sides of the line show little commitment to a common future with their Greek and Turkish Cypriot compatriots.

Conclusion

A final break-through at the negotiations requires trust. This trust cannot develop as long as historical disputes remain at the forefront and while negotiators and political leaders try to apportion blame for the present situation. The Cypriots will only be able to develop a common future if they are ready to leave behind the past and develop mutual trust. However, this can only spring from common collaboration. Important issues like property rights are being addressed during the initial phase of a settlement. But, as long these issues are considered to be more important than reaching a workable framework of mutual cooperation, no viable settlement can be found. Can the Cyprus Problem be solved? My answer is 'maybe'. However, if Greek and Turkish Cypriots fail to rebuild trust through cooperation, I am afraid that the language to describe future Cyprus talks might be constructed from the very same text blocks that have been used from 1968 to this day.

References and recommended reading

Asmussen, Jan, *Cyprus at War: Diplomacy and Conflict During the 1974 Crisis* (London: I.B.Tauris, 2008).

——, 'Conspiracy theories and Cypriot history: the comfort of commonly perceived enemies', in Rebecca Bryant (ed.), *British Colonial Cyprus* (Nicosia: University of Nicosia Press, 2011).

——, 'Cyprus – should the UN withdraw?', Issue Brief, European Centre for Minority Issues (ECMI), April 2011.

Clerides, Glafkos, *Cyprus: My Deposition*, 4 vols (Nicosia: Alithia Publishing, 1989).

Denktaş, Rauf, *Hatıraları* [Memoirs], 9 vols (Istanbul: Boğaziçi Yayınları, 1996–9).

Hannay, David, *Cyprus: The Search for a Solution* (London: I.B.Tauris 2005).

Ohnefalsch-Richter, Magda H., *Griechische Sitten und Gebräuche auf Cypern. Mit Berücksichtigung von Naturkunde und Volkswirtschaft sowie der Fortschritte unter Englischer Herrschaft* (Berlin: Dietrich Reimer/Ernst Vohsen, 1913).

Patrick, Richard A., *Political Geography and the Cyprus Conflict, 1964–71* (Ontario: University of Waterloo, 1976).

5

A Bizonal Federation is not Viable

Tozun Bahcheli and Sid Noel

Federations composed of only two units, while theoretically within the range of possible federal formations, are rarely found in actual practice. And where they have been attempted – as in Pakistan (pre-Bangladesh), Czechoslovakia, Yugoslavia (when reduced to Serbia-Montenegro) and Bosnia-Herzegovina, to cite a few examples – they have proven to be fragile, dysfunctional in operation and often short-lived, with the most common outcome being political deadlock followed by disintegration. The basic flaw of two-unit federations is their stark, inherently oppositional configuration, which allows no room to develop the shifting coalitions among members that in successful multi-unit federations serve to counter disintegrative tendencies. And this in turn encourages a political dynamic in which issues tend to be viewed as matters of 'us versus them' and policy outcomes as zero-sum.

Yet despite the manifest structural defects and sorry historical record of the two-unit federal model, it has been stubbornly promoted – by the UN and other intermediaries – as a solution to the Cyprus Problem since the division of the island in 1974 created a territorial basis for federation. It has also been repeatedly and exhaustively considered by both communities, and while it has been endorsed 'in principle' by both, their endorsement has had no practical effect because the two sides do not agree on what federation 'in principle' means, and neither side embraces federation as its preferred option. Instead, both sides have come to see it as a second-best option provided that satisfactory terms of union can be negotiated.

Futile search for a settlement

Since in democratic politics getting one's second preference is not necessarily a bad outcome, it might be thought that two democratically governed communities would have at least a fair chance of agreeing on a compromise settlement. With a view to exactly that end, mediators under UN auspices have spelled out – in ever-increasing detail – the terms of a supposedly possible settlement: in the 'Preliminary Draft for a Joint High-Level Agreement' of 1985, in the 'Set of Ideas' framework agreement of 1992 and in the most comprehensive and detailed proposal of all, the 'Annan Plan' of 2004. Yet on every occasion the result has been failure.

If the problem were merely one of finding the 'right' federal formula for Cyprus, it would likely have been solved long ago, given the extraordinary international pressure, expertise and resources that have been so single-mindedly devoted to the search. But it is not, and the principal obstacle that has stood in the way of every plan and initiative is the absence of sufficient desire on the part of the two Cypriot communities for federation.

Even if a genuine mutual desire for federation should somehow develop, there would remain the question of whether a two-member federation is a viable form of governance. A large number of countries are federations or quasi-federations of one kind or another. But almost none are two-member federations and the very few that do exist are problematical, with virtually nothing in their history, structure or operation that would make them realistic models for Cyprus. Belgium is sometimes cited as a possible model, but it includes Brussels as a third region and there are other profound dissimilarities: Flemings and Walloons do not have a history of violent conflict or partition, and while their complaints against one another may seem endless, they are of a different order of seriousness from those in Cyprus. There is no 'refugee problem' in Belgium, no 'property issue', no cries for 'justice' for past atrocities, no sense of intolerable loss. Bosnia-Herzegovina is an even more dubious model: its constitution was externally imposed and its defects as a federation are so numerous and manifest that it can serve only as an example of what to avoid. The Federation of St Kitts and Nevis (a union of two tiny, ethnically homogeneous, unilingual Caribbean islands) is arguably the world's only true two-unit federation – a configuration it acquired more by accident than design when in 1980 Anguilla, which had originally been included, broke away. In a 1998 referendum

62 per cent of Nevisians voted to secede but the result fell short of the required two-thirds majority. As far as can be determined, no one has yet proposed it as a suitable model for Cyprus.

The challenge facing those who promote the idea of a two-unit federation for Cyprus is to devise a federation that can overcome the basic and often fatal flaws in the generic design: namely, its built-in tendencies to produce zero-sum policy outcomes and a politics in which issues are chronically framed in 'us–them' terms. These tendencies create difficulties even where ethnic divisions are not a factor, as in St Kitts and Nevis, turning minor issues into major ones and making consensus a rarity. In places where territorial lines and ethno-national lines coincide, as in Bosnia-Herzegovina, these difficulties are compounded, and are compounded yet again when the two constituent units are in addition drastically unequal in population, wealth and territory, as would be the case in Cyprus.

Problems of asymmetry

The multidimensional asymmetry of the two Cypriot communities is one of the underlying reasons why so many past efforts to negotiate a federal settlement have failed. Outnumbered by at least three to one, Turkish Cypriots are apprehensive about the prospect of living in a common state with Greek Cypriots. While federation would leave them in control of their local affairs, as determined by the constitution, there is no escaping the fact that in the country as a whole the Turkish Cypriots would be a minority. And as in other federations, non-constitutional factors, such as the economic power of the majority population, are likely to be at least as important a determinant of majority–minority relations as anything written in the constitution. Greek Cypriots have demographic anxieties as well, though of a different kind. From their majority perspective, being long accustomed to majority rule in the operation of their own political system, any central government of the federation that does not recognise the majority's right to rule is inherently undemocratic – which makes dual-majority and minority veto provisions (such as those proposed in the Annan Plan) unacceptable in principle. Put simply, majorities and minorities think differently about federation and have understandably different goals and priorities.

The very large disparities in income and wealth between the two communities present no less of a challenge, although these have not been widely discussed in the public domain. Greek Cypriots' incomes are on average roughly double those of Turkish Cypriots and there is no reason to suppose that disparities in individual wealth and access to investment capital are not equally great. Cumulatively, given their vastly greater number, the Greek Cypriot financial advantage is potentially overwhelming. Without effective restrictions on the flow of money, on the ownership of property and on residency, Turkish Cypriots would be at risk of the richer Greek Cypriots buying up their properties and other assets and so fundamentally altering the character of nominally Turkish Cypriot areas. This is why the Annan Plan put strict limits on how many Greek Cypriots would be allowed to purchase properties and reside in the envisaged Turkish Cypriot state. Such restrictions, however, would deprive Greek Cypriot investors of what many regard as their legal right – and they have on their side EU rules that prohibit restrictions on the free movement of people and capital. Exemptions ('derogations') to those rules could be granted by the EU, but these would likely be time-limited rather than permanent, and if so could only delay the inevitable.

At the governmental level, assuming that each of the constituent states would be responsible for the same competencies, the basic asymmetry of the two states would soon become apparent. The government of the Greek Cypriot state, by taxing its more numerous and more affluent citizenry, would have the fiscal resources to provide comprehensive public services of a high standard. The Turkish Cypriot state, even with a smaller population to serve, would have much less fiscal capacity because its per capita tax revenues would be much lower – which would mean, inevitably, poorer and probably fewer public services. And if the government of the Turkish Cypriot state tried to make up the shortfall by imposing substantially higher rates of taxation on its citizens, it would create yet another disparity and could even reduce total revenue by encouraging a shift of economic activity to the Greek Cypriot state. In a federation, member states are not only partners, they are also competitors.

How then might the wide disparity in fiscal capacity be addressed? Other federations employ various forms of fiscal transfers that require the richer states to pay into a centrally administered fund from which transfers are then made to the poorer states. These transfers, however, are a common source of inter-regional friction even in multiple-member federations where the lists of contributing and withdrawing states can vary over time. In an asymmetrical two-unit federation, where every transfer must go straight from one community to the other – 'from Greek Cypriot pockets to Turkish Cypriot pockets' (at least for the foreseeable future) – they may be so politically contentious as to be practically impossible. Almost as contentious is the issue of allocating fiscal responsibility for the costs of the central government. The way the Annan Plan proposed to deal with this issue was rejected by Greek Cypriot opponents of the plan on the grounds that Greek Cypriot taxpayers would be stuck with the lion's share of the costs. Unfortunately, there is no practical remedy: to assign costs equally would impose an impossible fiscal burden on the Turkish Cypriots.

Constitutional and political obstacles

Apart from fiscal arrangements, there are constitutional and political arrangements that are essential to the successful operation of a federal system but are exceedingly difficult to organise and operate when there are only two constituent states. To take one of many possible examples, federations tend to be prolific generators of inter-governmental legal disputes that require adjudication, in the last resort by a Supreme (or Constitutional) Court. In a multi-member federation judges are generally drawn from several states, thus diffusing responsibility and making it possible for particular cases to be decided by judges whose home states are not party to the case in question. But in a two-member federation judges must be drawn from one state or the other and hence must rule on cases involving their home states, which leaves them open to charges of partiality and conflict of interest. The Annan Plan proposal was to have foreign judges appointed who presumably could cast the deciding vote whenever the Greek and Turkish Cypriot judges were deadlocked – a suggestion that provoked predictable outrage, particularly on the Greek Cypriot side, where opponents of the Plan denounced it as insulting and an intolerable interference with national sovereignty. Outrage, however, was not matched by credible suggestions as to how an impartial court might be established.

A second example may be found in the workings of the democratic political process. In all federations party systems play a vital role in that process; yet the manner in which they are structured is for the most part not something that can be constitutionally determined but must be allowed to develop freely. If the same or closely related parties compete for office and power in the central government and all or most states, this will normally have an integrating effect on the federation as a whole. In ethnically divided federations, such parties can provide valuable cross-communal links and sites for cross-communal accommodation. They may even be the main glue holding the federation together. But if parties develop that are singularly based in their respective states the effect on the federation will be mainly negative and disintegrative. One of the principal factors that has reduced the Belgian federation to a condition of chronic deadlock is the splitting of its major political parties into separate Flemish and Walloon parties that have no need to seek support outside their own ethno-linguistic bailiwicks. In Bosnia-Herzegovina, Serb, Bosniak and Croat political exclusivity has given rise to parties and leaders whose intransigence and mutual animosities have made constitutional power-sharing unworkable. The political dynamic of two-member federations leans relentlessly towards division, and there is no reason to think that same dynamic would not also apply in Cyprus.

In all federations there is a problem of constitutional obsolescence that must be dealt with. In spite of the inordinate amount of time and effort that often goes into the writing of federal constitutions, they quickly become obsolete and need to be adapted to changing circumstances through formal amendment, judicial interpretation or some other means. The process of constitutional change, however, is always difficult and frequently divisive. In a multi-member federation, the approach is generally to seek a broad consensus among the central government, the constituent states and the public at large, and even then some states and a significant portion of the public may be left out. But if most states and most citizens are behind a change, its legitimacy is difficult to dispute and controversy tends to die down. In a two-member federation, particularly one where even a seemingly minor change can upset a delicate ethnic balance, the process of constitutional change is considerably more difficult to manage successfully. And a proposed change that pits one state against another – which is hard to avoid when there are only two – is especially fraught with difficulty. For Cyprus, the Annan Plan's remedy was to make those parts of the constitution dealing with the structure of government completely unamendable and to require dual majorities for other, presumably less important, matters. On the question of how the proposed federation would adapt its system of government to meet the challenges of a changing world, it was discreetly silent.

Finally, in every federation there are issues of entry and exit, and in Cyprus these are matters of crucial significance. Entering into a federal union is a momentous step for any community and even after careful study and debate it remains largely 'a leap in the dark'. Is a razor-thin majority in a referendum ('50 per cent plus one') an adequate basis for entry? Or, to put it another way, what are the prospects of creating a stable, well-functioning, democratic federation – one that can work effectively to the benefit of all its citizens – when one or both of the communities are deeply and evenly divided over the issue? And the question of exit from a failed federation is no less acute. Is there to be a peaceful and orderly process of exit agreed in advance, such as holding a referendum at some future date on the possible dissolution of the union with a specified majority threshold that must be reached, as was the case in Montenegro's union with Serbia? Or is the federation to be declared 'indissoluble', as the Annan Plan proposed – which would make an illegal unilateral declaration of independence followed by secession the only means of escape, with all its attendant risks? There are no clear answers, unfortunately: to provide for legal exit could be tantamount to encouraging it, while not to provide for it could be seen as encouraging an illegal and possibly violent break-up. What has been made abundantly clear, by both Greek and Turkish Cypriots, is that federation is not their preferred system of government, and if they are somehow persuaded to enter into a federal union they will do so with reluctance and against the wishes of many in their respective communities. A poll conducted among Greek and Turkish Cypriots in 2010 confirmed what previous surveys have also found: that large majorities in both communities prefer other, non-federal options. Among Greek Cypriots, 92 per cent favoured a unitary state while among Turkish Cypriots 90 per cent favoured two separate states. It is of course the hope of those who promote federation and draft elaborate constitutions that it will all work out in the end. But if it does not, the conditions for an orderly exit are far too important to be left in abeyance.

Conclusion

Given the absence of a genuine popular desire for federation, and the fact that the only model on offer – a bizonal, bicommunal federation – is arguably the most failure-prone of all the many varieties of federation, it might seem prudent to try a different approach, such as proceeding by a series of steps to build a closer working relationship between the existing Greek Cypriot and Turkish Cypriot states, before attempting to negotiate a full-fledged federal agreement. However, such an approach would require direct collaboration between the Turkish Cypriot and Greek Cypriot governments, which is something the latter adamantly rejects on the grounds that it would confer legitimacy on the 'illegal Turkish invasion' and the internationally unrecognised 'Turkish Cypriot puppet state'. Hence small steps are as difficult to take as large ones.

The long-term failure to reach any kind of negotiated settlement in Cyprus raises questions about whether there are sufficient incentives to motivate either community to abandon its respective state for the uncertainty of a type of federal union that elsewhere has proven to be fundamentally problematical, if not utterly unworkable. The Republic of Cyprus, controlled solely by Greek Cypriots since 1963, is a success story on many counts. While not without problems, it is prosperous, democratic and internationally recognised. Its people would need to be given a very strong reason why they should trade all this for a dubious federal union with the Turkish Cypriots. The latter appeared to be more willing to gamble on such a union when they voted 'yes' in the 2004 referendum on the Annan Plan. However, their support was more apparent than real, for it had less to do with federal union as such than with the enticing prospect of becoming prosperous EU citizens and the ending of their international isolation. Since then, however, the EU has lost much of its lustre as a bastion of financial stability and land of economic opportunity, and its failure to deliver on promised financial and trade assistance (made in the heat of the referendum campaign to encourage Turkish Cypriots to vote 'yes') has been disillusioning. Meanwhile Turkey, which has enjoyed a decade of high economic growth and democratic progress, continues to provide the TRNC with financial aid and security. The Turkish Cypriots remain economically disadvantaged by their lack of international recognition, but the political and civil society institutions that they have created function well and democratically, not unlike those in Greek Cyprus. They too will need to be given a stronger reason than the prospect of a bizonal, bicommunal federation before they give up their familiar and valued institutions.

References and recommended reading

Bahcheli, Tozun and Sid Noel, 'Imposed and proposed federations: issues of self-determination and constitutional design in Bosnia-Herzegovina, Cyprus, Sri Lanka and Iraq', *Cyprus Review* 17/1 (2005), pp. 13–36.

—— and Sid Noel, 'Power sharing for Cyprus (again)? European Union accession and the prospects for reunification', in Sid Noel (ed.), *From Power Sharing to Democracy: Post-conflict Institutions in Ethnically Divided Societies* (Kingston and Montreal: McGill-Queen's University Press, 2005).

De Winter, Lieven and Pierre Baudewyns, 'Belgium: towards the breakdown of a nation-state in the heart of Europe?', in John Coakley (ed.), *Pathways from Ethnic Conflict: Institutional Redesign in Divided Societies* (London and New York: Routledge, 2010).

Duchacek, Ivo, 'Dyadic federations and confederations', *Publius: The Journal of Federalism* 18/2 (1988), pp. 5–31.

Franck, Thomas M. et al., *Why Federations Fail: An Inquiry into the Requisites for Successful Federalism* (New York: New York University Press, 1968).

Milne, R.S., *Politics in Ethnically Bi-polar States: Guyana, Malaysia, Fiji* (Vancouver: University of British Columbia Press, 1981).

Wheare, K.C., *Federal Government*, 3rd edn (London and New York: Oxford University Press, 1953).

6

The Party Politics of the Problem

GIORGOS CHARALAMBOUS

It seems paradoxical to many outside observers and diplomats that attempts to resolve the 'Cyprus Problem', especially the Annan Plan, have failed even though the two main Greek Cypriot political parties are officially in favour of a solution and have consistently stressed their willingness to compromise in discussion with the Turkish Cypriots. This is the subject I would like to explore in this chapter, not because it is more significant (causally, or otherwise) than other factors, but because few understand the significance of party politics, or lack thereof, in efforts to resolve the issue. For example, in a wider constellation of recent developments, there has been a total absence of substantive focus on parties in discussions about the Cyprus Problem. By this I do not meant that the normative aspects of their ideologies have not been studied. In fact, they have been the object of extensive (albeit also polemical) reflection. Rather, very little attention has been paid to their political behaviour, their relations with society and the institutional and the boundaries of the party-system that sees them frequently operating within their own closed spheres of activity.

Moreover, party behaviour in the context of the Cyprus Problem has tended to be a rather esoteric issue. It belongs firmly within the 'infamous' local dimension of ethnic division; a dimension which has been marginalised and overshadowed in dominant political debate about, and in, the island. Indeed, it has often been rather pushed into the background of UN rhetoric on the issue. (Interestingly, one could argue that the distinction between the local and external dimensions of the Cyprus Problem – and ethnic conflicts at large – can be useful in telling us what the Cypriots can or cannot do for themselves.) This is not to say that all the different aspects of ethnic conflict matter to the same extent. Some factors are more important than others; rather in the same way that some aspects of the problem are more easily solved, in terms of negotiation efforts, than other aspects. However, if we accept that Cypriot parties embody the significance of veto players in resolution attempts, not least of all because the Cypriot social and political arena is a deeply 'partitocratic' one, then briefly examining them can illuminate larger questions about the domestic elements of the Cyprus Problem and thus help refocus attention on things that can be changed, rather than ones that cannot. After all, the viability of any solution will largely depend on what happens domestically at the bicommunal level *before* the agreement is reached and ratified.

The power of history

Contrary to the arguments put forward by some specialists on the Cyprus Problem, the Greek Cypriot political parties are not the main cause of nationalism on the island. Instead, they merely reflect wider views. And neither is nationalism in Cyprus a phenomenon beginning or ending at the level of the parties. Nationalism flourished at a time when there was no party system in Cyprus and crystallised politically during the 1940s, when the ethnic social cleavage found political expression in the competing forces of AKEL (Progressive Party for the Working People – the Cyprus Communist Party), on the one hand, and the initially divided and unorganised right, on the other hand. Meanwhile, the Church has also been extremely influential. Its immense economic power – largely owing to the Church's financial empowerment during Ottoman rule and the transition to British colonialism – has been widely used either to divert attention from the perils of a de jure partition or to sustain the widespread social acceptance of policies that are essentially hostile towards reunification. It is here that Cypriot parties enter the picture. Growing out of social tensions and divisions revolving around both economic left-right issues and ethnic ones, political parties have inevitably carried with them ideological traits and political outlooks that bear the marks of the past, and thus also those of nationalism as a dominant ideological trait on the island. Shaking it off cannot be accomplished through their interaction with each other and their supporters in the electoral arena. On the contrary, such interaction only reinforces their existing identities and strategies.

Even AKEL's rejection of the Annan Plan, for example, can be understood within the context of its anti-imperialist identity that is widely ingrained among the party's social milieu. It is this same identity that renders the party patriotic in a sense that international peace alliances are approached as inherently biased to Turkey's benefit. A recent development that bears out such behaviour is the party's repeated rejection of an enlarged international conference, where Cyprus would participate alongside the other key players of the Cyprus Problem with the ultimate intention of solving the problem through an arbitrated give and take process. Consequently, AKEL has popularised among its members and followers the conviction that if the Greek Cypriots feel unready to concede certain things for the sake of a solution, then their desire should be respected above all, even if this means recurring stalemates.

Similarly, DISY's (Democratic Rally) internal divisions between liberals and nationalists reflect disagreements at the societal level that existed within the right since the 1940s; a time when there was no unified party. The schemes and chameleon-like behaviour of the right's leadership in the past two decades, which shifts speedily between appearing flexible on the hot issues of the Cyprus Problem negotiations and playing the nationalist card, echoes its entrapment within a wide constituency that includes both ultra nationalist, anti-communists on the one hand and Western educated open-minded liberals with a post-materialist orientation and a post-modern respect for human rights on the other. EDEK's (Movement of Social Democrats) intransigent stance can be explained to a great extent by the influence that the so called 'Third World socialism' had on its leadership and activists, and the composition of the party's electorate that was diverse from the beginning, spanning left and right. DIKO's (Democratic Party) approach, which is again deeply rejectionist, can be traced to its relations with, and the social conservatism expressed by, the ethnarchy.

The questions that arise from this are, I would argue, uncomfortable to answer. Can the parties of the centre, which are not independent from the Church, simply avoid the latter's influences and (perhaps) reconsider their course on the Cyprus Problem? Can the main party of the left, which has been more patriotic than anti-nationalist since its birth, completely avoid sliding into the traps of the anti-imperialist ideology that its social milieu has been so used to? Can the right risk alienating a core part of its constituency by trying sincerely to build solid bridges with the Turkish Cypriots? Can any party, right, left or centre, easily ward off Cypriot structural undercurrents and remain unaffected by the dominant social discourse of self-victimisation, selective amnesia and national liberation permeating the mind of the common person? All four questions can be answered with a 'no'. Path dependency should not be forgotten when examining the Cyprus Problem with reference to political parties. The power of history is a tremendous obstacle to ethnic conflict resolution attempts, especially when it is strongly institutionalised inside political parties and within the party system as a whole.

Furthermore, the socio-demographic changes of the Cypriot electorate have not led to political realignment or substantive independent thinking, although abstention rates have been climbing recently. Unlike in many other European countries, parties in Cyprus have inculcated in their followers a relatively strong group identity, which has not really worn away despite important changes in Cypriot social structure. Neither increased education nor shifts in occupational patterns have altered the partisan orientation of the Cypriot electorate. This is due to a range of factors that cannot be 'fixed' from the outside: institutional constraints, in the form of an electoral system that favours established parties; the ability of parties to adapt by incorporating new issues into their agenda and altering the particular emphasis they place on certain matters; well-developed patronage networks exerting control over the distribution of public resources; the prevalence of family-based voting; and strong organisational resources, provided by a range of ancillary organisations operating to the benefit of their parties, and feeding largely on the absence of strict regulations governing party funding. The fact that a post-materialist rubric has not yet emerged – the Green Party's extensive focus on the Cyprus Problem and its nationalist stance attest to this – is a further obstacle to the solidification of individual level ideological orientations that transcend the main cleavages, and are more open to bi-partisan or supra-partisan initiatives.

But what about reciprocity?

On other hand, parties are not simply products of cleavages or prisoners of their past. They are also active agents, contributing either to the perpetuation of division within society or to its gradual disappearance. Parties are affected by social divisions but they also mould the latter into shape, giving them an ideological and normative logic upon which to feed. They are composed of opinion leaders and influential politicians who have an ideological reach beyond their own constituencies; they contest elections strategically, shaping the choices available to the electorate; they are tied to the state and interact daily with its bureaucracy, dispensing favours in exchange for votes and thereby nurturing 'the social politics of convenience' that might be endangered through a consociational solution. In all, the relationship between parties and their history is a reciprocal one. Parties act in a manner that is consistent with their historical legacies, but they also have the capacity to manoeuvre around these legacies so as to satisfy short-term interests and respond to new social and political developments.

One of the most prominent features of Cypriot party politics is the one which is also systemic at the party system level: bipolarism – the deep social, ideological and political division between right and left. This has resulted in some of the lowest levels of electoral volatility in Europe. As already suggested, bipolarism in Cyprus is largely historically determined; the product of cleavages with firm roots in the 1940s. However, the very choices of political parties on given political situations, either related or unrelated to the Cyprus Problem, add a top-down dimension to the issue. The parties cultivate bipolarism. They contribute not merely to the consolidation of partisan identities and the passing of these identities down from generation to generation, but also to the utter vilification of those pro-solution sections of the opposite camp with which they would have to forge temporary alliances in order to shift public opinion towards a solution. Bipolarism prevents any kind of cooperation between the pro-solution elements of each pole as this would translate into shaking the hand of the eternal enemy in left-right terms.

Are there any common characteristics among the various ways in which Cypriot parties mobilise in response to new developments? A strategy of making decisions in accordance with historical and political lines of division, and not policy convergences, remains one of the chief traits of party strategy in Cyprus and is the particular strategy employed by AKEL. Most notably, in 2004, AKEL explicitly refused any cooperation or joint action with the liberal wing of

DISY, then still under the leadership of Glafkos Clerides. Its stance can be attributed to a decades-long line (reinforced after the party's bad results in the 1985 parliamentary elections, when this line was temporarily and partially interrupted) of absolutely no common initiatives with the right. This is part of the reason why, for almost half a century, AKEL has identified the centre parties, DIKO and EDEK, as the progressive forces with which coalitions are permissible. It is one of the most important explanatory factors for AKEL's support of Tassos Papadopoulos between 2003 and 2007.

A similar rationale explains why what was initially seen as a historic opportunity to resolve the problem – the simultaneous presidency of Dimitris Christofias and Mehmet Ali Talat in the South and North side of the island, respectively – did not lead to any significant changes in regard to public opinion on the problem. Christofias was trying very hard to deflect the accusations of the opposition that he was compromising too much at the negotiation table. The whole organisational machinery of the parliamentary left was focused on his defence in the political sphere. At the same time, as AKEL immersed itself into the corridors of political and governmental power, the number and diversity of its bicommunal initiatives have been waning; although the PEO trade union (Pancyprian Federation of Labour), which is organically linked to the party, does continue to hold events and rallies in favour of reunification jointly with Turkish Cypriot trade unions. To a certain extent, the party's youth organisation, EDON (United Democratic Youth Organisation), has also been active. But these moves are not enough to counterbalance the negative effects of an economically commanding nationalism, if not reinforced by AKEL's full mobilisation potential. Since 2003, when the party officially entered government (initially with four ministers and then under the presidency of its own leader, Christofias), its presence in bicommunal and pro-rapprochement initiatives has been significantly smaller than before. As its office and bureaucratic obligations have naturally increased due to its relation with government during the past five years, the attention it has been paying to contributing towards a pro-reunification consciousness has decreased.

Additionally, AKEL has become increasingly fearful of supporting any kind of bicommunal initiatives not endorsed officially by the party itself. Whether the excuse is that these are funded by foreign money and should be approached with suspicion, or that extensive societal mobilisation will shift attention from Turkey's blame to the local level and thus endanger the official negotiations and undermine the coherence of the Cyprus government's official position in diplomatic circles, little has been done at the government or party level to educate citizens about the advantages and nature of a bizonal, bicommunal federation, and the benefits of fighting nationalism, or portraying solidarity with the Turkish Cypriots. We have now reached a point when AKEL's support of the Turkish Cypriots is limited to the political arena in the form of rhetoric, bi-partisan contact with the Turkish Cypriot CTP and congressional decisions. Much of this can be attributed to the presence of a pivot party – DIKO – and the left's (as well as the right's) response to its pivotal position. The two-round presidential election system pushes left and right to maintain a friendly attitude towards DIKO voters so that they can potentially attract them to their side in the second round of the election. Similarly, once government is formed, DIKO is needed for a majority inside parliament to be sustained, albeit informally. Beyond ideology then, left and right have an electoral incentive to downplay flexibility in their Cyprus Problem rhetoric, colour it with nationalist or patriotic discourse and focus solely on Turkish inflexibility, thus downplaying the local dimension of the problem.

Like all pivot parties, DIKO is devoid of any real ideology that has a truly centrist content. Alongside clientelistic practice and the division of the party into a left and a right wing, themselves changing in composition according to circumstances, DIKO's ideological nucleus is nationalism. In an otherwise deeply fragmented party body, a rejectionist stance on the Cyprus Problem has been the only enduring policy ingredient on which the whole party converges. Depending on internal dynamics that favour one of these wings or the other, and most importantly driven by the intent to share government office and in this way keep afloat in the absence of a solid ideological orientation, DIKO tilts towards either AKEL or DISY. Every time it enters government or forms a government with the support of another party, its main demand (beyond what the party itself conceives as its fair share in government ministries) is focused on a 'strict' Cyprus Problem policy. The fact that this demand is easily accepted by its potential partners only for DIKO to leave the government, or kick its partners out shortly afterwards, because this demand 'was not respected' is ample proof of the corporatist mentality that prevails in Cypriot electoral politics, whereby the spoils of power constitute the main negotiating axis between coalition partners during the phase of government formation. Since ideological differences can be bridged temporarily so that a government can be formed, then no real effort needs to be made for substantive discussion or real engagement with society on Cyprus Problem policy.

Conclusion

It is widely recognised that in ethnic conflicts, domestic dynamics often tend to work against resolution. In Cyprus, these domestic dynamics are intrinsically related to the political parties and the ways in which they compete with one another. Overall, it is perhaps pointless to expect that the parties will push society towards the realisation that a resolution of the Cyprus Problem is both feasible and desirable. This would not only entail compromise in terms of their identities, but also a seismic shift in their environment that would involve uprooting them from the island's historical experiences in the political sphere. The possibility of either of these two things happening soon is very small. It should therefore be emphasised that the issue at hand is not so much that political parties have failed to change wider public attitudes. Rather, it should be understood that their very way of trying to engage with public opinion was either all but non-existent or was so entrenched in their intellectual and organisational habitats that it was never likely to bear fruit. Rather, we should expect that if the Cyprus Problem is to be solved in the short to medium term, or at least that the local dimension of the problem is to be given more public attention, then it will primarily be forces outside the parties' spheres of influence, or forces that are at least only partly dependent on the parties, that are likely to set off the chain of events leading towards a settlement.

No foreign interventions, diplomatic missions or rounds of negotiation can directly influence the parties' trajectories or their place within their broader environment. As domestic actors, they are affected mostly by their immediate surroundings and have strong identities that were shaped by events during their formative years. Put differently, political parties play on their own field when responding to external developments, rather than drawing on external influences to shape the political milieu on the island. From this perspective, the greater the encouragement of citizens (and even parties) to engage with the peace movement by those interested in resolving the problem, the greater the chances that strategic and historically entrenched political behaviours that remain the conflict frozen in time will gradually wither away, and allow the possibility for shifts in public opinion as well as in the outlooks of the parties themselves. Gradual, steady, but carefully crafted pressure that focuses on the necessity of bicommunal contact can only be for the best.

References and recommended reading

Charalambous, Giorgos, 'The February 2008 Presidential Election in the Republic of Cyprus: the context, dynamics and outcome in perspective', *The Cyprus Review* 21/1 (2009), pp. 97–122.

——, 'AKEL: A socio political profile of Cypriot Communism', in Nicos Trimikliniotis and Umut Bozkurt (eds), *Beyond a Divided Cyprus: A State and Society in Transformation* (Basingstoke: Palgrave Macmillan, 2012).

Christophorou, Christoforos, 'The evolution of Greek Cypriot party politics', in James Ker-Lindsay and Hubert Faustmann (eds), *The Government and Politics of Cyprus* (Oxford: Peter Lang, 2009).

Heraclides, Alexis, 'The Cyprus Gordian Knot: an intractable ethnic conflict', *Nationalism and Ethnic Conflict* 17/2 (2011), pp. 117–39.

Protopapas, Vassilis, 'The rise of a bi-polar party system, municipal elections 1940–1955', in Hubert Faustmann and Nicos Peristianis (eds), *Britain in Cyprus: Colonialism and Post-Colonialism 1878–2006* (Mannheim: Bibliopolis, 2006).

7

The Prospects of a Federal Settlement

ODYSSEAS CHRISTOU

The prospect of resolution of the Cyprus dispute on the basis of a bizonal, bicommunal federation has long been regarded as the most promising option for the Greek and Turkish Cypriot communities. It has formed the basis for negotiations since the 1970s and has been especially advocated by actors external to the conflict, including the United Nations, which has served as the primary mediating actor to the conflict. Yet, a historical tracing of the ways in which this concept of solution has been treated within each community reveals perplexing inconsistencies on both sides, partly derived from historically persistent preferences and partly because of the evolution of the dispute over the years.

Intercommunal negotiations and interpretations of federalism

The genesis of the bizonal, bicommunal federation (BBF) approach was the set of guidelines in the High Level Agreement between Makarios and Denktash in February 1977 under UN auspices, which called for an independent, non-aligned, bicommunal federal republic with territorial administration for each community. However, protracted negotiations ever since have failed to produce the necessary political convergence at the elite level that would harmonise the expectations of the two communities as to the specific form of such a solution. The various institutional components of constitutional arrangements that fulfil those criteria have been discussed for many years; yet the failure of the negotiation process can be more easily understood in terms of the ultimate goals of each community. Throughout this interminable process, one fact has remained constant: BBF has never been the highest in the rank ordering of preferences for either of the two communities. Greek Cypriots have traditionally favoured the unconditional return to the 1960 Constitution, which is characterised in the community as a unitary state – an inaccurate characterisation given the consociational configuration of that state, which contravened many of the conventions of an archetypical unitary state. On the other hand, Turkish Cypriots – having achieved increasing levels of self-determination since the breakdown of constitutional order in 1964, culminating with the unilateral declaration of the Turkish Republic of Northern Cyprus two decades later – have regarded BBF as less favourable than partition and the creation of two independent states on the island. Yet this rank ordering presents a perennial opportunity for reconciliation, assuming that the two communities are able to bear the inevitable intracommunal political cost that comes with rapprochement and compromise. The potential comes in the form of the realisation that the second-best option for each community – which is exactly what BBF is – may be the best, if not the only viable, option for both.

Major divergences have persisted in the interpretation of the constitutional specification of power sharing in the event of a solution to the conflict in the form of BBF. Since there is a wide range of power-sharing mechanisms that could potentially be implemented, the two communities tend to favour forms that best approximate their first preferences: a unitary state for Greek Cypriots and a two-state solution for Turkish Cypriots. Greek Cypriots would be more likely to agree to a unified federal Cyprus, where most power is reserved to the central government. Such a model is likely to exhibit a high degree of centripetalism in institutional design, whereby incentives would be provided for politicians to transcend ethnic lines in order to attract votes, leading to the creation of aggregated, integrationalist political forces in the form of parties and/or coalitions. Yet even though official support for BBF has been upheld since the 1970s, opposition to such a solution is strong and, if anything, on the rise among the Greek Cypriot community; aided and abetted by several influential elements such as the Orthodox Church, as well as increasing nationalist pronouncements by traditionally centrist political parties. In fact, the trend in recent years has been a pronounced polarisation over BBF together with an accompanying politicisation of the issue. This is largely aimed at delegitimising BBF as a viable option. Such has been the enduring legacy of the 2004 Annan Plan that it is difficult to see how the trend can be reversed when the rejection of the Plan has been elevated to an act of heroism among the centre and centre-right parts of the Greek Cypriot political spectrum. The election of Nicos Anastassiades of DISY (the right-wing party which supported the Annan Plan) to the presidency in February 2013 raised hopes for a more conciliatory approach, but these were almost immediately dashed by the ongoing banking and financial crisis, which will inevitably be prioritised over the negotiation process.

On the other hand, Turkish Cypriots would tend to favour decentralisation of power, even to the degree where the resulting unified state exhibits confederal traits. For the Turkish Cypriot community the maintenance of a certain threshold level of autonomy is paramount, due to its accordant sense of security. The institutional distinction between federal and confederated systems is beyond the scope of this piece, but it should be noted that in the dominant discourse on Cyprus, the term confederation is used with generality and imprecision to refer to a federal arrangement with a high degree of decentralisation and constituent state-level autonomy in decision-making processes. The complex sovereign implications of a true confederated approach are typically absent from the political debate.

The post-Annan Plan negotiating framework

This polarisation is a recurring trend that reveals much about the inherent ambivalence in the bargaining dynamics between the two communities: it is very easy for political elites on both sides to fall back on intransigent nationalist rhetoric that stands in direct opposition to the official status of negotiations, since the political cost of bringing the negotiations to a standstill is negligible. In fact, the opportunity cost of not playing the nationalist card may be realised in the form of ethnic outbidding by political opponents within each community. Thus, while the technicalities of the negotiation process deal with specific aspects of BBF, the rhetoric on both sides regresses to the politically expedient themes of maximalism, thereby reinforcing a zero-sum characterisation of the process that is by now deeply ingrained in the sociopolitical psyche of each community. At the same time, the contradictory attitudes of the political elites of both communities contribute to the lack of both inter- and intra-communal trust.

The characterisation of the framework of interaction between the two communities has been fundamentally altered by the precedent of the Annan Plan through the process of decision making via dual and simultaneous referenda. Moving the decision-making calculus from the elite-level bicommunal negotiations that had been the norm since 1977 to the community-level implementation through the use of referenda entails that the situation cannot be analytically explained through the preferences of elite-level actors; rather, the preferences of the two communities have to be accurately reflected in a revised framework if it is to stand any chance of being accepted. Thus, while the process is still elite-driven in the negotiating stages between the communities, ultimately it is the citizens who will be making the decision to cooperate via the referendum process.

The impact of the Annan Plan on the perceptions of federal arrangements by the two communities cannot be overstated. As an actual implementation of the BBF model, the proposed plan came to define, whether realistically or not, possible future iterations in the minds of all Cypriots. Thus, while the Annan Plan was not binding and subsequent attempts need not be path dependent, the expectations of any such attempts in both communities will necessarily be framed with the Annan Plan as a reference point. Numerous studies since 2004 have attempted to explain the failed outcome of the Annan initiative. Quite simply, the question was: why did the Greek Cypriots reject BBF while the Turkish Cypriots endorsed it? There is no shortage of explanations at various analytical levels. However, at the community level the answer is simple: the Annan Plan did not provide sufficient incentives to the Greek Cypriots to forgo the alternative of unilateral accession to the European Union, since unification of the island was not set as a precondition to accession. The fundamental problem in the bargaining structure between the two communities remains: neither side can realistically expect to bring about their most desired outcome through negotiation – a unitary state for Greek Cypriots and a two-state solution for Turkish Cypriots – simply because the other side would never agree to such a development. Therefore, why do the two sides not simply agree to their second-best alternative, which is BBF? What would it take for Greek Cypriots to agree to a revised framework, given that they were the ones to reject the previous one?

Part of the answer lies in Greek Cypriot opposition to specific power-sharing arrangements under negotiation, such as a presidency that rotates between the two communities. Yet, this is not a sufficient explanation. In other words, tweaking the elements of a comprehensive settlement is not enough to shift the negotiations from the current stalemate. A reevaluation of the incentive process illustrates that not much has changed for the Greek Cypriots: the lack of progress is not sufficiently costly to induce cooperation, as was the expectation of some analysts in the wake of the Annan Plan failure, through the expected chastisement of Greek Cypriots and reward of the Turkish Cypriots by the international community. The recent development of the discovery of hydrocarbon deposits in the Exclusive Economic Zone of the Republic of Cyprus has been hailed as a facilitating condition that can bear fruit in renewed negotiations. However, it may simply be another example of the application of the same logic: if Greek Cypriots can unilaterally gain the benefits of hydrocarbon exploitation, why would they acquiesce to sharing them? It is possible, of course, for Turkey, and possibly the international community, to compel Greek Cypriots to cooperate, but this would only reinforce the growing perception among the community that Turkey – rather than the Turkish Cypriot community – is their actual counterpart in the management of the conflict. The situation is further complicated by the ongoing economic crisis, which is likely to fuel the sense of isolation and powerlessness in the Greek Cypriot community, thus pushing them further away from the negotiating table.

The other possible outcome at any given stage of the bargaining process is the continuation of the status quo, which has typically been the outcome of elite-level stalling due to a lack of urgency to make real progress in the process. However, recent research by the Cyprus 2015 Initiative illustrates that the possibility of indefinite perpetuation of the status quo – similar to the unresolved situation between the Republic of China in Taiwan and mainland China – has been slowly gaining ground as the preferred 'solution' to the conflict within both communities. If the status quo becomes preferable to BBF and thereby the second-best alternative to the unattainable first options of the two communities, a resolution to the conflict through any negotiated settlement will seem increasingly unlikely. In the event of a mutual rejection of a future BBF-based proposal, it is likely that the international community will divest itself of the Cyprus imbroglio due to a lack of sufficient political will on the part of both communities. The situation in Cyprus has exhibited a number of windows of opportunity over the years; but if there is no political will for compromise either at the political elite or at the communal level, then all windows may close for good.

A trizonal, bicommunal federation as an alternative approach

Given the entrenchment of the BBF discourse, neither its usage in the 2004 Annan Plan nor the longevity of the negotiation process the consideration of alternative approaches seem very probable in the case of Cyprus. However, such an approach could yield heretofore disregarded potential benefits in terms of post-solution normalisation of relations between the two communities. The approach proposed in this chapter is the creation of a trizonal, bicommunal federation (TBF), which is an improvement over the BBF model in various ways. The TBF model would be implemented through the creation of an additional zone centred on the capital Nicosia; in this way, this region would be analogous to a federal or capital district, which is a common feature of federal systems worldwide.

This approach would contribute towards the development of trust between the two communities through the demonstration of peaceful coexistence as well as the facilitation of the federal system in various ways. First of all, such a system would reunite the divided capital of Nicosia, which would remain divided under a BBF arrangement. Beyond the symbolic gesture of tearing down the Green Line, which has persisted since the 1960s, creating a united capital city would also benefit the federal structure in terms of administrative efficiency. Additionally, and more significantly, this arrangement would contribute towards rapprochement between the two communities. Given the reinforcing nature of cleavages between Greek Cypriots and Turkish Cypriots – ethnicity, language and religion – the prevalence of the zero-sum characterisation of the bargaining structure is easy to justify analytically. The implementation of a BBF system would entrench this mutually exclusive dichotomy in institutional arrangements, thus begging the question: where would each community find the source of trust in the other in order to develop a common identity down the road? The creation of a federal district could provide an answer to that question by creating an area where existing bicommunalist tendencies are allowed to flourish. Given the linguistic barrier to communication – especially since knowledge of each other's language is remarkably low and increasingly on the decline since the separation of the communities – it is to be expected that in a unified Cyprus, English would be elevated to a lingua franca, which would not be encouraged by a bizonal arrangement wherein each side would perceive its own mother tongue as the only legitimate means of communication. Unfortunately, such a proposal is unlikely to find much support among the political elite of the two communities since it contains the potential to dilute political control over their respective communities and lead to unpredictable developments.

Conclusion

Repeated studies of public opinion of both communities reveal that a pervasive and mutual sense of mistrust is a sufficient explanatory variable for the lack of development; not only on the general level, but also in terms of the specific attributes of power sharing. This sentiment is exhibited at the level of the political elite as well as throughout each community. This is an environment susceptible to an infinite regress of stagnation. Trust is necessary for political accommodation and yet, in the absence of such accommodation, it is difficult to develop. The remedy suggested for this predicament has been the implementation of confidence-building measures that will illustrate in practice the willingness to cooperate in mutually beneficial ways. Nevertheless, initiatives to implement such measures – for instance proposals for the opening of the Varosha region, of which there have been many – typically falter. The reason for this recurrent failure is quite simple: neither side is willing to relinquish long-term bargaining chips for a short-term gain such as an increased perception of credibility in the eyes of the other side. Such qualitative benefits are difficult to rationalise within their respective communities, and may even carry political cost if concessions are characterised as appeasement. The way forward is through the disaggregation of the 'Cyprus Problem' into a variety of tangible, tractable issues, some of which bear little political cost to either community. For example, cooperation on cultural, economic or educational issues need not be politicised, and can take place even in the absence of political convergence at the elite level, through the involvement of a variety of previously unengaged stakeholders. Such an approach can foster grassroots organisational cooperation with the participation of new actors and a strengthening of the existing civil society structure that has flourished on both sides of the divide in recent years, but has found it difficult to shape the hearts and minds of Cypriot society at large. If sufficient levels of social and political trust are not cultivated in the two communities through such measures, any amount of constitutional engineering – be it in the form of BBF or otherwise – is unlikely to yield a favourable outcome.

References and recommended reading

Bahcheli, Tozun, 'Searching for a Cyprus settlement: considering options for creating a federation, a confederation, or two independent states', *Publius* 30/1 (2000), pp. 203–16.

Cyprus 2015, *Solving the Cyprus Problem: Hopes and Fears* (Nicosia: Interpeace and Cyprus 2015 Initiative, 2011).

Fisher, Ronald J., 'Cyprus: the failure of mediation and the escalation of an identity-based conflict to an adversarial impasse', *Journal of Peace Research* 38/3 (2001), pp. 307–26.

Hadjipavlou-Trigeorgis, Maria and Lenos Trigeorgis, 'Cyprus: an evolutionary approach to conflict resolution', *The Journal of Conflict Resolution* 37/2 (1993), pp. 340–60.

Richmond, Oliver P., 'Ethno-nationalism, sovereignty and negotiating positions in the Cyprus conflict: obstacles to a settlement', *Middle Eastern Studies* 35/3 (1999), pp. 42–63.

Tocci, Nathalie, *The 'Cyprus Question': Reshaping Community Identities and Elite Interests within a Wider European Framework*, CEPS Working Document No. 154, September 2000.

8

A Cypriot's Problem

COSTAS M. CONSTANTINOU

What's our problem? What's in a problem?

There is an old joke that participants at Cyprus conflict seminars have probably heard more than once. It pokes fun at a peculiar Cypriot fixation, still highly topical, and goes like this:

> Three men are sentenced to death in a faraway country: an Englishman, a Frenchman and a Cypriot. On the day of their execution they are asked to name their last wish. The Englishman asks for a cigar; the Frenchman for a glass of wine. The Cypriot asks to be granted a last opportunity to talk to the execution squad about the Cyprus Problem. On hearing this, the Frenchman and the Englishman change their last wish and beg to be shot before the Cypriot starts talking.

We know, at least since Sigmund Freud's seminal work, that a joke is never just a laughing matter. It can have a social function, publicly releasing repressed ideas and feelings that often remain unconscious or unstated. To that extent, psychoanalysis combined with hermeneutics can account for the euphoria and offer insight to some participants and not others. Why and how is a joke funny or not funny? What ways of life (and what ways of death, as in the joke above) does it consciously or unconsciously ridicule or celebrate? And for our purposes in this short chapter, how can a joke inform the current 'problem' in Cyprus, which is not just political but psychological?

Those who find this joke funny seem to delight at the exposure of a long-established Cypriot obsession with debating the Cyprus Problem ad infinitum (more than 40 or 50 years depending on when one thinks it started); not just negotiating locally but pestering unconcerned foreigners at every opportunity, seeking to educate those who don't seem to 'get it' after all these years. They laugh at the discreet charm of the Cypriot, his total lack of measure or sense of proper time and place for advocating his rights and explaining his suffering. And they laugh at the narcissistic pleasure the Cypriot seems to take in being didactic about his problem, so much so that he appears oblivious of his other real problem, i.e. that his life is soon to reach an abrupt end.

Those who don't find this joke funny don't necessarily lack a sense of humour. Some, especially Cypriots who may also feel the urge to talk and lecture others about 'the problem', can sympathise with the man's commitment to publicise his small country's big problem. They see in his behaviour at most a tragic irony, not a matter to be derided. Others may read in the joke (not unjustifiably) elements of colonial humour, the civiliser's so-called burden with the native's problem, even after the latter's emancipation from the master. Isn't it a sign of Western civility not to bother others with one's problem and a sign of Oriental emotivism to seek to bother them at every opportunity? From this angle the joke is tasteless, not least because the colonialist may have contributed to the creation of the problem he now complains about. Also, the joke's emplotment encourages us to view the end-of-life indulgence in one's private pleasures as normal (smoking a cigar, drinking wine), whilst the indulgence in collective or socially meaningful goals as abnormal or vain. In short, those who find it funny as well as those who don't may themselves harbour narcissistic tendencies by positive or negative association.

Narcissism, nationalism and existential anxiety

Post-Freudian psychoanalysis has viewed narcissism as a 'semi-pathological phenomenon'. It identified a healthy narcissism, stemming from the 'primary narcissism' of the child and necessary for ego protection and self-respect. But it has also studied the narcissism that exceeds normal ego development and leads to destructive and aggressive behaviour, physical or discursive. With respect to the latter, Erich Fromm (1977) spoke of group narcissism that is associated with nations and nationalism, suggesting that ethno-nationalist conflicts also entailed a clash of narcissisms. Though one must be careful not to reduce all aspects of a conflict to psychological phenomena, the role of egocentricity and self-love should not be ignored.

Concerning their conflict, Cypriots are caught in a narcissistic game whose stakes are extremely high. Group narcissism psychically functions to produce a collective 'ego ideal' which members of the group (however this is defined) are expected to live up to and, if they do not, they are then castigated. This speaks not only of Greek Cypriot and Turkish Cypriot nationalism but equally of neo-Cypriot nationalism that is supposed to be pro-reconciliation, yet reproduces a Cypriot superego vis-à-vis the 'primitive' Greek and Turkish ones. Group narcissists of this type ceaselessly talk and lecture about 'the problem' through idealised and romanticised images of the Self (Cyprus, Greece, Turkey), and deride and attack those who fail to live up to the expectations of their superego. Tragically, because the beautiful image they have fallen in love with is confirmed by others in their group, they view their behaviour as normal and are therefore less likely to accept it as pathological. There is an aesthetic certitude and erotic excitement when talking about their collective ego, its destiny and its problems.

We think of the Cyprus Problem in the way that we do primarily because of the way we talk about it. And the way we talk about it is deeply connected to the meaning this discourse gives to our lives, the status it grants to our individual and collective selves. It does not take much for narcissists to move from healthy group narcissism – necessary for social cohesion and solidarity – to pathological group narcissism which brings with it a crusading spirit against threats to one's Self image and, as such, perpetuates conflict. It only requires a link that politicians are keen to make and which the mass media amplify on a daily basis: namely, defining any questioning and negative depiction of the group's Self image (either from inside or outside the group) as existential threat, which in turn threatens the individual's erotic excitement and pleasure. Sublimated as patriotism, it triggers individual existential anxiety; denying someone's routine pleasure is akin to denying one's reason for being. The group's problem becomes the individual's problem, larger than life, and sometimes (when exacerbated by lack of other pleasures or erotic objects) even the actual meaning of life. Among highly mobilised activists, the group's problem acquires an erotic qua ethical significance at the same time as it is reduced to a pathetic game of collective image management and branding. Thus the need to constantly talk about the beloved, to struggle to enhance or correct the collective ego's image before eponymous and anonymous others; even before one's executioners, for others will follow the ethico-erotic struggle of the protagonist.

What the most famous Cypriot politician said with reference to his own struggle is pertinent here: 'Even if Makarios dies, one thousand Makarioses will continue the struggle.' Meaning, the struggle is bigger than me and will outlive me. But also the struggle will continue (for many years, if not forever – *makrochronios agonas*) because it is so (morally) seductive, because the collective ego is so beautiful, and by extension I – valiantly fighting for it – am also beautiful and worthy of love. From this perspective, the joke's protagonist on Death Row is not a mere comic narcissist but a paradigmatic figure. He deals with his existential anxiety by unconsciously resorting back to daily routines that have been meaningful to his social life in Cyprus, i.e. talking about and publicising the trite dramas of the Cyprus Problem, and through them, in effect, also talking about his life and himself.

The psychical significance of humanity's search for existential meaning is associated with the so-called Third Vienna School of Psychotherapy, which is based on the innovative work of Viktor Frankl. Following from Freud's theory that psychic conflicts are the result of an unconscious 'will to pleasure' (First Vienna School) to Alfred Adler's theory that psychic conflicts are caused by an unconscious 'will to power' (Second Vienna School), Frankl (1984) developed an existentialist scheme tracing psychic problems to an unconscious 'will to meaning'. His theory, also known as logotherapy, was developed out of his own experience in Nazi concentration camps, where death was imminent, life stripped of any value or meaning, yet survivors managed to linger on by having or constructing a logos, a reason for being. Frankl argues that 'the meaning of life' is not universally the same and cannot be answered abstractly or given to an individual by someone else. It is rather the product of a self-discovery, something that is 'revealed' to humans in the everyday acts of living and social routines that are peculiar to their individual circumstances. The meaning of life helps individuals to overcome their existential anxiety and it is especially comforting in dire circumstances and when one comes closer to one's death.

To that extent, any personal task or mission, including commitment to the resolution of the Cyprus Problem or other problems, can be given existential value and elevated to a meaning of life. If so, it can serve as a sedative in the face of death or as a stimulant under different circumstances.

The Cyprus Problem and the meaning of life

The Cyprus Problem has a peculiar connection to the Third Vienna School of Psychotherapy. Frankl's book *Man's Search for Meaning* was translated into Greek and introduced to (Greek) Cypriot society by a controversial political figure, the Cypriot psychiatrist Takis Evdokas. It was translated while Evdokas was in prison for publishing an article titled 'Machiavelli to Makarios', considered by the court as hubristic and libellous to the Cypriot President. Evdokas was the only person who, a few years earlier, had dared to challenge the incumbent in the 1968 Presidential election (an election that was delayed due to the intercommunal violence in 1963–4 and the breakdown of the bicommunal constitutional order that allowed Makarios to declare a state of emergency and rule under the doctrine of necessity). Though himself a respectable figure who in the past had also been a personal friend of Makarios, his candidacy was not taken seriously and in the end received less than 4 per cent of votes compared to 96 per cent plus for Makarios. Others more prominent than Evdokas in the opposition camp declined to formally challenge Makarios, given the climate of intimidation against them, which popularly associated dissent with undermining not just the leader but the national cause and struggle.

Evdokas recalls that it was after reading Frankl's book (in one go, in one single night!) that he gathered the necessary courage and literally made up his mind to challenge Makarios. 'Frankl's book helped me to clear any doubt that I had', Evdokas says, and points to 'the happiness and internal satisfaction that I felt because I was dedicating myself to a struggle for freedom and democracy' (2007: 48–9). The Cyprus Problem, for Evdokas, was inextricably linked to Makarios' psychological problem, his narcissistic rule. Evdokas wrote a book about it with the revealing title, *'I Am Cyprus'*, referring to Makarios. Rescuing Cyprus from the narcissism of its leader was elevated to a new-found meaning of life, thus launching an interesting but short-lived career in Cypriot politics. It was the mental stimulant that helped the young Cypriot psychiatrist to overcome his existential fear ('not to take into account death any more': 48), including implicit and explicit threats against his life and social status in Cyprus.

The Cyprus Problem as a meaning of life, as sedative and stimulant, has not just personal but social implications of which Evdokas was aware and which perhaps explain his subsequent early retirement from 'active politics'. One's problem will always extend beyond oneself. Defining the meaning of life through a political objective may give a person 'happiness and internal satisfaction' but that can be attained at the expense of social unhappiness and external dissatisfaction for others. This goes beyond one's political opponents or others who may pursue equally legitimate counter-objectives; it can also affect sympathisers of the cause and people close to the one whose life is totally consumed by a political struggle, including one's family. ('The cry of Winnie Mandela' as Njabulo Ndebele put it (2003), the personal and social expectations of being associated with a man whose life is his struggle, however noble that struggle is, meaning that one must always be judged by the moral parameters of the struggle.) The question consequently is, who is left outside the mirror of admiration one holds before one's individual or collective self and what ethical responsibility is owed to those who are left out?

Note that for Frankl, associating the meaning of life with narcissism, with the 'pursuit of an achievement' (scientific, monetary, social, political or counter-narcissist, as in the case of Evdokas) is one way but not the most interesting or spiritual way of dealing with existential anxiety. He warns about the danger of fanatically pursuing pseudo-values or ideals and idealisations that are only a cover up for one's internal conflicts. He is especially critical of vain self-expressions and pursuits that create temporary existential comfort for one but remain unconcerned about the existence and spiritual ambitions of others. Frankl is more interested in the small practices of everyday life, the openness to everything that exists around one, the experience of nature or culture, the love and care for those close to someone. This is not to belittle political causes or the fact that some may require total commitment, and indeed healthy narcissism. The problem lies with the kind of life commitments that this creates and which impose upon others a realm of moral edicts and social expectations, a realm normalised and naturalised by seeing the political cause as legitimately life-consuming.

Are we then stuck in a psychodrama of competing narcissisms and life-meaning soap operas? Are conflicted humans inescapably bound to their ethico-erotic struggles (a Freudian 'sad disclosure for the moralist') or can they redeem themselves from their psychological and self-inflicting problems? The task is not at all easy – not only for conflicted Cypriots but more widely for modern subjects. The difficulty lies in that, through extreme love of the ego, modern humans have lost not just the meaning of life but the love of life, including the Nietzschean recognition that to live is to be at risk. Fromm argues that the freedom modern humans currently have is highly ambivalent. The freedom gained from the bonds of mediaeval society has created insecurity, anxiety and ultimately powerlessness with regard to what to do with it, the freedom to be *this* or *that*, to do *this* or *that*. Besides fear of death, modern humans have developed a fear of life. Individuals often manage this fear of life, Fromm suggests, by 'escaping from freedom', by submitting to established routines, economies of logic and social expectations about what kind of life or problem is or must be meaningful. To that extent, they appear unwilling to socially experiment with or risk ways of living that they are not used to or told they are not feasible from a short-sighted egocentric angle. The Shakespearean motto 'to be or not to be' is not posed as a real question and difficult quest but as an edict to most people: to be is *not* to be. Life is only possible with this option, not with the other; whereas the love-of-life approach that is lacking suggests that life is also possible with the other option, and that in any case life always entails more than one option.

Concluding thoughts

There is more than one way of seeing and resolving the Cyprus Problem as well as living with it. Often persuaded that they are only safe with one way, Cypriots talk and talk about the problem rather than genuinely experiment in resolving or learning to talk less and live around or beyond the problem. All kinds of other problems are sidelined because of the problem: e.g., legal exceptionalism, protection of minorities, environmental issues, etc. A look at the largely comfortable lifestyle both North and South of the Buffer Zone and 'the problem' pales in comparison to serious problems around the globe. Partly because of this comfort, Cypriots have become too precious about principles that they think support their case, elevate their problem into life-meaning ideology and tie it to a variety of narcissistic discourses. A way out appears unlikely, even if a settlement is found, as its 'difficult' or 'partial' implementation may be the start of a 'new problem' for the narcissists. For any hope of redemption the struggle needs to be internalised; that is, for the thousand Makarioses that continue the struggle – Greek and Turkish alike – to realise their own complicity in the making of the problem.

Nonetheless, and though the problem has remained intractable for decades, its non-settlement is being transformed or 'solved' through other means. Specifically, people on the ground are negotiating and resolving their own personal 'Cyprus Problem', through permanent or temporary arrangements with the de facto or de jure authorities as well as individuals across the divide, enhanced by European Union accession and European Court of Human Rights rulings. For example, we have had an increasing number of cases of compensation or exchange of immovable property; purchasing of immovable property through overseas companies; partial restitution and right of return of certain groups of people (e.g. Cypriot Maronites); business partnerships and trade across the ethnic division; bicommunal non-governmental educational and cultural initiatives in the Buffer Zone and across the island; inter-ethnic cooperation for the restoration of heritage or for dealing with emergencies; and so on. In short, with regard to the Cyprus Problem we are currently experiencing the privatisation of its settlement – meaning *à la carte*, cross-ethnic settlements by Cypriots from all communities transgressing the divide, without authorisation by or consent of their respective authorities, as well as without these authorities having the ability to stop or control them.

To be sure, these settlements take place within the problematic 'states of exception' established on the ground, and which severely restrict rights, options and bargaining leverage for individuals. Furthermore, a lot of people still suffer the material and psychological effects of the forceful division of island, thus of the failure to reach a final and comprehensive settlement. Consequently, this deep psychological wound will not easily heal. It will remain a source of anxiety and conflict, of stories and anecdotes – comic but also tragic ones.

References and recommended reading

Constantinou, Costas M., 'On the Cypriot states of exception', *International Political Sociology* 2/2 (2008), pp. 145–64.
——, 'Multidirectional diplomacy and the privatization of settlement', *Peace Review* 24/4 (2012), pp. 454–61.

Diez, Thomas and Nathalie Tocci (eds), *Cyprus: A Conflict at the Crossroads* (Manchester: Manchester University Press, 2009).

Evdokas, Takis, *'Ego Eimai i Kypros': I Proti Periodos tis Kypriakis Dimokratias* [*'I Am Cyprus': The First Period of the Cyprus Republic*] (Nicosia: Tamasos Publications, 1990).

——, *Politikos kai Psychiatros* [*Politician and Psychiatrist*] (Athens: Diodos, 2007).

Frankl, Victor E., *Man's Search for Meaning: An Introduction to Logotherapy* (Boston, MA: Beacon Press, 1984).

Fromm, Erich, *Escape from Freedom* (New York: Henry Holt, 1965).

——, *The Anatomy of Human Destructiveness* (London: Penguin, 1977).

Freud, Sigmund, *Jokes and their Relation to the Unconscious* (London: Penguin, 1991).

——, 'On Narcissism: An Introduction' in, *On Metapsychology: The Theory of Pyschoanalysis* (London: Penguin, 1991).

Ndebele, Njabulo, *The Cry of Winnie Mandela* (Oxford: Ayebia, 2003).

9

Hydrocarbons Can Fuel a Settlement

HUBERT FAUSTMANN

Within five years of the invasion and partition of the island, the formula for the solution of the Cyprus Problem in the form it assumed after 1974 seemed to have been found. The leaders of both communities signed the High Level Agreements of 1977 and 1979, which provide for a bizonal, bicommunal federation as the framework for any solution. All efforts by the international community in the form of UN mediation have since focused on this approach and, in all likelihood, will continue to do so. The obvious questions to ask are: why has such a settlement failed to materialise, and can its causes be overcome? Given that such a federation has been elusive for almost 40 years, one needs to ask: is the status quo or an alternative approach a more likely scenario?

The unpopularity of a bizonal, bicommunal federation

One basic obstacle in the way of a solution is the lack of agreement about what kind of solution both communities want. This is in part due to the vagueness of the bizonal, bicommunal federation solution formula. Since its inception, the two sides have differed considerably as to what this means. The High Level Agreements provided only for basic parameters of a settlement. They left the specifics open to interpretation. Therefore the leaderships on both sides have read it as closely as possible to their preferred solutions and have transmitted their views to the wider population. During the talks, the Turkish Cypriot side has favoured a loose federation, or even a confederation, of two largely sovereign states, whereas the Greek

Cypriot side has, so far, preferred a strong central government within a federal system.

Since 1979, the vague principles of the High Level Agreements have been translated into more and more detailed proposals. However, it was not until the Annan Plan of 2004 that a fully-fledged solution model was presented. It came as a shock to a public that had been continuously exposed to maximalist interpretations of the High Level Agreements. Nevertheless, the Annan Plan, with all its real and alleged flaws, did not appear from nowhere. It was the result of 30 years of negotiations. Moreover, even though it is despised by a majority among the Greek Cypriots, it still serves as a reference point in the negotiations. The changes agreed in the ongoing talks since 2008 have modified the content of a bizonal, bicommunal federation and have again provided a relatively precise framework for the reunification. So much so that some say the Cyprus Problem could be solved over a long weekend if the three sides – Greek and Turkish Cypriots as well as Turkey – really wanted to reach a deal. (Greece will support any solution that is acceptable to the Greek Cypriots.) Even on the unresolved core issues – including the particularly thorny issues, such as territory, property, security, Turkish Guarantees and military presence, return of Turkish mainland settlers, to name just the most contentious – there are plenty of models and ideas available. And yet these issues still have the potential to wreck any deal because they often revolve around mutually exclusive goals and are highly emotionally charged. Compromises on these points will inevitably be unpopular.

Indeed, even a grand compromise on the overall structure of a solution is unpopular. Since Turkish Cypriots prefer a twostate solution, whereas Greek Cypriots want a unitary state based on majority rule, the compromise of a bizonal, bicommunal federation is a second best option. Consequently, for all three main parties involved, any solution will face various degrees of opposition and criticism. This will work as a domestic constraint on any final agreement. The situation is made all the more difficult by the mass media in Cyprus. In this context, and in their majority, the media is part of the problem, and not part of a solution. Opposition to a solution will also be strengthened by the fact that plenty of the arguments put forward by opponents of a settlement will have a certain degree of validity. At the same time, the essential viability of a compromise solution can be called into questioned. Any bi-ethnic federation based on political equality will be very difficult to operate. The historic record of post-conflict, bi-ethnic federations is poor. A post-solution Cyprus will in all likelihood function little better than today's Belgium, at best; hardly a prospect to look forward to.

The presence of spoilers

Another reason for the intractability of the dispute is the fact that, for most, if not all, of the period since 1974, there has been at least one spoiler at the negotiating table. At least one of three negotiating parties had no interest in a negotiated settlement and was paying only lip service to the High Level Agreements and to the feasible solutions on offer. Rauf Denktash was the most notorious of these spoilers. He pursued, more or less openly, an agenda of preserving the status quo and promoting separatism from 1974 until he was sidelined in 2004. Until the AKP government came to power in 2002, he was backed by Turkey. Whether the Turkish side became genuinely committed to reaching a solution after changing its official policy in 2003 from 'the Cyprus Problem has been solved in 1974' to 'the Cyprus Problem needs to be solved' is disputable. However, Ankara did officially back the Annan Plan in 2004. At the same time, the majority of Turkish Cypriots endorsed it in the referendum. (They then voted the moderate Mehmet Ali Talat into office as Prime Minister, in 2004, and President, in 2005.) Meanwhile, the Greek Cypriots have also produced their own spoilers. One need only consider Spyros Kyprianou (1977–88) and Tassos Papadopoulos (2003–8). Both pursued policies aimed at maintaining the status quo in preference to any feasible solutions on offer. At least during the presidencies of George Vassiliou and Glafkos Clerides (from 1988–2003) the Greek Cypriot leadership genuinely sought a solution.

    The only time that there appeared to be a genuine commitment by all three sides to a solution at the same time – and, again, this is open to dispute – was during a brief period from 2008 until 2010, when two leftist moderate Cypriots, Demetris Christofias and Mehmet Ali Talat, led the two communities. However, since 2010, the Turkish Cypriots have again appeared to adopt a rather more hard line by voting for Dervis Eroglu; a known rejectionist of the Annan Plan, who only continued to negotiate because he was instructed from Ankara. Having said this, the Turkish Cypriots are the least likely to pose problems in a solution attempt. Those Turkish Cypriots who do not want to become a minority in their own 'state' are particularly desperate to see a settlement agreed. Any scenario that is based on political equality and addresses their vital interests – such as security, territory, property – is potentially attractive for a sufficient number to vote yes. But in order to get another yes vote, a considerable number of naturalised Turkish immigrants in the North will also have to be convinced. This is likely to happen through a settlement that allows most of them to stay, a concession already made by the Greek Cypriot side, thus providing them with EU citizenship.

Christofias, too, was playing for time; neither exhibiting the courage to bring the negotiations into a final phase nor willing to defend the painful concessions required to reach a comprehensive settlement – with the exceptions of the right of residency for 50,000 settlers and a rotating presidency based on cross voting. Instead, he preferred to advance at snail's pace until the negotiations stalled during the EU presidency of the Republic of Cyprus. On top of this, since 2008 Turkey has not made any move that would allow a breakthrough. It has shown almost no interest in solving the dispute now. This is in stark contrast to 2004 when the AKP government was desperate to gain a date for EU membership negotiations. At that time, it saw EU accession as the best way to protect itself from the secularist deep state and, in particular, from the military. However, since the AKP government has now won the internal power struggle, and EU membership is not a realistic option for Turkey in the foreseeable future, the incentives for Ankara to solve the Cyprus dispute have all but disappeared.

Another problem is that in the South the political system and party politics are structurally hostile to any solution of the Cyprus Problem. As a general rule, the two large moderate parties (though DISY, in particular, includes a strong 'hard line'/rejectionist segment) need the support of the smaller parties to win the presidential elections. The problem is that these small parties routinely denounce any concessions as excessive, if not acts of treason – even though they are never willing to provide realistic alternatives. Therefore, any serious attempt to solve the Cyprus Problem would inevitably lead to the collapse of the ruling coalition. At the same time, it would also mean that the incumbent president is left with little chance of re-election. Once in power, few presidents have been willing to challenge these small parties. Thus, in the end, any president going for a solution will have to overcome the opposition of DIKO, EVROKO (European Party), The Greens and EDEK. On top of this, there will be a considerable segment of both DISY and even AKEL who are likely to vote no. This not only makes it very difficult to reach a solution, even if DISY and AKEL were able to overcome their longstanding hostility towards each other and line up in favour of a settlement in a formal or informal coalition; it also means that it is hard to see any agreement gaining the necessary popular support needed to bring it into force.

However, while none of the feasible scenarios is very attractive to the Greek Cypriots, and it seems as if it would need a political miracle to bring about a favourable settlement (which is nowhere on the horizon), all is not lost. The avoidance of something worse than the status quo, which is at least acceptable, if not comfortable, could still bring about majority support for a settlement. One such negative development is the ongoing Turkification of the North. But because this happens gradually and, at the same time, the available solution options are unattractive from a majority Greek Cypriot perspective, Turkification has failed (and will, in all likelihood, continue to fail in the future) to create a moment of truth or a deadline which could create enough pressure to make Greek Cypriots 'desperate' for change. In the meantime, Taiwanisation – the recognition of the North by some states and at least functional recognition by others – is another important factor. Without a solution, Taiwanisation is a likely development that would put considerable pressure on the Greek Cypriots to accept a deal. But, again, such recognition will probably happen gradually. Moreover, it is not an option for the EU member states and many other members of the international community. All things considered, only a second Greek Cypriot 'no' in another referendum could trigger the recognition of the North by a considerable number of states in the foreseeable future. Recognition by some Muslim states remains a prospect. However, it is not realistic to assume that Greek Cypriots could be bullied into a settlement given that they have de facto already lost the North and probably will not be willing to give up the security of their own homogenous state just to avoid further formalisation of the existing situation.

Another factor that has increased the chances for a settlement is the possibility that the Greek Cypriots, under President Nicos Anastasiades, might pursue a loose federation as a new basis for a solution. This is probably more viable as a starting point for reunification, because it minimises the issues on which both sides have to agree. It seems, therefore, to be a better option for Greek Cypriots as well than the strong federation they envisaged so far. Since it is much closer to the solution designs of the Turkish side, this would be a promising policy shift that might serve the interests of all three sides. One cannot yet tell if Anastasiades will really pursue such a model, nor how the vague formula of a loose federation will be interpreted by the wider Greek Cypriot society (or even if Anastasiades would be willing and able to sell the idea to the Greek Cypriots). His political strength, however, has been undermined by his controversial role in the bailout agreement for Cyprus with the Troika (consisting of the European Commission, the European Central Bank and the International Monetary Fund) in March and April 2013. It is as yet unclear to what extent his position in the Greek Cypriot community has been severely weakened, or, if so, for how long, and if the prospects of settling the Cyprus dispute will become collateral damage of the bailout agreement aimed at avoiding the bankruptcy of the Republic. Presiding over a country in severe economic depression and having to implement harsh austerity measure might very well torpedo any chance for him to push through a settlement.

Hydrocarbons as the way out

So, is there a thinkable scenario in which all three sides have a strong incentive to overcome the status quo? The hydrocarbon findings and the current financial and economic crises in the South might be a decisive game changer. For Turkey, only EU accession and now the supply of cheap natural gas from the Republic of Cyprus (and the Eastern Mediterranean) might provide a sufficient incentive to pursue a solution. Otherwise, non-solution has so far been Ankara's preferred choice. Given the absence of a realistic EU accession perspective, the hydrocarbon issue is now widely understood to be the only factor that has the potential to bring about a solution to the Cyprus Problem. If Turkey were willing to settle the issue, it could dramatically facilitate the export of natural gas from various Eastern Mediterranean countries, including Cyprus, Israel, Lebanon, possibly Egypt and maybe even one day Syria. All of them could export their energy via a pipeline across Turkey to Europe. This would make Turkey, and Cyprus, extremely important energy hubs. Turkish-Israeli talks about the export of Israeli gas to Turkey are already taking place.

Meanwhile, the discovery of natural gas off the coast of Cyprus can create a win-win situation for all three sides to the Cyprus dispute. It is conceivable that the only way the Greek Cypriots will be able to export their rich gas, and possibly oil, reserves in a politically and economically viable way is by solving the Cyprus Problem and exporting the gas via a pipeline to Turkey. In the light of huge new finds globally, due to improved technology (including fracking), it is very possible that gas prices will be too low for many years to make the idea of exporting liquefied gas (LNG), an option favoured by Greek Cypriots, economically viable. LNG plants are notoriously expensive to build. But even if a plant were to be built, there is always the possibility that Turkey would take steps, including military measures, to block the Greek Cypriots from exporting their hydrocarbons without a solution. In such a case, the highly indebted Greek Cypriots could find themselves in a desperate situation where a solution of the Cyprus Problem might become necessary for economic reasons and therefore 'worth the risk'. The trouble is that under such circumstances the Greek Cypriots would be negotiating from a position of weakness. According to this calculation, there is a good argument to be made that they should seek a settlement sooner rather than later. Alternatively, if the Greek Cypriots are able to export oil and gas profitably via other routes – the feasibility of such an option becoming apparent in the years ahead – without obstruction from Turkey or the Turkish Cypriots, then it is quite possible that the hydrocarbon issue is likely to hinder a solution. The Greek Cypriots will have not strong incentive to change the status quo and thus share revenues with Turkey and the Turkish Cypriots. This will naturally lead to increased tensions with Turkey and the Turkish Cypriots. Meanwhile, it is also unclear if the Turkish side will be willing and able to make use of this opportunity by making concessions as well (in particular within the security aspect of the settlement – Turkish right to intervene and Turkish military presence on the island). Judging from the developments so far, it would seem that the oil and gas issue is more likely to serve as a bone of contention deepening the dispute rather than act as a catalyst for a solution.

Conclusion

The combination of the Greek Cypriot economic crisis and the discovery of hydrocarbons have given rise to cautious optimism regarding the solution of the Cyprus Problem. This is further aided by the election of Nicos Anastasiades, who has a record of support for 'realistic' solution scenarios like the Annan Plan, and could be politically strong enough to strike a deal leading his community to another referendum. Should he be able to overcome the obstacles he now faces as a result of the financial crisis, then the natural gas issue could provide the most promising constellation for a settlement since 2004.

However, for this all to be worthwhile, a solution needs to be reached relatively soon. Moreover, a lot of things have to happen to make a settlement a reality. Unfortunately, the domestic and regional circumstances remain too volatile to give much reason for hope. Given the historic record of settlement efforts since 1963, and 1974, one therefore has to end on a rather pessimistic note. The continuation of the status quo remains clearly the most likely scenario. Keeping the situation as it is does not require a decision for which any political leader has to take political risks, or pay an immediate political price. Moreover, the status quo is stable and sustainable for many years to come if need be. Most probably, at least one of the three sides will remain unwilling to settle for a price that is acceptable to the other parties. Consequently, Greek Cypriots are likely to end up with a de facto, and maybe one day de jure, Turkish (not Turkish Cypriot) North. The Turkish Cypriots have long lost control over their own fate and depend on Turkish willingness to give up its loot from 1974. Their future is that of a disappearing community, unless the Cyprus Problem is solved.

As long as a Cyprus Problem exists, there will be actors who will try to do something about it – or at least pay lip service to such attempts. But the likelihood of a reunification decreases with every failed attempt and the passing of time. The Taiwanisation of the North with recognition by some states remains then the most likely scenario. It is difficult to see how the division will not become formalised one way or another 20, 40 or 100 years from now. The Cyprus Problem in its current form has been with us for almost 40 years. It can easily last another 40 years and longer, if it comes to that.

References and recommended reading

Faustmann, Hubert, Ayla Gurel and Greg Reichenberg (eds), *The Hydrocarbon Wealth of Cyprus: Equitable Distribution and Regional Politics*, PRIO Cyprus Centre Report 1/2012 (Nicosia: PRIO/Friedrich Ebert Foundation, 2012).

——, 'Hydrocarbon findings off the coast of Cyprus: showdown in the Eastern Mediterranean or a chance for local and regional reconciliation?', *Mediterranean Politics* (forthcoming).

Gürel, Ayla, Fiona Mullen and Harry Tzimitras, *The Cyprus Hydrocarbon Issue: Context, Positions and Future Scenarios*, PRIO Cyprus Centre Report 1/2013 (Nicosia: PRIO, 2013).

International Crises Group, 'Aphrodite's gift: can Cypriot gas power a new dialogue?', Europe Report Number 216, 2012.

Ker-Lindsay, James and Hubert Faustmann (eds), *The Government and Politics of Cyprus* (Oxford and Bern: Peter Lang, 2008).

Varnavas, Andrekos and Hubert Faustmann (eds) *Reunifying Cyprus: The Annan Plan and Beyond* (London: I.B.Tauris, 2009).

10

Gas Can Become the New Lost Opportunity

Ayla Gürel and Harry Tzimitras

In general, history shows that discovery of natural resources may equally well contribute to prosperity or lead to conflict. Hydrocarbons may easily be a curse rather than a blessing, or be a curse before they become a blessing. Hydrocarbon disputes are frequent, not only in relation to ownership of oil and gas reserves, but also in terms of the safety of sea-based transportation, and the location and tariffs for pipeline transportation over land. However, conflict is of course by no means an inevitable outcome of hydrocarbons development. Every extraction project could potentially offer an opportunity for peaceful cooperation between stakeholders. Hydrocarbons can have a great socio-economic transformative ability. At the same time, they can certainly become a problem, before serving a good cause. Situations can easily get out of hand, expectations can be raised irrationally, and things can be taken for granted, leading to diminished incentives for cooperation or, worse, increases in confrontation.

The discovery of hydrocarbons off the shores of Cyprus holds the potential for being a game changer. Hydrocarbon exploration around Cyprus has been an ongoing issue for some years now but its significance has increased since the Republic of Cyprus (RoC or Republic) launched its first sub-sea drilling South of the island in September 2011. This was when a long-running dispute about maritime borders and ownership of offshore hydrocarbons involving the Greek Cypriots, the Turkish Cypriots and Turkey turned into a crisis. This crisis subsided in the subsequent months. However, the hydrocarbons exploration issue continues to exacerbate relations between the Greek Cypriots, on the one hand, and the Turkish Cypriots and Turkey, on the other. Thus, the issue has now become a factor that cannot be ignored when assessing the prospects of solving the longstanding 'Cyprus Problem'. It is a development of strategic, political, economic and social significance. Indeed, given that it has also coincided with a period of economic and political crisis for Cyprus and the EU as a whole, it has become a national issue in Cyprus – or at any rate comprises a new phase of the traditional one. For the RoC, hydrocarbons development has become the vehicle for the promotion of the national cause against Turkey; the way out of the economic crisis; the reaffirmation of the RoC's legitimacy; the means of cementing of bilateral relations with a number of states; and the securing of an economically, politically and strategically viable future.

The discovery of hydrocarbons around Cyprus

Major discoveries of offshore natural gas by Egypt in 2003 and Israel in 2004 led to enhanced efforts in hydrocarbon exploration by the Eastern Mediterranean countries, which until then were thought to possess no such resources. After Egypt and Israel, the first serious attempt at exploration in the region came from Cyprus. The Greek Cypriots began preparing the ground for offshore hydrocarbons exploration in the early 2000s. In their capacity as the internationally recognised RoC, they signed 69 (EEZ) delimitation agreements with Egypt in 2003, Lebanon in 2007 and Israel in 2010. These agreements demarcated the outer limits of a 51 km² exploration area in the sea South of the island, which is carved into 13 blocks. During 2006 seismic surveys were carried out in the area, and based on the data from these initial surveys, in 2007 the RoC launched its first international tender for exploration licences. There were only two bids in this initial tender, and in 2008 the US-based Noble Energy was awarded a three-year licence in Block 12. After further seismic surveys, Noble was authorised by the RoC to carry out the first exploratory drilling in Block 12. Drilling began on 20 September 2011, and in December 2011 Noble announced the discovery of an estimated 5 to 8 trillion cubic feet of natural gas (with 'estimated gross mean resources of 7 trillion cubic feet').

In February 2012, the RoC announced its second round of international tender for exploration licences in the remaining

12 blocks. Encouraged by Noble's findings in Block 12, this time numerous international companies and consortia – some of them 'big' names in the energy industry – participated in the tender. Early in 2013 the RoC signed agreements with ENI-KOGAS (an Italian-South Korean consortium) for blocks 2, 3 and 9 and with the French firm Total for blocks 10 and 11.

These are hugely important positive developments for Cyprus given that currently the island as a whole is almost completely dependent on oil imports for its energy needs. It is estimated that the gas discovered in block 12 alone is enough to meet Cyprus' energy consumption for over a century. Moreover, gas that is not domestically consumed can be exported. Given this, a PRIO Cyprus Centre report published in February 2013 estimates that block 12 gas could generate, over a 25-year supply period, a revenue somewhere between \$50–70 billion, depending on the export method employed. Such a sum of money would obviously be a huge boon for the island, especially when one considers that this is more than double the combined GDP of the Greek Cypriot and Turkish Cypriot economies. It is also particularly welcome given the current dire state of the economies on both sides, but especially for the Greek Cypriots who have now signed a bail-out agreement with the EU following a severe financial crisis in early 2013. And the Turkish Cypriots are unable to survive without Turkey's financial support. However, this ostensibly hopeful picture turns gloomy as soon as one remembers that Cyprus is not a normal country. The Greek Cypriot pursuit of hydrocarbons is in fact antagonising the Turkish Cypriots as well as Turkey.

The positions of the parties

The Greek Cypriots argue that their actions are compatible with international law because they are, as accepted by the international community, the legitimate government of the RoC, which is recognised as formally encompassing both the Greek Cypriot and Turkish Cypriot communities. As such, the RoC is entitled to an EEZ; can sign delimitation agreements with other states; and enjoys exclusive sovereign rights to explore and exploit the natural resources in its EEZ. This Greek Cypriot position also has the strong backing of the international community, including the five permanent members of the UN Security Council and the EU. As regards the distribution of revenues from hydrocarbons found in Cypriot waters, the Greek

Cypriot position is that the Turkish Cypriots, as citizens of the Republic, will enjoy the benefits of any natural resource wealth *within the framework of a united Cyprus*. As the then President Christofias put it on 25 September 2012, 'in a reunified Cyprus the natural resources, including hydrocarbons, will be common wealth for all Cypriots, Greek Cypriots and Turkish Cypriots alike'. However, pending a solution that will reunify Cyprus, the RoC's sovereign right to explore and extract hydrocarbons lying in its EEZ is, as one Greek Cypriot official put it, 'inalienable and non-negotiable' and not conditional on a Cyprus solution. More specifically, the exercise of this right is not a bicommunal issue for negotiation with the Turkish Cypriots at present, in other words before a settlement.

The Turkish Cypriots and Turkey dispute the Greek Cypriots' and the international community's perception of the situation in Cyprus. Their fundamental contention is that the Greek Cypriots alone cannot legitimately represent the RoC as this would be contrary to the 1959–60 Cyprus Accords and Constitution. In their view, since the breakdown of the bicommunal power-sharing structures of the RoC, in the early 1960s, no single authority has existed on the island that is constitutionally competent to represent Cyprus as a whole; that is, the Greek Cypriots and Turkish Cypriots together. On this basis, they object to all Greek Cypriot actions relating to signing of bilateral maritime delimitation agreements, the issuing of hydrocarbon exploration licences to international firms, as well as the authorisation of drilling operations off the coast of Cyprus. The Turkish Cypriots, together with Turkey, regard such actions as involving exercise of sovereign rights at the international level, which the Turkish Cypriots and Greek Cypriots *jointly* possess by virtue of their being the equal constituent communities of the 1960 Republic of Cyprus. For the same reason, the Greek Cypriots and Turkish Cypriots are co-owners of the island's natural resources and should both benefit from any exploitation of such resources. From this perspective, any unilateral Greek Cypriot action in the absence of an agreement between the two sides – either on the question of resources, or in terms a comprehensive settlement of the Cyprus Problem – amounts to ignoring the legitimate rights and interests of the Turkish Cypriots. Moreover, according to the Turkish–Turkish Cypriot stance, the unilateral Greek Cypriot initiatives in question are inconsistent with the spirit of the UN-sponsored negotiations for a solution the Cyprus Problem. In addition, they say, these initiatives create *faits accomplis* that prejudice the terms of a prospective solution to the disadvantage of the Turkish Cypriot side and serve only to complicate matters at the negotiating table. Thus, they are promoting a proposal that either all hydrocarbons development activities offshore Cyprus be suspended, or alternatively conducted by a bicommunal authority operating under UN supervision. This bicommunal authority will also have the power to decide how the two sides will share the revenues.

At the same time, the Turkish Cypriot–Turkish proposal also includes a suggestion to export the natural gas to be extracted offshore Cyprus via a pipeline to Turkey and from there to European markets. This is another important question affecting the issue. For example, a recent article published by *The Economist* stated that 'Cyprus's creditors [in the context of the bailout the RoC is seeking from the EU] may press for the faster (and cheaper) option of building a pipeline to Turkey: something that, with settlement talks with the Turkish Cypriot North stalled, Greek Cypriots would find hard to swallow'. While the present RoC government rules out such a prospect until after the settlement of the Cyprus Problem, there are apparently signs that Nicos Anastasiades is not ruling out completely the idea of piping Cypriot gas to Turkey. Moreover, Chrysostomos II, the Archbishop of Cyprus, recently made a surprise statement that a Cyprus gas pipeline could pass via Turkey if that would serve Cyprus' national interests.

The Greek Cypriot side is refusing to consider these ideas on familiar grounds: that, as things stand, the RoC has a sovereign right to explore and exploit the natural resources in its exclusive economic zone, a fact that is recognised by the international community, and that the exercise of this right is not a bicommunal issue for negotiation with the Turkish Cypriots. Therefore, despite the continuing protests from Turkey and the Turkish Cypriots, the RoC carries on implementing its hydrocarbons development plans in the waters South of Cyprus. With the Greek Cypriots determined to continue on their own exploring for hydrocarbons, the Turkish Cypriots and Turkey collaborated in restoring the political balance, as they saw it, by taking 'reciprocal steps of equal significance'. In response, the Turkish Cypriots, with support from Turkey, have been taking steps towards conducting their own exploration in Cyprus' waters. In September 2011 they signed an agreement demarcating the continental shelf between the island's Northern coast and

Turkey, and the Turkish Cypriot authorities granted to the Turkish national oil company TPAO hydrocarbons exploration licences for sea areas in the North, east and South of Cyprus (with some areas in the South and east partly overlapping the RoC exploration area). These 'reciprocal steps' amount to the Turkish Cypriots' claiming what they consider to be their equal share with the Greek Cypriots in rights concerning maritime jurisdiction and hydrocarbon exploration, notwithstanding the lack of a negotiated settlement.

Meanwhile, in addition to the intercommunal dimension of the energy issue, Turkey itself has another reason for opposing the Greek Cypriot pursuit for hydrocarbons: its continental shelf claims in the Eastern Mediterranean clash with the EEZ proclaimed by the Greek Cypriots. Turkey disputes the RoC-Egypt EEZ boundary agreement, insisting that this agreement ignores Turkey's continental shelf rights in the area to the west of longitude 32° 12' 18". The continental shelf that Turkey claims in this area covers almost all of the EEZ that the RoC claims in the west and partially overlaps some of the Greek Cypriot concession blocks in the island's Southwest. Of course, this issue of overlapping claims is also related to the Cyprus Problem. For pending a solution, and as long as Turkey does not recognise the Greek Cypriot government as legitimately representing the RoC, it is difficult to see how the claimants can come together to discuss a negotiated solution or resort to an international adjudicative mechanism or tribunal for a resolution of their claims.

In light of these developments, it is hardly surprising that the last three reports by the UN Secretary-General to the Security Council concerning the UNFICYP (United Nations Peacekeeping Force in Cyprus) contain very similar comments about the issue of natural resources. Thus on 7 January 2013 he expressed concern about the continuing '[t]ensions and rhetoric in and around Cyprus related to the exploitation of natural resources', and on 5 July 2013 he noted that:

> It is important to ensure that any new-found wealth, which belongs to all Cypriots, will benefit both communities. Without doubt, the discovery of offshore gas reserves constitutes a strong incentive for all parties to find a durable solution to the Cyprus Problem. It is my hope that the discovery may engender a deeper cooperation for the benefit of all stakeholders in the region.

The UN Secretary-General's references in these UNFICYP reports on the hydrocarbons issue – which has no apparent relevance to UNFICYP – have been interpreted by some commentators in the Greek Cypriot press as an indication of 'the aim of more or less making it appear as a bicommunal issue'.

Can the hydrocarbons help to bring the two sides together?

Notwithstanding the serious political differences described above, the Greek Cypriot discovery of significant natural gas deposits has led many people to talk about the possibility of these valuable reserves expediting a solution in Cyprus. Not just *any* solution, of course, but an enduring one that will unite the island by bringing the Cypriots communities together under the roof of a common federal government.

One idea is that prospects of natural gas extraction offer strong incentives for the two Cypriot sides to seek cooperation. Cooperation on as vital an issue as this should also help to build trust between them which would in turn ease the way towards a solution. Such cooperation, as one expert described it, is the 'mother of all confidence building measures'. The Greek Cypriots and Turkish Cypriots stand to gain here because an environment of cooperation rather than dispute implies geo-political stability which would make Cyprus a more attractive place for investment on the part of oil and gas companies, hence enabling Cyprus to negotiate more profitable contracts with them. So there is here, for the Turkish Cypriots, the incentive of receiving their share of the wealth to be made and, for the Greek Cypriots, more revenue than would be likely without cooperation. Moreover, it would be possible to export the gas to Turkey via a pipeline. Experts confirm that this is the cheapest, quickest and most profitable way of monetising the Cyprus gas. Thus not only would Turkey be there as a ready market; it would also be possible for the Cyprus gas to reach the European market via the prospective transit pipelines already planned to carry Caspian gas through Turkey to Europe. Turkey, which is hungry for energy, would certainly welcome such a development.

But what chance is there for this to happen? Not much it seems, unless a settlement is reached first. Pending a solution of the Cyprus Problem, the hydrocarbons controversy appears to have exacerbated the two sides' more fundamental disagreements regarding where sovereignty lies in Cyprus under the present circumstances, i.e., prior to a settlement, and the related question of how 'a new state of affairs would come into being' under a political settlement. The two sides' very different, indeed mutually exclusive, views about these issues were succinctly described in a report dated 1 April 2003 presented to the UN Security Council by the then UN Secretary-General Kofi Annan. According to Mr Annan, for the Greek Cypriot side, 'the exercise [of creating a new state of affairs] was the writing of a new constitution for the existing, internationally recognised, and continuing Republic of Cyprus, to transform it into a bicommunal, bizonal federation, the Turkish Cypriot community essentially being reintegrated into that state'. The Turkish Cypriot side, on the other hand, perceived 'the exercise' as 'the founding of a new state by two pre-existing sovereign states or entities, which devolved some of their sovereignty to that new state but otherwise retained sovereignty in their hands'.

It is obvious that the two sides still strongly adhere to these incompatible positions and that their preoccupation with defending them is essentially what informs their stances vis-à-vis the hydrocarbons issue. The Turkish Cypriot proposal – calling for the two sides either to suspend all exploration activity prior to a solution, or alternatively to cooperate in such activity pending a solution – appears to the Greek Cypriots as simply an attempt to strengthen the Turkish Cypriot side's hand at the negotiations: either by creating a precedence of the RoC not being sovereign enough to explore alone Cyprus' seas or by challenging 'the sovereignty of the Republic' and putting 'on an equal par the unrecognised TRNC with the legitimate state, the Republic of Cyprus, which is internationally recognised' (as the RoC government spokesman Stephanou put it on 6 October 2011). Conversely, the Turkish Cypriots have always perceived the Greek Cypriot determination to continue to explore unilaterally as being connected with their desire to have confirmed once again (as happened when it was allowed to join the EU in 2004) that there is nothing problematic about the RoC as a sovereign independent state and their position that the RoC should be preserved under a settlement. In other words, the hydrocarbon controversy is perceived by both sides as yet another episode of the fundamental conflict of principle between them and thus has already turned into 'a zero-sum game'.

Conclusion

The issue of hydrocarbons has emerged as a major new factor in the Cyprus Problem. While everybody – the Greek Cypriots, Turkish Cypriots, Turkey and the international community – seems to be in agreement that the natural resources of the island belong to all Cypriots, the agreement ends there. The Greek Cypriots maintain that any sharing of the revenues from natural resources can come only after a solution. The Turkish Cypriots and Turkey argue that not only are the island's natural resources jointly owned, but so is the right to explore and exploit them, irrespectively of whether there is a solution. The international community, which clearly supports the RoC's – in other words, the Greek Cypriots' – right to explore and exploit the island's natural resources, has nevertheless made it clear that all eventual earnings should be shared. As we saw, this has been emphasised in the UN Secretary-General's last three Cyprus reports.

The conclusion seems to be that, rather than cooperation over natural gas serving as a way in which to boost confidence between the two communities, there needs to be a political solution first. For this the two sides will need to compromise on their fundamental positions. Can they be persuaded to do that? Hydrocarbon finds can perhaps be used to drive the parties towards a compromise because only in the event of a solution will there be circumstances making cooperation possible and hence enabling everybody fully to benefit from these resources. The incentives are all there, but where are the political leaders who will make the case for a compromise solution? Especially between two peoples in both of whose languages, incidentally, compromise (*symvivasmos/uzlaşmak*) has only a negative connotation.

References and recommended reading

Darbouche, Hakim, El-Katiri, Laura and Fattouh, Bassam, *East Mediterranean Gas: What Kind of a Game-changer?* (Oxford: The Oxford Institute of Energy Studies NG 71, 2012).

Faustmann, Hubert, Gürel, Ayla and Reichberg, Gregory (eds), *Cyprus Offshore Hydrocarbons: Regional Politics and Wealth Distribution* (Nicosia: Friedrich Ebert Stiftung and PRIO Cyprus Centre, 2012).

Giamouridis, Anastasios, *The Offshore Discovery in the Republic of Cyprus: Monetisation Prospects and Challenges* (Oxford: The Oxford Institute of Energy Studies NG 65, 2012).

Gürel, Ayla, Mullen, Fiona and Tzimitras, Harry, *The Cyprus Hydrocarbons Issue: Context, Positions and Future Scenarios* (Oslo-Nicosia: Peace Research Institute Oslo PCC Report 1/2013).

Stocker, James, 'No EEZ solution: the politics of oil and gas in the Eastern Mediterranean', *Middle East Journal* 66/4 (Autumn 2012), pp. 579–97.

11

A Gender Perspective

Maria Hadjipavlou

In 1997 I was invited to Princeton University to participate at a panel discussion on the Cyprus conflict. One of the American panellists, Matthew Nimitz – who had, in the late 1970s, been an envoy of President Carter to the island – started his presentation by saying: 'The Cyprus Problem has become an industry, the amount of people involved to solve this problem exceeds the number of people living on that island.' I remember then my impulsive reaction was, 'Who are you to judge and evaluate the situation in my country?' On second thoughts his statement brought home the deep-rootedness and intractability of the conflict (something that continues to this day) and also the fact that the persons involved in trying to solve the problem have all been men at the local, national and international fora. What does this tell us about today? That patriarchy, sexism and male dominance are doing well on the island and that there are no prospects for a solution on the horizon. In view of the present economic crisis, the question of a solution has been put aside, even though there have been informal and formal statements connecting the economic crisis and the natural gas issue in a way that sees a solution as an interrelated opportunity for working out a settlement that would benefit all interested parties in a win-win situation. However, this could only happen with insightful and visionary leadership willing to work outside 'the box'. The role of unofficial processes and civil society would also be crucial in such an eventuality. The polity needs to be prepared in the culture for a solution amidst changing local and regional realities. The role of women and the integration of a gender equality mentality should be part of this new state of affairs.

In fact since the beginning of the most recent history of Cyprus it was Greek Cypriot men who took the decisions on what kind of 'colonial struggle' or means to undertake and who to include and who to exclude, and it was men who signed the agreements for the 'reluctant independence'. The same applies to the Turkish Cypriot community either at the TMT (Turkish Resistance Organisation) levels comprising all men or at the building of the new state in 1960 (Hadjipavlou and Mertan 2010). Women's exclusion from public affairs in both Cypriot communities is deeply rooted in the patriarchal mentality. There was no woman in the Cyprus Republic legislature until 1982. It is exclusively men who have been negotiating the plans and future solution for almost half a century. What is really going wrong despite the professed statements that the two sides are working for a solution? In the last 20 years there have also been numerous citizens' conflict resolution efforts with which I have been involved that have worked to challenge and change the status quo (Hadjipavlou-Trigeorgis 1998, Hadjipavlou 2004). This chapter will deal with these themes. How have women been used in the conflict culture primarily, but not only, as victims? How have Cypriot women also mobilised to project their subjectivity and agency and articulate a different voice?

Cypriot women's critical voice

> Many officials (all men) and non-officials knew the truth about our beloveds and we ask again today why they did not tell us for the last 35 years? The state has exploited politically our pain... (Greek Cypriot woman with a missing husband since 1974; interview, 2008)

> I brought up my children without a father. He has been missing since 1963 and we don't know to this day what happened to him. If he is dead, where is he buried and who killed him? (Turkish Cypriot woman with a missing husband since 1963; interview, 2008)

The above quotes from Cypriot women's narratives are loaded with anger and complaints at the inadequacy of the state's responsibility to respond to their right to information and to stop using their pain and suffering as instruments to serve its own ethnicised national project. The women want to be treated as citizens with rights beyond any hierarchical opposition. This is also an example of the impact of protracted conflict on the lives of ordinary citizens and new generations. This human female protest – together with other unaddressed issues of gender inequality, women's exclusion and victimisation – still continues on the island with very limited public debate (Anthias and Yuval-Davis 1992).

A gender perspective in the context of conflict situations means paying close attention to the special needs of women, girls and men (note, not as homogeneous social groups) during both the peace negotiations and the peace-building processes, including disarmament, demobilisation, repatriation, resettlement, rehabilitation and reintegration to the social fabric in conditions of safety as well as taking measures to support local women's empowerment. As a feminist I view armed conflict and warfare not as isolated instances but as a continuum of violence that flows through peace and war, pre-war and postwar periods. In Cyprus we might not have armed violence (but frozen conflict), as in other protracted conflicts, but we do have high levels of structural violence – especially gender-based violence. It is also important not to forget that gender identity is only one of many other social identities, and is closely connected to class, race, ethnicity, sexual orientation, age, etc. Such a complex web of relationships has not been taken into account when drafting most international documents or national peace agreements, let alone the participation of women in the negotiation processes. This despite the United Nations Security Council Resolution 1325 (2000) on *Women, Peace and Security*, which recognised for the first time that women are disproportionately victimised in wars and has called upon all parties to armed conflict to take special measures to respect women's rights, to protect women from gender-based violence and to end impunity for crimes of violence against women and girls as well as including women at the negotiating table. This resolution is pertinent too in Cyprus, where, in the decades' old negotiations, no woman has sat at the table despite the fact that the Cyprus Republic endorsed not only Resolution 1325 but many other similar resolutions and conventions such as the Convention on the Elimination of all Forms of Discrimination and Violence against Women (CEDAW) and the Beijing Plan of Action of 1995–2010. Women stereotypically are depicted as victims and men as perpetrators, thus essentialising gender differences. Ignoring women's experiences contributes not only to their exclusion but also to a process of self-selection that results in an overwhelmingly male population both at the centre of foreign policy and in the executive where issues of decisions on war and peace, development and allocation of budgets are taken. Thus this androcentric view of politics deprives the new state of a plurality of voices and diverse discourses.

Dichotomies and bipolarities

In ethno-national conflicts like the Cyprus conflict, members of opposing parties are called through dominant national narratives, which are patriarchal, militaristic and oversimplified, to choose their side and locate themselves on the conflict map. Issues such as victimhood, truth, human rights violations and justice acquire a monofocal, masculinist meaning according to the processes of constructing memories and forgetting which enter into what Volkan aptly termed 'chosen glories and chosen traumas' (Hadjipavlou 2006). Thus the dominant national narratives on each side of the divide as well as the societal beliefs (myths, enemy images, history textbooks, dehumanisation of the other, etc.) reinforce the continuation of the conflict and its non-solution. What are the implications of this bipolar scenario for women and conflict resolution and reconciliation groups who view the political and ethno-national conflict in Cyprus as having a multilayered texture? Does a conflict culture, as it is defined by dominant andocentric discourses and a patriarchal mentality, one of whose many tasks is that of 'enemy construction', allow space for the development of alternative options and analyses?

Cypriot society is a hierarchical society characterised by both sexual, racial and generational oppressions where the private/ public divide – which is often used as an excuse to exclude women from public life based on binary sexual biological differences – still prevails, and most of the research confirms both this divide and the gender stereotypes that define the choices men and women make (Hadjipavlou 2010). As one of the Turkish Cypriot women mentioned in a dialogue session among women from the Cypriot women's non-governmental organisation Hands Across the Divide, 'I want a solution [of the Cyprus conflict] to bring a culture of inclusion, everyone having a voice, everyone having an opportunity to contribute to change. I want an end to all divisions.' Another Greek

Cypriot woman remarked with urgency, 'I also want a settlement to gain freedom from fear of renewed violence, freedom from male suppression, freedom of movement, freedom to choose my own direction in life beyond social pressures and patriarchal impositions, and gender stereotypes...' Women's desires tell us that we cannot achieve gender equality without peace and we cannot achieve peace without democratic participation of women in all levels of public life. Thus peace for women means concrete new daily social conditions that have to do with choices, safety, empowerment beyond ethnicity and nationalism.

The Cypriot women's struggles are part of the global women's agenda for implementation of human rights as women's rights, democratic participation visibility of women's presence and empowerment. The Republic of Cyprus was obliged to harmonise its laws pertaining to social issues, work and family matters with EU laws, which are progressive but have yet to become owned by grass-roots women; they still remain an elite project. There are, however, bicommunal women's groups who engage in both activism and research projects to develop alternative understandings and analysis of the Cypriot conflict experience from a women's and a gender perspective. Here I mention selectively the bicommunal groups Hands Across the Divide (HAD) and the Gender Advisory Team (GAT). HAD is a bicommunal Cypriot women's non-governmental organisation that came together in 2001 during a two-day seminar titled 'Communication in Divided Societies: What Can Women Do?' Two years ago HAD registered as an NGO in the Republic of Cyprus. The underlying worldview of HAD is that 'we all believe in the values of democracy, which for us means an open market of ideas and freedom of speech, gender equality, equal access to resources and opportunities for development and we aspire to live in a reunited, federal homeland!' In its 12 years of activism, HAD has promoted reconciliation across the divide and sought to analyse the Cyprus experience from a gender perspective. It has also organised conflict resolution workshops, staged street protests and called on Cypriot negotiators to integrate UNSC Resolution 1325 in the peace negotiations, as well as many other activities. Meanwhile, GAT consists of women, scholars and activists from across the divide and has been meeting since 2009. Having identified that the context of the Cypriot negotiations lack a gender perspective and thus fails to address gender equality issues, GAT, with the support of the UN

Good Offices in Cyprus, has communicated to the negotiators the need to incorporate women's concerns into the solution agenda and the gender equality provisions in the future constitution. Another success for GAT was that the two negotiators appointed a gender focal point each in their office. The gender focal points have been in close communication with GAT. In highlighting these two groups, I do not underestimate all other political party women's organisations, which I see as restricted by, and closely linked to, the male agenda of their political parties and which unfortunately have not developed a separate agenda on women's rights and issues.

As mentioned before, the overwhelming dominance of the economic crisis and the 'national problem' as the dominant discourses have now marginalised all other issues, including women's equality issues, minority rights, health, migration and environmental issues, sex trafficking and gender-based violence, etc. In this respect the structure of patriarchy becomes mediated with nationalist politics to keep particular agendas visible while marginalising others. We see this also reflected in the plethora of books and articles produced on the 'Cyprus conflict' from an international relations perspective as well as on the international proposed plans to resolve it. (I wonder if any of the Cypriot politicians read any of these books.) Hardly ever do the mass media, in either community, invite women on to prime time discussion programmes to talk about what the continuation of the problem and its non-solution mean for women, and what suggestions they may have. Even with the economic crises, the media almost only ever invite men to speak as experts on economic and banking issues, despite the fact that we know that those who suffer the consequences of unemployment are primarily women, not just because of their low-paid status but also because of the curtailment of welfare and social programmes on which women and their children depend. However, such issues are not of interest to the Cypriot media!

Cypriot women's representation and participation in the legislature, the executive and the judiciary is among the lowest in the European Union, which is surely an omission of participatory democracy and violation of women's human rights. In such conditions it was impossible to establish an independent feminist movement on the island, both prior to the 1960s and to this day, that could have networked with women's movements in the region and form alliances across borders. The reasons for this absence are historical (colonialism, nationalism, militarism, national problem), political and structural (patriarchy, religion and education), as well as more specifically to do with party dominance, cultural gender stereotypes and gender prejudices (Hadjipavlou and Mertan 2010).

Critical engagement

Women with a gender agenda have a different voice and understanding of the issues under discussion at the negotiating table. That is why their participation will enrich the outcome. I give examples of how members of GAT understand the citizenship issues, amongst others, through a gender lens and would like to see it included in a mutually acceptable agreement and in a future federal constitution. These ideas derive from our desire to implement Resolution 1325. As GAT we believe that two major principles should underlie citizenship rights in a new federal Cyprus: citizenship rights should be accessible on a non-discriminatory basis at all levels, including gender; and, measures to ensure that the experience of citizenship is based on equal opportunity for participation in all spheres of life including the right of women to affirmative action for the purposes of redressing the imbalances created by history, tradition or custom. With regard to access to citizenship, GAT notes that: citizenship rights should not be treated as a unitary bundle; transferability of rights between the two constituent states should be provided for and different categories of rights should be accessible in both constituent states in a non-exclusive basis (e.g. the granting of political rights in one constituent state should not exclude access to cultural rights in the other constituent state). The right of choice in exercising each of these rights should be recognised. Provisions should be incorporated into the law to allow minors the ability to enjoy all rights in both constituent states. It is also of paramount importance that non-discriminatory provisions be included, such as that citizenship should not be presumed on ethno-national hetero-normative bases and should not be modelled on the performance of militant violence. Moreover, discrimination at all levels (on the basis of ethnicity, race, class, age, sexuality, pregnancy, marital status, language, political belief or ideology, religion, culture, physical and mental ability, and place of birth) should be criminalised in both constituent states and at federal level and in both civil and military legislation. The protection of women's and children's rights should be equally guaranteed in both constituent states as well as at the federal level. Protection of minority rights in each constituent state (cultural, educational and social) should be guaranteed. In addition, appropriate monitoring mechanisms should be set up to scrutinise violations of anti-discrimination legislation in the mass media and any other public information mechanisms (including parliamentary debates and speeches).

GAT also proposes that gender mainstreaming should be prioritised at all levels of institutions and mechanisms should be set up to ensure that it will be actively pursued. Institutions pertaining to social and economic rights (e.g. ombudsperson offices, trade unions, equality bodies, monitoring bodies, etc.) should ensure equality of protection in both constituent states. Those institutions pertaining to equality should be staffed by professionals with expertise in intersectional gender issues and provisions for ongoing training should be included in the law. All levels of education in both constituent states should include gender awareness, reproductive health issues and cultural pluralism, including the institutionalisation of both languages in the educational system, and the purging of discriminatory language and incitement to hatred. GAT has prepared similar recommendation with regard to governance, property and the economy and has submitted them to the negotiator's advisors and the UN.

Trapped in the past and party politics?

Can Cyprus be solved? The easy answer is 'No' based on the prevailing conflict culture and negotiators' mentality and inability to include the other, as well as on the approaches the third parties have been using. Even when they are made to shake hands the image they project is of mistrust and sadness. The opening of checkpoints along the ceasefire line in 2003, has been an opportunity that could have been utilised by both leaders to promote citizen's diplomacy and re-rapprochement and connect this momentum to the macro-level negotiations. Yet, on the whole, the state has remained absent (Demetriou 2007). It could also have been a moment to show leadership and redefine the problem as a shared problem to be solved cooperatively. Instead, there followed political party politicisation and exploitation of the momentum to circulate fears and questions about the political correctness of crossing. People's desires to see their homes and come to terms with pain and loss remained unaddressed. The fact that no violence occurred, and that there was so much international coverage, meant that this could have been turned into a moment of euphoria to push for civic peace building and facilitate the solution processes. People were ready to embrace a different discourse. It was an opportunity to dispel myths, stereotypes and mutual fears and connect the Cypriots across class and ethnicity.

Then there were the referenda, in 2004. This constituted another lost opportunity and the 'us' and 'them' dichotomy re-emerged even deeper. Polarisation ensued, especially in the Greek Cypriot community. People who had been working unofficially for years for a solution on both sides felt betrayed. In fact, those who voted 'yes' in the Greek Cypriot community were suspect and were labelled unpatriotic. Some of us, including this writer, were called before the House of Representatives Ethics Committee accused of having been given money by the UNDP (United Nations Development Programme) to promote the 'Yes' vote! (This is an example of how democracy works in an intractable conflict situation.) Glimmers of hope reappeared when Christofias and Talat – two 'comrades' – led the peace talks. The 'Cyprus solution by the Cypriots for the Cypriots' slogan seemed to have carried some meaning at least for some of us who interpreted it to mean that 'finally the Cypriots take responsibility and will be accountable for the success or failure of the process'. The appointment of technical committees by Cypriots – although women were almost excluded – gave hope for joint thinking and collaboration on shared interests. Soon these hopes died off and the old blame game ensued. The momentum was over. Mistrust, fears about partition, helplessness and reference to past grievances abound today despite the fact that the UN in private tells us that many convergences have been reached on most of the issues but 'only if good will and mutual trust [are] there'. Would it be different if women with a peace and women's agenda participated in the peace process along with men? My previous discussion would give a positive answer and it is something that has not been tried. Many women from HAD and GAT have been involved in peace-building work and reconciliation and have had experiences which should be of value to the official peace processes. Women's insights into how to reframe the deadlocked peace negotiations and broaden both sides' perspectives to validate the bottom-up contribution and its linkage to macro-, meso- and micro-level politics on the island should be used.

In February 2013 the people of the Republic of Cyprus elected a new president, Nicos Anastasiades, who inherited a severe economic crises and the unresolved problem. The peace negotiations have taken a back seat. Questions have arisen of whether the way the negotiations have been conducted need to be redesigned to include the natural gas opportunity on the agenda and also whether the UN should suggest a timeframe for the conclusion of negotiations. In the meantime, certain confidence-building measures and the strengthening of civil society should be promoted.

Conclusion

Today the crossings to and from continue and joint businesses, educational, health and environmental projects need to be encouraged much more and the learning experiences should inform the content of the peace process. There is also a valuable bicommunal social, intellectual and political capital that needs to be utilised and integrated into the vision of a future Cyprus. The grassroots' voices and bicommunal groups' experience of decades' old reconciliation efforts to reach out to the other, and the human needs of other 'others' as well as their concerns, fears and perspectives should be taken into account and integrated into building a new civic culture. These discourses have been generated on the island beyond the 'old familiar politics' and have something new to propose on how to build a culture for a solution. This shift might provide a new text and site for moving forward. It is an indispensable ingredient in any gender-sensitive and participatory democratic system whose citizens aspire to live in peace and it is their right to contribute to a new visionary solution with many possibilities for growth for all its citizens, men and women.

References and recommended reading

Anthias, Floya and Nira Yuval Davis, *Racialized Boundaries: Race, Nation, Gender, Colour and Class and the Anti-Racist Struggle* (London: Routledge, 1992).

Bryant, Rebecca, *The Past in Pieces: Belonging in the New Cyprus* (Pittsburg, PA: University of Pennsylvania Press, 2010).

Demetriou, Olga, 'To cross or not to cross? Subjectivization and the absent state in Cyprus', *Journal of the Royal Anthropological Institute* 13 (2007), pp. 987–1006.

Hadjipavlou-Trigeorgis, Maria, 'Different relationships to the land: personal narratives, political implications and future possibilities in Cyprus', in V. Calotychos (ed.), *Cyprus and its People: Nation, Identity, and Experience in an Unimaginable Community* (Boulder, CO: Westview Press, 1998).

Hadjipavlou, Maria, 'No permission to cross: Cypriot women's dialogue across the divide', *Gender, Peace and Culture: A Journal of Feminist Geography* 13/4 (2006), pp. 329–351.

——, 'Multiple stories: The "crossings" as part of citizens' reconciliation efforts in Cyprus?', *Innovation* 20/1 (2007), pp. 53–73.

——, *Women and Change in Cyprus: Feminisms, Gender in Conflict* (London: I.B.Tauris, 2010).

—— and Mertan, Biran, 'Cypriot feminism: an opportunity to challenge gender inequalities and promote women's rights and a different voice', *The Cyprus Review* 22/2 (2010), pp. 247–68.

12

Civil Society Can Reinvigorate the Peace Process

Yeshim Harris

Since the beginning of the Cyprus conflict there have been a number of direct and indirect negotiations between the Greek Cypriot and Turkish Cypriot administrations. Even after so many years, these attempts have failed to formulate an answer that satisfies both sides. Following the failure of the latest negotiation talks in the spring of 2012, the situation now seems more intractable than ever before.

In May 2012, and again in May 2013, civil society leaders from both communities came to London and gave a series of talks. These meetings took place in the UK parliament and at the London School of Economics with mixed audiences of parliamentarians, academics and NGO representatives and members of the Cypriot diaspora (and were initiated by the UK All Party Parliamentary Group on Conflict Issues and Engi Conflict Management). The aim was to create a new platform for discussion and to reconsider the meaning of a 'Cypriot-owned, Cypriot-led' peace process and how that could include the wider Cypriot society rather than just the political elite.

The speakers represented different constituencies, covering a wide range of issues from women to youth, from education to business. They argued their points from different perspectives, different interests, different ethnicities and age groups – but they shared one single conviction: that the peace process called for more transparency; and that civil society needed to be a part of it. They suggested a process in which civil society groups from both communities could take part, a system that embraced public consultation and made people feel heard and understood.

A top-down approach

Many polls have been carried out over the past decade to get a better understanding of the two societies' views on the peace process. One of the most striking outcomes of these is the sense of despair, in both the South and the North of the island. According to one study by Cyprus 2015 (a bicommunal research organisation), people in both communities strongly desired a settlement (60–70 per cent) and yet very few believed that a settlement would actually be achieved (only 15–20 per cent). One of the reasons for this pessimism is the big difference between the two communities' desires for a satisfactory settlement, and the subsequent lack of progress so far. Another reason, however, could be the realisation that whatever the level of enthusiasm, civil society's and the wider public's input would not make an impact on the result of the talks.

So far, settlement and peace building negotiations in Cyprus have largely consisted of bringing the political leaders, the UN and the guarantors to the negotiating table. In essence, all efforts to reach a settlement for a sustainable, peaceful co-existence have been guided by a traditional top-down approach, i.e. the elected leaders reach decisions on behalf of their communities, and once the talks are complete, then the leaders bring the communities along in support of the agreements or disagreements. Over the years, there have been attempts at engaging the two communities in the process, but these have been ineffective. For instance the creation of technical committees for consultation in 2008 was a step in the right direction but their work faded away over time in the absence of a coherent system. Another example is the series of open public meetings held during the last two settlement negotiations by the leaders, their representatives or the UN; however these were mostly in the form of question and answer meetings held on an ad-hoc basis, rather than designed to garner regular feedback.

Based on their experience, the group told their listeners that people on both sides of the divide have now moved on towards more organised civil society participation, but the formal negotiation methods have remained stuck in the old approaches. Involving communities at the end, rather than during the process, has made communicating the need for a compromise solution difficult.

Not clearly understanding the reasons behind failing to achieve 'convergences' (the term used in Cyprus negotiations) has made the positions of the negotiators detached from their communities.

Involving civil society

The first question that arises is: how does involving civil society and the wider public help with negotiations? Political leaders may sometimes be unable to adequately address the multifaceted and forever shifting relationships between the communities in conflict. With the best of intentions, negotiating behind closed doors may distort perspectives and leaders may find themselves lagging behind the changing dynamics at grassroots level.

In a conflict where two communities, as well as the broader regional or international actors, are involved, the overall picture becomes very complex. This has always been the case for Cyprus given its geopolitical position and the long history of the conflict. It is therefore understandable that those decisions that would potentially have particularly complicated implications would need a degree of confidentiality and diplomacy and may have to remain confidential until they reach a mature point in discussions. However, this does not necessarily have to entail absolute secrecy until the very end of the process. A comprehensive consultation mechanism could be designed which ensures that throughout negotiations, leaders are open, informative and accountable to their public without compromising the inevitable sensitivities.

The next question that needs to be addressed is whether Cypriot civil society is ready to take on this task. The development of civil society requires time, effort and resources; and its effectiveness depends on a range of factors. For instance, the level of acquaintance with democracy, participation and the concept of organised civil society would determine the attitudes of the community groups towards the peace process. The extent of leadership and the availability of resources ensure that appropriate advocacy skills, as well as technical capacity, are adequate: donor groups, the international community and political leaders have a role in and significant responsibility for these areas.

Up to a decade ago, civil society activities in Cyprus consisted primarily of academic or diplomatic events to facilitate contact between the two communities. Since then, with the increase of resources, these activities have grown appreciably. Even if it only involves a small number of people, they have become more institutionalised, and more focused on reconciliation and long-term change in society. There are currently a number of bicommunal initiatives aimed at improving cooperation and building confidence, such as regular cross-border gatherings, chambers of commerce and other professional membership associations carrying out joint projects, trade unions working together on specific issues, etc.

There are also monocommunal initiatives in the South and the North but the CSOs (Civil Society Organisations) in general need further capacity building. The activities on each side of the island are similar and mostly led by membership-based establishments, such as unions and professional organisations. Concern about issues such as environment, health, gender, peace and education are fairly new to the island and therefore CSOs promoting these are not very effective, but with the support of the EU, UNDP and other funders, they are becoming more institutionalised and organised. Nonetheless, while civil society development is being encouraged with the help of these significant resources and is gradually improving its capacity, it remains cut off from the peace process and ongoing negotiations. Although many proposals have been put forward in the past for how to engage the civil society of both communities (for example, through the creation of a Consultative Body, a Social Reconciliation Commission, etc.) none of these has yet been implemented. The absence of community-level participation in decisions means that there is still a lack of strong momentum and motivation.

Civil society breaking the log jam

How could an inclusive peace process help with the log jam? Polls show that, despite the absence of violence on the island, the two societies remain deeply divided and guarded towards each other. The provision of limited access through the checkpoints in 2003 offered an opportunity for contact across the divide. Following this, the island saw a set of bicommunal activities, which continue to date. However these activities are attended by a small group of 'committed regulars' and do not reach the hardliner end of the spectrum. Fundamental inter-community trust is still to be established between both sides.

If there is any chance of reaching a satisfactory and sustainable settlement, these issues need to be addressed before and during, not after, the negotiations are complete. As James Ker-Lindsay from the LSE points out, the failure to engage with civil society during a peace process would ill-prepare that society for an eventual settlement package. It would also open up space for hardliners and rejectionists who will happily play on the poorly informed fears and concerns of the communities. By the time an agreement was presented to the public, the damage would already have been done. Without the opportunity to understand and shape ideas and decisions, people will not feel a part of the process and, consequently, will not be confident enough to vote positively.

An example of the lack of public involvement and its consequences was the Annan Plan in 2004. There are a number of factors which resulted in its failure. One of these was that the plan was prepared with limited consultation or communication; and the absence of a joint awareness campaign caused counterproductive speculation and the development of mistrust. When the plan was presented, many people found it difficult to understand, and to trust and own its proposals.

Kaymak, Lordos and Tocci argue in their article 'Building confidence in peace' (2005: 3):

> The need to engage public opinion and listen, inform and discuss the peace process publicly and transparently is thus key to achieving, first, positive referenda results, and second, the actual implementation of a peace agreement on the ground. It is essential that debate and communication be established between local leaders and the public and for the peace process to be as open and participatory as possible in order to maximise its chances of success.

Experience from other conflicts shows that broadening the dialogue to include a wider range of opinions, especially from relevant civil society groups, can loosen up negotiation deadlocks. It helps the society involved to move towards long-term social change, and builds the capability to endure a peaceful co-existence in a number of ways. First, providing a better dialogue and understanding between divided communities may improve public support for the negotiations. Second, identifying and bringing to the surface root causes and hidden sensitivities can help the leaders to address these in the 'settlement package'. Third, building confidence by creating an informal and safe space for communities to engage with each other would prepare the ground for a sustainable peaceful co-existence. Fourth, educating the wider public about considering different perspectives challenges their perceptions about distorted or incomplete views of history and the beliefs about the 'facts and causes' of the conflict (the Association of Historical Dialogue and Research has comprehensive work on this). Finally, influencing the media positively encourages them to provide balanced reporting of both progress and obstacles.

Celia McKeon, in her article 'Civil society: participating in peace processes', gives specific examples where civil society action was accepted by the leadership and led to participation in formal negotiations. She points out three cases as examples. In the case of Mozambique, she states that the mediation provided by three representatives of the religious Community of Sant'Egidio to the opposing sides played a key role in the peace process. Because they did not have any political stake in the outcome of the process and were not influenced by international actors or multilateral institutions, they had strong credibility and were able to provide a fresh approach. In Northern Ireland, the quiet mediation work provided by Peace and Reconciliation Group between the British security forces and the Irish Republican Army led to a de-escalation of armed conflict in Derry/Londonderry. This was a turning point in the building of trust between the opposing sides. The resolution of border disputes between Ecuador and Peru in the Andean region of Latin America was significantly helped by the opening of channels of communication by civil society groups from both communities. She suggests that their dialogue and subsequent work provided an awareness and understanding among the affected communities and contributed to the sustainability of the peace agreement.

Conclusion

According to the polls by Cyprus 2015 there is a clear need for improved CSO existence and the introduction of a system whereby the public have a greater say in the peace process. The resources available from the UNDP, the EU and other donors could in theory enable this. However, a culture change also needs to take place for these to be passed on into real life. Only a paradigm shift can break the old patterns; a shift where 'peace process' is understood as something which concerns the whole of society, not just the political elite. Working towards engaging not only key people but also different types of groups and wider society through a number of targeted actions is the first, essential step. Influencing the policy making process and policy makers should go hand-in-hand with this.

During the presentations, the visiting group made a number of suggestions for improving the current style of the Cyprus Peace Process. Progress reports at each step would increase the 'hope' factor. For example (despite the cost implications), mini referenda on separate issues in discussions during – not after – the peace process could be held. This would also increase public interest and engagement in that process. Trying to achieve a total agreement first and then holding one final referendum might only highlight the failures by undermining the successful parts of the negotiations. Transparency and media reporting during the talks, as well as regular feedback from the civil society representatives of the wider population would reduce speculation and misunderstanding and increase trust.

To achieve all these aims, structural reform of the peace process is needed, in order to allow a harmonious collaboration of the leaders, civil society and the wider public. At each level, representatives would have to be appointed whose sole task would be to liaise with the key members of civil society. CSOs on the island should form consultative bodies, with the purpose of enriching the Track 1 negotiation process. The wider public could be given a seat at the negotiations table through specialised polling, where the acceptability of alternative proposals would be tested. This could include groups that cut across the dividing line (such as women, youth and business groups).

South Africa and Northern Ireland provide good examples for Cyprus to learn from. In both cases extensive engagement took place with a wide range of political groups and civil society. After years of efforts and talks on these seemingly intractable conflicts, the leaders realised that an agreement without an inclusive process would not be sustainable. There is no doubt that many other factors contributed to the success achieved in these two conflicts; but it can be reasonably argued that inclusivity was one of the key components.

Every conflict has its own unique characteristic and therefore needs its own unique solution, but there are important lessons Cyprus can learn from other peace processes, which can then be tailored according to its specific needs. Northern Ireland, for example, benefited significantly from the South African experience despite the deeply different nature of the two conflicts.

Paradigm shift and culture change are notoriously difficult to achieve. They certainly don't happen overnight, but, as frankly admitted by one of the leading figures of the Northern Ireland peace process, Jeffrey Donaldson, during the Q&A session at the meeting, they are possible:

> I initially resented the interest/involvement of civil society. I thought; what do they know? I'm elected to do the job. Just keep out of it and we'll sort it out. But that was just a foolish perspective and I came to realize as a politician that we needed civil society to support the settlement and help prepare the ground and change the mindsets that are such an important part of any conflict/divided society. It is humans who are in conflict, not pieces of land. The soil does not rise up in Cyprus and have a fight with itself, it is the people who live on the Island who are in conflict so it is a human solution that must be found and civil society has an important role to play in that.

Note

The visiting group who gave the presentation consisted of Michalis Avraam (NGO Support Centre); Bulent Kanol (Management Centre); Alexandros Lordos (Cyprus 2015); Meliha Kaymak (EDGE); Marios Epaminondas (Association for Historical Dialogue and Research); Rana Zincir (UN Gender Advisory Team in Cyprus); and Katerina Antoniou (Youth Power).

References and recommended reading

Association for Historical Dialogue and Research, 'A proposal on the reform of history education' (Cyprus, 2012).

Barnes, Catherine, 'Democratising peacemaking processes: strategies and dilemmas for public participation' (Conciliation Resources Accord Series, 2002).

Cyprus 2015, 'Bridging the gap in the inter-communal negotiations: an island-wide study based on polls and extensive research' (Nicosia: Interpeace/Cyprus 2015, 2011).

Engi Conflict Management, 'Cyprus: tired of talking? civil society to bring life to a stagnant process' (London, 2012).

Kaymak, Erol, Alexandros Lordos and Nathalie Tocci, *Building Confidence in Peace: Public Opinion and the Cyprus Peace Process* (Brussels: Centre For European Policy Studies, 2005).

Ker-Lindsay, James, 'Peace efforts in Cyprus must involve civil society if there is to be any chance of success where so many others have failed', *European Politics and Policy (EUROPP) Blog*, London School of Economics, 28 May 2012.

McKeon, Celia, 'Participating in peace processes', in Paul van Tongeren, Malin Brenk, Marte Hellema and Juliette Verhoeven (eds), *People Building Peace II: Successful Stories of Civil Society* (London: Lynne Rienner, 2005).

NGO Support Sentence and the Management Centre, 'An assessment of civil society in Cyprus: a map for the future' (CIVICUS: Civil Society Index Report for Cyprus, 2011).

The Peace Exchange, 'Making the case for change on the road to peace in Cyprus'. Available at http://peacexchange. wordpress.com/tag/cyprus-civil-society/ (last accessed 29 May 2012).

Pope, Hugh, 'Cyprus: six steps toward a settlement', *International Crisis Group*, Europe Briefing No. 61 (2011).

Social Development Department Sustainable Development Network, 'Civil society and peacebuilding potential, limitations and critical factors', World Bank Report No. 36445-GLB (2006).

13

Cyprus in the Doldrums

Alexis Heraclides

The establishment of a federation of two politically equal constituent federated states, with each community in charge of one federated state – what has been known in Cyprus since 1977, as a 'bizonal bicommunal federation' – is the most obvious solution for reuniting the island and resolving the Cyprus Problem. Today more than ever before since the dramatic summer of 1974 such a solution is urgently needed and if the two parties do not arrive at an agreement soon, they will both be in dire straits. Yet the 'Cyprus led Cyprus owned talks' that started in March 2008 (with the UN as a facilitator) have been at stalemate and in danger of collapsing since early 2010.

In the mid-2000s, during the rejection by the Greek Cypriots of the Annan Plan (24 April 2004) and its aftermath, a case could be made (at least convincingly to the majority of Greek Cypriots) that there was no urgency for such a solution, that once in the EU, the Republic of Cyprus (RoC) would be in a far better position to bring about a resolution more favourable to their side. However, this has proved to be wishful thinking and neither the EU nor the UN, for that matter, are prepared to put pressure on the Turkish Cypriots to be so accommodating as to render the Greek Cypriots predominant in a reunited Cyprus. This is seen as unfair and unjust (and rightly so) given the history of the Cyprus conflict with the Greek Cypriot side as culprit from December 1963 until June 1974. In any event a solution that left the Turkish Cypriots 'unequal' would be totally unacceptable to Ankara, and if Turkey is not taken on board, resolution and reunification are simply impossible. But as long as the island remains divided and the problem is not resolved by way of a bizonal bicommunal federation, the Greek Cypriots' worst nightmare will become the only reality: the permanent partition and permanent presence of the daunting 40,000 Turkish Army in the island. Moreover, Anatolian Turks will continue to arrive in Cyprus even if Turkey discouraged it (which it does not) for purely economic reasons.

The present predicament

Recently the great shock of Cyprus's near default (due largely to mistakes of its own) has made the need for reunification more urgent than ever before for reasons of sheer survival. Only in a reunified Cyprus will the island become a thriving economy once again, with the appropriate exploitation (for the benefit of both communities) of its newly-found hydrocarbon resources in the seabed. If the island is not reunified and if the de facto partition becomes in all practical consequences de jure, the outcome would be disastrous for both parties. The Turkish Cypriot state (TRNC), even if nominally independent, would be reduced to a province of Turkey (even more than it is today) – indeed to a backwater of Turkey. As for the RoC, as long as reunification does not take place it will continue the downward trend of shrill nationalism and ethnocentrism which has sullied its democratic culture.

According to opinion polls, were a federal reunification plan to be put to a referendum today (mid-2012), 51 per cent of Greek Cypriots would vote against, with only 18 per cent supportive. As for the Turkish Cypriots, 31 per cent would vote against as against 42 per cent in support of the plan. In the present talks there has been some convergence on governance, power sharing, economic affairs and EU aspects, but very little on property, territory and international security guarantees. (The last issue is to be settled with the inclusion in the talks of the three guarantor powers, Greece, Turkey and the United Kingdom. However, the RoC does not want these three as guarantors, especially Turkey). However, given the overall negotiating principle in the present talks, that 'nothing is decided until everything is decided', their two publics are not aware of these convergences and initial agreements and both sides and a new administration can cast doubt on the convergences at any time. From September 2011 another issue has arisen to mar the atmosphere, the hydrocarbon perspective, which, instead of becoming an incentive for an acceptable reunification of the island, has become yet another bone of contention leading to mutual recriminations.

The main reasons for the impasse yesterday and today

To begin with it is worth stressing that no other ethnic conflict in the contemporary post-1945 world has led to such a plethora of mediations, and sustained ones at that, especially on the part of UN Secretary-Generals (in fact all the Secretaries-General starting with U Thant in 1964 have been actively involved). Yet all these mediation and facilitation attempts have come to naught. The end result is that UN mediation has almost earned a bad name, especially in the Greek Cypriot community, as trying to impose a settlement, a case in point being the Annan Plan. Furthermore there have been intermittent official talks between the two communities since January 1968, again with no settlement in sight.

No other ethnic conflict has been non-violent for so long (for more than four decades) but despite this lack of armed violence there is no solution in sight. The Cyprus Problem has been on ice since September 1974 but the two sides have not mellowed, with very few exceptions at leadership level only, as in the 2008–10 talks between Christophias and Talat. But even then the two leaders did not dare clinch a deal.

The root cause of the Cyprus conflict since it made its entry onto the world scene in 1950 is that both parties in their majority felt – and continue to feel – primarily Greeks and Turks respectively, and secondarily Cypriots. Characteristically the preferred flags on either side of the green line are the Greek flag and the Turkish flag respectively and the national hymn of the Republic of Cyprus is the Greek national anthem.

With the passage of time a huge psychological barrier was put in place in Cyprus, almost as forebidding as that between Palestinians and Israelis or Albanians and Serbs. Nicosia is not only, anachronistically, the last divided city in the world, it also happens to be the only city in the world with two museums of 'barbarity' regarding the other side's deeds. The sense of victimisation and trauma runs very deep. Turkish Cypriots remember and constantly refer to their treatment at the hands of the Makarios administration (discrimination as well as various atrocities) in the period 1964–74, while the Greek Cypriots remember and constantly refer to what they suffered at the hands of the invading Turkish Army in 1974, with Turkish Cypriots diehards assisting them in their atrocities.

The reigning mutual suspicion and demonisation has led to an array of misperceptions. Historically, the most pernicious mutual misperception is the view regarding *enosis* (union with Greece) and *taksim* (partition and union of the Northern part with Turkey), respectively. Until this very day it is regarded as the hidden agenda of the other side, incredible as this may seem. Thus, for instance, even the accession of the RoC to the EU is seen by the Turkish Cypriots (and many in Turkey) as indirect *enosis* with Greece; and as for the Greek Cypriots (and many in Greece), any concept of federation is seen as stepping stone to *taksim*. In fact the great majority of Greek Cypriots and the great majority of Turkish Cypriots abhor *enosis* and *taksim* and, incidentally, are not particularly attached to their so-called 'motherlands' in the same way as they were from the 1940s until the early 1960s. The very opposite is the case – dislike and distrust for the mainland Greeks and Turks. But is this mutual dislike and distrust (at times even resentment), which is shared by both communities, enough to glue together the two parts of divided Cyprus?

Another vital element against reunification is that despite the direct talks between the two sides that are now in their fifth decade (they have been going on since 1968) which imply that the two sides recognise each other, this was not the case in substance (save perhaps for a fleeting moment during the Christophias/Talat talks of 2008–10). Each side continues to reject the other's chosen identity and self-definition. For the Greek Cypriots the Turkish Cypriots are merely 'Turks', 'puppets of Ankara', 'late comers' and 'foreigners' in an island which is 'Greek since time immemorial'. The TRNC is called by almost every Greek Cypriot (and mainland Greek) the 'occupied areas' and their secessionist state, a 'pseudo-state' run by a 'pseudo-government' under the thumb of Turkey. When the Greek Cypriots refer to 'Cypriots' they mean only the Greek Cypriots, as if the Turkish Cypriots do not exist or could be wished away. The Turkish Cypriots return the compliment in their own way. They claim that the Greek Cypriots are not Greeks or descendents of the Ancient Greeks, but a motley collection of peoples who chose to call themselves Greeks for obvious reasons; they are a former subject people of the Ottomans, whose rule was a blessing for the island. Thus they disparagingly call the Greek Cypriots *Rum* (a Greek Orthodox designation from the days of the Ottoman Empire) and not Greeks (*Yunan*). As for the RoC, it is dubbed 'the Cyprus Administration' that 'usurped power' in 1964 and should not have been recognised by the UN as a sovereign independent state and member state of the UN (this has also been the official line of Turkey since 1964).

The predominant view in the wake of the 1974 mega-crisis in Cyprus still persists until today: that the Cyprus conflict is inherently 'win-lose'. The great majority of Greek Cypriots favour a unitary state and not a federal one. It is as if the 1974 crisis had not taken place and the island is not divided into two parts, as a consequence of the Turkish intervention that followed the Greek Junta's intervention. The Turkish Cypriots, for their part, favour two independent state members of the UN and EU; However, they could accept a federation as a compromise solution. Apparently the present division of the island, however unsavory (especially for the Greek Cypriots), is preferable to any conceivable peaceful settlement or power sharing. 'No solution is a solution', but each side, for different reasons, does not acknowledge this openly. The absence of 'a hurting stalemate', to use the concept coined by I. William Zartman, is also a potent obstacle, in the sense that neither community is sufficiently dissatisfied with the existing situation to make the difficult switch in order to resolve the conflict. Thus there is no urgency to reach a settlement and the alternative is not attractive but a source of Angst. Both sides as clearly seen in opinion polls (and and as noted by UN Secretary-General Ban Ki-moon) are absolutely convinced that a solution, though desirable, is impossible, and that even if a solution was somehow reached at leadership level it would not be implemented by the other party.

What constitutes a just solution is yet another minefield. For the Greek Cypriots a just solution should include: (a) the departure of all the Turkish soldiers, to the last man; (b) the departure of all the 'settlers' (immigrants from Turkey); (c) the Greek Cypriots to regain their properties and resettle in their original homes; and (d) power to be handed to the Turkish Cypriot federated state and the territory of each federated state to be analogous to the percentage of the population (that is, not much more than 20 per cent for the Turkish Cypriots). Clearly in any mutually accepted settlement none of the above can be taken on board as such. Even the Greek Cypriots realise that they are unattainable. It could well be that these unachievable goals are put forward (consciously or unconsciously) so as not to allow any reasonable settlement, making 'no solution the solution' by default, as it were. The Turkish Cypriots' view of a just solution includes the retention of part of the Turkish Army as a guarantee against the Greek Cypriot nationalists; the departure of only a minority of the immigrants from Anatolia; and power and territory to be based on a power sharing.

The creation of a bizonal bicommunal federation is the generally accepted blueprint for a solution since the Makarios–Denktash agreement of February 1977 (reiterated by the Kyprianou–Denktash agreement of 1970 and two joint statements by Christofias and Talat in 2008). Yet the federal model has been unable to capture the hearts and minds of most Greek Cypriots, who from 1977 until today have viewed it with deep suspicion. It is seen, at best, as a bad solution but with nothing else available for reunifying the island. The main reason for this posture is the fear that a Turkish Cypriot federated state would merely pave the way for eventual partition and annexation by Turkey. Another reason that makes federalism so unpopular to the Greek Cypriots is that it was a Turkish idea to begin with (back in August 1974). It is seen as accepting the *fait accompli* of the Turkish 'invasion'. Turkish Cypriots adverse to reunification regard a federation as disguised domination by the Greek Cypriots leading to a unitary Greek-dominated state. But by and large the federal blueprint is more popular among Turkish Cypriots.

According to recent opinion polls, the majority of Greek Cypriots could accept as a compromise 'a federation without restrictions on settlement and property ownership throughout the whole island'. Obviously such a federation would undermine the basis of a bizonal bicommunal federation of two politically equal constituent states and communities, as the Greek Cypriots would become the majority in both states, swamping the Turkish Cypriots. The restrictions on settlement and property ownership, as advocated by the Turkish Cypriots, is obviously the only way forward if the island is to be reunited, yet it is rejected by the great majority of Greek Cypriots.

Now let us hark back to the wider setting of 1999–2004 and compare it with that of today. The period 1999–March 2004 offered an unprecedented window of opportunity for resolving the Cyprus Problem. The following factors coalesced: a strong desire by the RoC for accession to the EU; the genuine desire of Turkey for accession to the EU; the sudden amelioration of relations between Greece and Turkey; the sustained interest of the UN, US, Britain, the EU and the G7 for a final workable solution; the energetic role of Greece under

Simitis for a solution; the huge effort put by Secretary-General Kofi Annan, which was unique in the annals of UN mediations in ethnic conflicts; the gradual de-legitimation of the intransigent Denktash in his constituency, with a concomitant rise of support for reunification in the North; and from mid-2003 onwards a veritable volte face on the part of Turkey under the Erdoğan government in support of Annan's efforts (though this switch had come late, when the intransigent Tassos Papadopoulos was in full control in the South).

Today by contrast the overall landscape is not encouraging. Turkey has lost interest in the EU, so it has little incentive to be accommodating regarding Cyprus. As for Greece it is in its worst-ever situation economically and prestige-wise and is out of the picture; the EU's influence in both Turkey and Greece is limited and it is immobilised by none other than the RoC as a member state (the RoC, for instance, does not allow the EU to make good its 2004 promise to halt the isolation of the Turkish Cypriots); and as for the US, it stands aloof and has other pressing priorities to address. Furthermore, Greek–Turkish relations are troubled and in their worst state since the 1999 thaw. As for Erdoğan, he has abandoned his previous line that Ankara would always be 'a step ahead' on the road to reunion and resolution. In a trip to the TRNC he went as far as stating that the return of territory as envisaged by the Annan Plan was unacceptable to Turkey. More alarmingly as far as its neighbours are concerned, Turkey seems to be under the spell of Ahmet Davutoglu's incredible geopolitical vision, the belief in all seriousness that Turkey (a 'neo-Ottoman Turkey') can become the leader of the Islamic world and a world power, on a par with the US, Russia and China.

One of the fundamental problems of Cyprus, seen in the case of the Annan Plan but also today in the talks, is that deep down the Greek Cypriots in their majority find equality with the Turkish Cypriot very difficult to swallow. After having monopolised the Cyprus state for almost 50 years, the Greek Cypriots are loath to abandon exclusive control of the state and opt for power-sharing. Power-sharing is seen as unjust and unfair by the majority of Greek Cypriots, given the percentages involved, 80 per cent as opposed to 18 per cent. The difficulty here, compared to, say, Belgium, is that the percentages involved are not very helpful. But I dare say that the real problem is not only that the Greek Cypriot regard power sharing as unjust. Most Greek Cypriots regard Turkish Cypriots as culturally alien as well as inferior. Clearly this is hardly the ground for 'remarriage' of two equal partners based on mutual respect, let alone 'parity of esteem', to use the apt wording of the Good Friday Agreement on Northern Ireland.

Conclusion

So, what is to be done? In all probability the present talks that started in 2008 will not bear fruit, at least not in the foreseeable future. The two communities have, with their attitude, placed themselves in a Catch 22 situation: no move is acceptable to them and sheer immobility is also unacceptable. Clearly the gains from a settlement of reunification are not appreciated by most members of the two communities who, when the chips are down, appear to prefer separation to reunification. On the other hand, the present situation is equally unacceptable yet they are not ready for the necessary compromises of reunion, when only reunion can jolt both communities to prosperity and a functioning liberal democracy. Both sides have themselves to blame for the miserable impasse but their gut reaction is to blame everything on the other side (and in the Greek Cypriot case on Ankara in particular) and on 'foreign conspiracies'. But the RoC is in a state of shock given its tragic economic situation and in no mood for compromise or for addressing the solution of the problem.

Given this unhappy state of affairs, I see three procedural possibilities. The first is to continue with the talks, but not to beat about the bush. To call a spade and spade and include the 'velvet divorce' as an option, with a return of some 7–8 per cent of territory to the Greek Cypriots. The outcome could be a confederation so as to enhance cooperation and assure that the North does not become part of Turkey in all but in name. The second option is to change the format to a peace conference which would include the EU, the UN, Greece and Turkey with two options ahead: first a loose bicommunal bizonal federation (the Annan V model without improvements) and if it fails, a velvet divorce. The third option is to abandon the talks for the time being so as to allow for in-depth reflection and soul-searching within each community for a period of one or two years. So long as the stalemated talks continue with no progress in sight they will be discredited, rubbing in the fact that a solution is unattainable. In the course of this hiatus in talks it could well be that a deus ex machina might appear or a level 'conflict transformation' as in the period 1999–2002. During this gap the two parties need not remain idle but could take one or more positive steps that could create momentum for eventual settlement, such as: (a) opening the Famagusta Port and the Tymbou (Ercan) Airport; (b) opening the fenced ghost city of Varosha to its inhabitants; (c) lifting the isolation of the Turkish Cypriots; (d) normalising RoC–Turkish trade relations without Turkey formally recognising RoC; and (d) opening the locked chapters of the Turkey–EU accession talks.

I would favour the third procedural solution, to buy time for the federal solution before it loses all its remaining attractiveness. Only after a sincere internal soul-searching could talks be resumed. These resumed talks should have a clear timetable, ending with reunion or permanent separation. In this final stage of the talks the positive role of Turkey (as back in 2003–4) and of a hopefully invigorated Greece is essential. At the moment, however, and for the foreseeable future the situation is dismal with no solution in sight for several years.

References and recommended reading

Anastasiou, Harry, *The Broken Olive Branch: Nationalism, Ethnic Conflict, and the Quest for Peace in Cyprus*, vol. I, *The Impasse of Ethnonationalism* (Syracuse: Syracuse University Press, 2008).

Asmussen, Jan, *Cyprus at War: Diplomacy and Conflict during the 1974 Crisis* (London: I.B.Tauris, 2008).

Bryant, Rebecca and Yiannis Papadakis (eds), *Cyprus and the Politics of Memory: History, Community and Conflict* (London: I.B.Tauris, 2012).

Faustmann, Hubert and Emilios Solomou (eds), *Independent Cyprus 1960–2010: Selected Readings* (Nicosia: University of Nicosia Press, 2011).

Hannay, David, *Cyprus: The Search for a Solution* (London: I.B.Tauris, 2005).

Ker-Lindsay, James, *The Cyprus Problem: What Everyone Needs to Know* (New York: Oxford University Press, 2011).

Michael, Michalis Stavrou, *Resolving the Cyprus Conflict: Negotiating History* (Basingstoke: Palgrave Macmillan, 2009).

Papadakis, Yiannis, Nicos Peristianis and Gisela Welz (eds), *Divided Cyprus: Modernity, History, and an Island in Conflict* (Bloomington, IN: Indiana University Press, 2006).

Pericleous, Chrysostomos, *The Cyprus Referendum: A Divided Island and the Challenge of the Annan Plan* (London: I.B.Tauris, 2009).

Varnava, Andrekos and Hubert Faustmann (eds), *Reunifying Cyprus: The Annan Plan and Beyond* (London: I.B.Tauris, 2009).

14

The Catalytic Role of Regional Crisis

ROBERT HOLLAND

'Can the Cyprus Problem be solved?' is the puzzle set for contributors to this volume. Insofar as this implicitly means solved by negotiation alone, the answer must be no. There is no likely feasibility that a lasting settlement could come about through the clever permutation of constitutional formulae or 'golden words'. If this had been possible, it would have happened long before now. In this regard the failure of the Annan Plan in 2004 represented the line in the sand. It has, of course, been followed by a more 'Cypriot-owned process'. What 'Cypriot-owned' has meant in this context is a negotiation part and parcel of a more general manoeuvring for advantage, rather than an authentic effort to thrash out a workable consensus. Cynics will think that the show goes on merely because it gives a sense of self-importance to the international and Cypriot personnel involved. There is enough truth in this at least to be uncomfortable.

Parallels have been made between the situations in Cyprus and Northern Ireland. The foundational Good Friday Agreement of April 1998 and what has followed in Ulster provides some optimism that a similar 'coming together' of two hitherto alienated communities and traditions might be engineered in Cyprus. But the circumstances are vitally different. In Ulster there was always a middle class straddling lines of religious division. The Good Friday Agreement had the imprint of overlapping social forces for which the prospect of shared prosperity massively trumped continued fetid bickering. Although bitter division remains in Ulster, it now festers within enclosed and dwindling working-class ghettos, both

Catholic and (perhaps especially) Protestant. In Cyprus there is no mainstream social process spanning core communities.

At the same time, the essence of the paradox surrounding putative Cypriot solutions must be clear. The balance of ethnic power internal to the island has long been obverse to that prevailing in the external and regional spheres. This is why Anthony Eden, the British statesman, remarked in his memoirs that seeking solutions to Cypriot problems is like one of those board games where a lot of little balls have to be coaxed into holes. No sooner do you get the last ball nearly into place than all the others get displaced, and the game starts anew. Whether you start at the internal or the external ends of the puzzle in Cyprus, sooner or later the basic contradiction upsets all expectations of a satisfactory outcome. This remains as true today as it was in Eden's very different context.

The missing ingredient

Whether in its pre-independence or post-independence formats, the most basic missing ingredient in Cyprus has been goodwill. With goodwill the 1960 constitution might have evolved without foundering. Amendments to improve its operability could have been introduced over time, possibly under a broad consensus, whereas in the event President Makarios' premature and communitarian power-grab in late 1963 swiftly stalled. Even then the inter-communal talks after 1968 might with goodwill have reset a path away from the abyss of 1974 had they been something more than a tactical parenthesis within the larger struggle. There are those who believe that the creation of such goodwill will never come through the actions of self-interested governing cadres, but that a more lasting method is provided by the dissemination of reconciliationist ideals by non-governmental organisations and civic endeavour. An industry of this kind is now engaged in such activities as the rewriting of Cypriot history books. It is easy to cast aspersions on such hopes, pointing out that much of the time this consists of preaching only to the converted, lubricated with donations by nice people from Scandinavia. All one can say is that the evidence points to an ebbing of goodwill rather than the reverse amongst ordinary Cypriots, both Greeks and Turks, in recent years. Certainly amongst Turkish Cypriots there has been a regression of the tendencies at work during the climax of the Annan process, which led to an unavailing acceptance of the proposals on their own side, whilst amongst Greek Cypriots a sense of hubris after the Plan's collapse – and the prosperity that then ensued for other reasons – only deepened a frank lack of interest in fellow-inhabitants of the island that had always characterised a good deal of Greek Cypriot political culture.

It is relevant to reflect on why Greek Cypriots rejected the proposals put to a referendum in 2004. At a popular level there was not that *yearning* for an end to the status quo that characterised feelings in Ulster, for example, at the start of the new century. This in itself is not surprising. In the Irish case existing conditions were bleak and sometimes bloody, whereas in Cyprus the physical clarity of division after 1974–5 had prevented day-to-day ructions and the occasional 'spectacular' outrage. It is probably true to say that most Greek Cypriots by 2004 were more preoccupied with what they might lose through a compromise settlement than by what they might gain. But what ordinary Greek Cypriots thought in 2004 was not much to the point. It was the Greek Cypriot decision-making elite – existing within their intellectual and material bubble – who shaped outcomes on their own side, above all through its domination of the press and media; and from their perspective, the context created by Cyprus' unimpeded accession to the EU, far from being conducive to an immediate settlement, made it all the more imperative to contemplate no such thing.

The reason for this was that ultimately the process of EU accession, and a settlement of the island's divisions, ran athwart each other, the complete opposite, that is, of the expectation held by ill-informed outsiders. Through its membership, the Republic of Cyprus was handed what appeared to be an unparalleled opportunity to gain the high ground in securing its most fundamental aspiration: not just to ameliorate the effects of 1974, but to completely reverse them. At last, and perhaps unexpectedly, the internal and external balances of power could be seen approaching a new equilibrium, and one that this time favoured the Greek side. It was entirely rational to conclude that to sign on a dotted line for a settlement before the effects of EU membership – highly differential in its benefits between the two main island communities – had worked themselves out over a prolonged period was madness from the Greek vantage-point.

In fact this has not happened yet, and in the meantime one necessary element in the calculation – the pressure point constituted by Turkey's own desire to be part of the European Union – has seemingly almost evaporated. But this is not to say that eventually the configuration within the island will never slide in such a way as to ensure an effective Greek power-monopoly of the sort Makarios always aimed at. If the only real structural solution to the current crisis of the Eurozone, that is a full 'political union', comes about, inevitably coming to embrace foreign as well as economic policy, the ability of the Republic of Cyprus to affect broader European decision making in the eastern Mediterranean might well be enhanced in critical ways. Such a capacity would certainly be leveraged to impact on the island's internal balances. The potential exploitation of natural resources in the maritime region clearly enters the future reckoning at this point (though currently it must be said that oil for European consumers is already starting to flow from Iraqi Kurdistan via Turkish pipelines, whilst surplus Cypriot energy, even if it exists in commercially viable form, is still years away). Nevertheless, all this speaks to a profound, and in many ways understandable, Greek Cypriot preference for a continuing 'long struggle' over any negotiated compromise.

The uses of forgetfulness

The trouble with this approach is how long can a piece of string be? Thinking historically, it seems to this writer that there are two ways that 'solutions' in deeply divided polities come about, and neither has anything to do with grey-suited men sitting around desks devising finely-balanced schemes, or with earnest academic and civic activists drawing on a play-book of inter-communal harmony. The first way is that eventually everybody apart from an antediluvian hard core 'forgets', or forsakes, what the struggle was all about in the first place. People, and societies, simply move on as other considerations and imperatives intrude. Contexts mutate in ways that make previous animosities seem not just outdated, but actually ridiculous. Such a transformation has been under way in Ireland for some time, to such an extent that in May 2011 the Queen was feted in Dublin, something previously unimaginable during the lifetime of this author. With devolution unfolding in the British Union, the English and the Irish will probably end up once again just as enmeshed as the English and the Scots, whatever the outcome of the Scottish referendum in 2014 (and as has always really been the case anyway sociologically-speaking, as any Londoner can tell you). Who knows, one day Ireland may even rejoin the Commonwealth, though of course not the long-deceased 'British' Commonwealth. Along this trajectory the line of physical division blurs, then distinctly fades and in the end becomes a subject of merely antiquarian curiosity.

For all sorts of reasons, such a sequence is especially difficult to simulate in Cyprus. It certainly cannot happen in quite the same way. Still, elements of it may be identified. The Greek Cypriot political class is having to confront an enormous challenge. All its default positions have been defined by the existing physical division, the legacy of 1974. Yet as issues of solvency, unemployment, economic growth and maintaining public services come increasingly to the fore, a different set of political priorities will inevitably develop. The election for the presidency in 2013 reflected such a tendency even before the economic implosion added a new intensity. Given the seepage of decision-taking – not least affecting the crucial matter of budgets – to Brussels, Frankfurt and ultimately to Berlin, the Republic will be hard pressed enough to maintain sovereignty over its current *de facto* responsibilities without having much time spare to devote to 'the Cyprus Problem'. The new President has recently assured one of the main Greek Cypriot diaspora organisations that 'the Problem' as traditionally understood remains the core priority of government, but this is the sort of empty rhetoric that political diasporas feed off; there is no cost in letting them have it. In practice, partition will always remain an offence in the eyes of Greek Cypriots, as it always will be to many Ulster Catholics, but compared to other dangers to the good life it will become less and less important as the years go by and new generations shift their angle of vision. In this vein the division in the island would not so much go away as drift steadily into irrelevance. For any Cypriot born in recent years, 1974 will as they grow up become what World War II was to the European generation brought up in the 1960s and 1970s: the sort of thing old 'fogeys' go on about, but actually little to do with real contemporary life.

The impulse of fear

There is another way in which change happens, however, one which cuts, often brutally, across the *longue durée*. This is when the status quo is broken up through external crisis, and *force majeure* imposes a fresh pattern. Under such circumstances fear, not goodwill, rudely pushes protagonists into accepting a different order of things. When one looks back over modern Cypriot history, regime change has normally happened as a by-product of regionwide crises involving Turkey. The end of effective Ottoman rule in 1878 came about in the wake of Russo–Turkish war; British annexation in 1914 occurred in the immediate aftermath of Turkey's belligerency alongside the Central Powers; the pre-independence deadlock over the island was only lifted when a medley of crises involving Iraq, Syria and the Lebanon in the summer of 1958 – impacting on Turkish frontiers – threatened the general stability of the area and made a viable solution in Cyprus far more urgent. It is a fair bet that, if real change comes about once more, it will ultimately be courtesy of an external shock, with seemingly intractable divisions overwhelmed by the after-spill of events elsewhere. Such a metamorphosis is likely to happen out of the blue, just like the Zurich–London agreements of February 1959 which were the true harbinger of an independent, if not absolutely self-determining, Cyprus.

Presently intimations of a systemic crisis have not been so audible since the Arab-Israeli war of 1973. Threats to the regional order, such as the Israeli-Hezbollah confrontations in 2006 and 2009, were contained, if with difficulty. However, it is now clear that something far more fundamental is going on. The so-called 'Middle East', the sovereign tramlines of which were laid down under Anglo–French supervision after 1916, and which anyway was always something of a confection, is cracking apart. A War of Arab Succession (not an 'Arab Spring', that convenient but superficial instant narrative for the media) is in motion defined mainly but not exclusively by Shia–Sunni divisions. If such a desperate saga unfolds there will be no way to disentangle existential struggles internal to countries in the region and those that are purely external. Cyprus has a good track record of avoiding – perhaps through luck as much as judgement – being sucked into such vortexes. It had, for example, a relatively peaceful existence throughout World War II; the quiet life is always to be preferred in dangerous eras. But the 'risk on' instincts of the Greek Cypriot political class, which were a fatal factor in driving up the stakes even before independence, seem as visible as ever in the current desire to link the Republic's strategic fortunes to favoured protagonists, above all Israel, and this at a time when the Israeli position itself seems weaker than at any time probably since 1968. Overall, amidst an impending Middle Eastern breakdown some very rapid footwork, 1959-style, might be required to help seal it off from drastic implosions elsewhere.

A distinctive aspect of recent developments, however, has been a refocusing of tensions configured not so much in the Middle

Eastern terms so characteristic of post-1945 regional politics, but one resembling an older pattern of rivalry in the Levant. Russia's hyperactive desire to get involved underlines such a sense. Cyprus is even less on the margins of an essentially Levantine phenomenon than it would be in a specifically Middle Eastern crisis. The discovery of hydrocarbons and the disputes surrounding this development have become the pivot. Predictably, foreign navies have shown a penchant for making their appearance and 'showing' their respective flags (so very nineteenth century!). Local politicians seek to draw attention to themselves by making provocative statements and uttering ambitious predictions. Amongst the motives is a desire to leverage future gas revenues to regain a financial and economic independence that was so painfully lost by the 'bail-out' of summer 2013, and which no slow and hard-won conventional recovery, such as improved tourist numbers, is likely to restore. In this way all sorts of issues are getting entangled with each other. It can only be assumed that Turkey will use any opportunities arising over time to pressurise the Greek Cypriot position, though with what degree of ruthlessness will depend on unpredictable factors.

What brought about the unexpected 'settlement' leading to independence in 1960 was that a sudden burst of pressure operated simultaneously on all three of the main protagonists: Britain, Greece and Turkey. Of these, the British were the least important then, and are much more marginal, even irrelevant, now. As in 1958–9, and so today, arguably the most basic requirement is that Turkey should feel the heat of circumstances before a new configuration can take shape. In principle at least this does not take much imagining in the light of incipient events. The old unified Syria looks beyond saving in any form, and one of the entities emerging from its ugly death is almost bound to be another Kurdish polity on Turkey's own border. Turkey has enjoyed great economic success in recent years, but harder times appear to lie ahead for emerging economies amidst the great sucking sound of the United States Federal Board ingesting dollar resources (the famous 'tapering' of bond purchases) rather than creating new international liquidity. India's pain today could be Turkey's tomorrow, with the lira following the rupee downwards. The palmy days of AKP successes may be behind it, and as problems mount the party's popularity may ebb away as did that of the Democratic Party as the 1950s progressed; certainly Tayyip Erdoğan shows a sensitivity and authoritarian streak rather similar to that of Adnan Menderes after 1956/7. Neither a proud, brazenly confident Turkey, nor a desperately weakened one, is likely to embrace a Cyprus agreement again as it did in 2004. But a newly uncertain and anxious Turkey might. Of course, the very factors we have mentioned might well point in a completely different direction so far as Turkish pliability is concerned, depending on the actions of others and the sheer contingency of events. This is where any precise prediction trails off into inconsequence.

The 'Anglo-Americans' and Europe

There are two other factors to put into this mix. The first concerns Greek Cypriot interaction with the 'Anglo-Americans', who they blame for many of their worst travails (the fact that such a devoted Anglo-Saxon couple has never really existed, and certainly does not exist now, we may pass over here). Greek Cypriot diplomacy has tried very hard to diversify its diplomatic partners in recent years. Again, the heady management of gas exploration contracts indicates just one aspect of such a process. The Cyprus Republic has invested a great deal of effort in constructing some sort of 'special relationship' with France; this has had a cultural dimension, too, so that Cyprus has become a member of *Francophonie* (a new Franco–Cypriot school in Nicosia is just another minor expression). This may well produce significant benefits one way or another. But if one believes in a 'big bang' theory of ultimate Cypriot settlement-making, much depends on whether third parties are likely to prove reliable when the decisive moment comes. After all, 'solidarity' may be problematical not only on financial matters, and the price of being found wanting when most needed even steeper. Certainly Washington's engagement with internal Cypriot issues is currently very much at arm's length. Meanwhile, although the social and, as it were, 'human' interaction between the United Kingdom and Cyprus continues as ever, the fact is that politically and diplomatically the connection is lukewarm on both sides. For younger states, old connections can be irritating and smack of a detested past dependency, alleged betrayals along the way keenly resented. But before cutting completely loose one needs to be entirely sure of the firmness of any new footing.

The other variable brings us back to Europe. The basic assumption of Greek Cypriot officialdom until recently was that there lies ahead a two-speed Europe in which Cyprus will be in the 'fast' lane. In such a brave new world, the crisis-management capacity of the Republic, and its ability to manipulate European leverage to its own advantage, could be seen advancing steadily and even exponentially. Recent events have been a rude blow to expectations about Europe, though the new government of President Anastasiades is striving to put the pieces back together again, since no alternative vision appears to exist. It may be that renewed Eurozone pressures in late 2013 and 2014 will at last compel Germany to make a leap in the dark towards full European Union. In what – to this writer – seems the all too likely eventuality of a major eastern Mediterranean crisis, possibly a war, during the course of the next two or three years, the Greek Cypriots may then still, for all their economic weakness, be able to present themselves as constituting the 'last bastion' of stability on Europe's exposed frontier. However, what, on the European front, seems most probable is not an a new centralised super-state, but a more flexible and variegated European Union, since the increasingly rigid phenomenon that presently exists will simply guarantee a slide down the hierarchy of the world system, not least commercially. This – including a role as the permanent master-subsidiser of Southern Europe – is not a future the Germans relish for themselves. *De facto* political union in the narrower Eurozone, if it happens, will therefore surely first do so within a Northern core, simply to ensure that the experiment does not this time fail almost as soon as it has got under way. Europe at the outer edges will remain frail, vulnerable and in key respects un-sovereign. No current EU or Eurozone member will be allowed to drop into a void. But some will be stuck in limbo, enjoying at best mediocre economic growth, and with an ambivalent relationship to further developments in integrated institutional machinery. Just how the Republic of Cyprus fits into whatever dynamic does emerge will determine how well or otherwise it is placed to look after its own interest, including on the matter of reunification.

Conclusion

The truth is, anybody who predicts with any certainty how the Cyprus issue is likely to pan out in the next few years is delusional. But the instinct of this commentator, based on rather messy historical knowledge, is that the Cyprus Problem will either end up being engulfed in a fog of forgetfulness – say, like the Schleswig-Holstein Question of the mid-nineteenth century – or, instead, events external to the island will threaten an uncontrollable denouement that none of the leaderships involved will want and force them collectively to make decisions that had previously been impossible to swallow. The trick will be to act before the eruption wreaks its full havoc, or to divert it into a more stable path, as the key leaders did at Zurich and London in early 1959. Highly improvised, no doubt illogical, and inevitably provisional compromise will then become the new and permanent reality. Under such a scenario, the resulting compromise will almost certainly share a good many of the provisions of the Annan Plan of 2004, though of course great care will be taken to allow the tracks to be covered.

But here there is for the historian perhaps an ultimate paradox. From the 1950s onwards amongst key non-Cypriot protagonists in the island's affairs there was a firm belief that an unfettered independent republic was in fact 'worse than *enosis*' with Greece simply because it would be an uncertain and maverick proposition, and thus a threat to international peace. This anxiety came to be heightened by President Makarios's gambling predilections. Outside protagonists did not themselves principally create the fault lines of 1963–4 and 1974, which resulted from the actions of local political cadres carried away by an inflated sense of their own capacity to shape events. But those events had a silver lining, albeit one that could not be admitted, for some external actors in putting off a day when a truly unified, independent and self-confident Cyprus might come into being. Perhaps, against the odds, it may one day indeed come about, though under the aegis hopefully (though again predictions are hazardous) of bicommunal leaders equipped with resources of political intelligence and genuine goodwill superior to those of an earlier cohort who squandered the opportunities that self-government in 1960, for all its anomalies, brought with it.

References and recommended reading

Bew, John, Peter Gibbon and Henry Patterson, *Northern Ireland: Political Forces and Social Classes* (London: Serif, 2002).

Hatzivassilou, Evanthis, *The Cyprus Question, 1878–1960: The Constitutional Aspect* (Minneapolis, MN: University of Minnesota Press, 2002).

Holland, Robert, *Britain and the Revolt in Cyprus, 1954–59* (Oxford: Clarendon, 1998).

Stefanidis, Ioannis, *Isle of Discord: Nationalism, Imperialism and the Making of the Cyprus Problem* (London: Hurst, 1999).

Yiangou, Anastasia, *Cyprus in World War Two: Politics and Conflict in the Eastern Mediterranean* (London: I.B.Tauris, 2010).

15

Adopting a Piecemeal Approach

Erol Kaymak

Cyprus is still known for its infamous 'Cyprus Problem', which now spans nearly half a century. Perhaps one day in the not too distant future the monopoly will be broken, and Cyprus will also be known to subsequent generations as part and parcel of the unfolding Eurozone crisis. For now, as far as the 'international community' is concerned, the salient problem remains the division of the island.

The most recent round of settlement negotiations is on life support, courtesy of the United Nations Secretary-General Ban Ki-moon and his Good Offices mission to Cyprus. Whereas it is clear that these 'Cyprus-led' talks have failed, the UN remains reluctant to declare it and to issue a death certificate for yet another process. Sadly, it is the members of the Good Offices mission who appear more affected by failure than Cypriots themselves. The first step in remorse is denial. If the stop-gap effort to bridge the current impasse with renewed negotiations in 2013 and 2014 proves but an interlude to the ultimate termination of talks, then there will be a sober reassessment of what ails Cyprus, hence alternative remedies.

We are approaching a deja vu moment, insofar as the UN has shut down its Good Offices before, even while speculating as to whether federalism remains a mutual objective of the sides. Ban's predecessor, Kofi Annan, had called upon the Security Council to reconsider Resolutions that served to isolate the Turkish Cypriots from the international community despite their having voted 'yes' to a fateful referendum on reunification in 2004. However, Annan's report was never adopted as a Resolution, so the international status quo remained. At the time there was still optimism that a new round of negotiations could be held in short order.

This chapter argues that a comprehensively negotiated settlement to the Cyprus Problem is unlikely, even if against the odds an international conference is eventually held. The UN and the international community need not hold their collective breath anticipating the outcome of these extended talks. Whereas the method of ratification through referenda may serve to consolidate any deal, public opinion polls demonstrate that there is the real prospect of any package being rejected by one or both communities, which would lead to further complications. Yet the United Nations Security Council can only offer its Good Offices service, which in turn is bound by Resolutions that foresee a power-sharing federal arrangement as the basis of any negotiations.

Ultimately, insistence on a 'comprehensive' take-it-or-leave-it package approach must be abandoned. Instead a piecemeal approach should be adopted in order to normalise relations between the communities (or states) in Cyprus, on the one hand, and deal with the international dimension, on the other. Alternatives to the UN mediation framework are complicated by the decision making processes in the European Union, where the Greek Cypriots have insisted that Protocol 10 of the Accession Treaty requires unanimity, but without normalisation the UN framework will not produce results. This chapter first assesses the current round of talks and argues that UN mediation has inadvertently served the ulterior motives of the sides. Solving the Cyprus Problem would require a new approach that engaged all interested parties in an integrated way, while allowing for innovative piecemeal solutions upon which to build (and learn) cooperative practices.

The fate of the (suspended) talks

Despite the impasse in the current round of negotiations, the UN remains committed to resuscitating the talks through proxy negotiations on what the Secretary-General's Special Advisor Alexander Downer dubbed 'the way forward'. Essentially, the UN averted a crisis in the spring of 2012 by first noting de facto political deadlines, including Cyprus' EU presidency in the latter half of 2012, but then extending the shelf life of the talks when the sides could not make substantive progress. So, whereas talks were effectively downgraded to a technical level, the Secretary-General did not shut down his Good Offices mission. Crucially the UN Security Council was spared the responsibility of producing any resolutions that could have singled out one of the sides for blame. The upshot was that the UN did not blame the Turkish side for 'leaving the table' as of 1 July 2012, when Cyprus assumed the EU presidency. Nor did the UN accuse any of the sides of dragging their feet at that stage.

Few Cypriots are in mourning or overtly concerned about the ultimate demise of the talks. The indifference is striking in contrast with the UN's anxiety. The nominal 'Cyprus-led' talks were never owned by the people and the talks could not spark public imagination. In a round of negotiations where the Cypriot sides were, for the most part, left on their own to build a consensus on their own terms, the result has been a spectacular sham. Even in the absence of mediation powers, much less the authority to arbitrate, Downer was the target of sustained campaigns among Greek Cypriot opposition parties due to his alleged partiality towards the Turkish side, thus foreclosing any real opportunities to expedite the process. For his part, the Greek Cypriot negotiator from 2008 through 2012, President Dimitris Christofias, remained reluctant to divulge details of convergences and resisted efforts to introduce deadlines and binding negotiation schedules. Whereas discreetness has its virtues, it meant that the talks became reclusive and the leaders introverted, allowing for opposition groups to exploit their roles as 'spoilers' in public opinion. The Turkish side, during the tenures of both Mehmet Ali Talat and Dervis Eroğlu, tended to push for deadlines in the absence of convergences in key dossiers, in an attempt to internationalise the talks. But similarly to the Greek Cypriot stance, the Turkish side also adhered to the principle that 'nothing is agreed to until all is agreed to', hence the need for a comprehensive, consensual package that has proven elusive. While this sequencing tactic is part of the mediator's toolkit, it has clearly backfired in Cyprus. In order to break the impasse the UN utilised summit diplomacy designed to reassure the Greek Cypriots that convergences were key to progress while demonstrating to Turkish Cypriots that the international community understood that talks could not be open-ended and would not be allowed to flounder indefinitely. Two Greentree summits hosted by the Secretary-General ended in what even the UN has described as failure. Against this, the respective sides were relieved that the UN has not engaged in ultimate attribution against one side or the other.

At the time of writing, it remains to be seen what turn Cyprus talks will take. Depending on how existential the Eurozone crisis proves to be, there is the distinct possibility that the Cyprus Problem could be crowded off the top of the agenda. Meanwhile discourses on the Turkish side suggest that most Turkish Cypriots speak of the future of their entity and the need for sustainability without regard to reunification. Overall, the lack of anticipation and concern for the negotiations contrasts with previous rounds where interest was much higher.

Paradoxically, this outcome appears to be a failure of the UN and not of the sides' 'Cypriot-led' approach. After all, each side has its own 'best alternative to a negotiated settlement' (BATNA) yardstick by which to judge the outcome. The failure of the talks apparently has only limited consequences for either community. Apparently is the key word, since such assessments are always filtered through subjective lenses. This is more acute for the Greek Cypriot side, where EU membership came at no cost and where any settlement will prove unpopular, if not unworkable. But for the Turkish Cypriot side there are also misgivings about a process where consensus is required. Significantly, many Turkish Cypriots are jaded following the aborted Annan Plan blueprint as a result of the Greek Cypriot 'no' in the fateful referendum of 2004. Most Turkish Cypriots anticipate another 'no' in the event of a subsequent referendum, reinforcing a sense of injustice due to political asymmetry. As a result, the Turkish leadership has been emphasising (perhaps ill advisedly, if not prematurely) a 'plan B' as an alternative to a negotiated federal agreement. Moreover, the Turkish Cypriot stance is affected by Turkey's diminished ambitions and opportunities to join the EU. The relationship between Ankara and Brussels reached a nadir during the Cyprus presidency in 2012.

Ultimately positive inducements may not outweigh objections to a compromise solution. This dovetails with a line of argument that discounts the potential for future conflict and risks. There are numerous accounts of officials downplaying the potential for trouble in the Mediterranean regarding the extraction of fossil fuels. Similarly, the uncertainty associated with another failed round is disregarded. Few entertain ideas about the consequences of the UN withdrawing from Cyprus *in toto*. However, if Greek Cypriots and Turkish Cypriots do not feel the urgency or otherwise lack the incentives to conclude a compromise package, then there is the very real risk that the UN and others will eventually reconsider resources devoted to the unrewarding task of reunifying Cyprus through negotiations. Against this, imposing settlements can be more costly and divisive. Given the fluidity of events associated with unrest in the Middle East and the conflict among Security Council members regarding resolution, the relative stability of the Cypriot 'frozen conflict' must be better than its alternatives. It is this calculus and dilemma that leads the UN to conclude that life support is preferable to pulling the plug.

Externalities of UN Good Offices

Although the UN continues to push for a renewed round, this is indeed an opportune moment to ask whether the Cyprus Problem can ever be resolved. Based on the foregoing the obvious answer is that the Cypriot side, independent of outside prodding and assistance, cannot be relied on to achieve a diplomatic breakthrough. Even were such a hurdle overcome, then the question would be whether there would be sufficient good will and trust to implement a complex settlement, replete with transitions that could easily trigger crises.

If there is a glimmer of hope it is in the growing acknowledgement that somehow negotiations would also have to involve Ankara and other actors. Indeed, if the UN remains committed to a negotiated settlement it must be harbouring the hope that a Greek Cypriot leader will emerge with the political will to conclude the talks successfully, assuming that the Turkish leadership is similarly inclined. Aside from committing to an international conference, the UN will also hope that deadlock in the governance dossier where Christofias was deemed stubborn could be overcome, paving the way for a genuine give and take across substantive chapters, including property and territory. As the UN Secretary-General has outlined, an international conference would be held to conclude negotiations on the international aspects of the Cyprus Problem, namely Turkey's role and security provisions.

Yet the much-anticipated international conference has not materialised precisely because normalisation on the island between the communities and their respective regimes must coincide with concrete acts to reconcile Turkey with the Greek Cypriot-led Republic of Cyprus. Remarkably this has not happened in the years since Cyprus' EU accession, even under conditions where Ankara has legal obligations to include Nicosia in customs union and the EU has a mandate to engage with Turkish Cypriots in lieu of a political settlement.

If anything, the UN talks have served to justify that stalemate. It is no coincidence that the current round of talks can be traced to a deal brokered by the UN in 2006 known as the Gambari process. In reiterating commitments to a bizonal, bicommunal federal settlement, the sides effectively preempted agreement on trade, the ghost city of Varosha and the opening of Turkish ports to Republic of Cyprus vessels under the Ankara Protocol. With the ongoing negotiations, Turkey was not obliged to recognise the government of the Republic of Cyprus, nor were Greek Cypriots obliged to agree to the 'Taiwanisation' of Northern Cyprus. As a result, the focus on comprehensive settlements prevailed over normalisation and other confidence-building measures (CBMs) that could have led to greater integration and normalisation. Since the commencement of fully-fledged negotiations in 2008 the emphasis on a comprehensive package has become even more acute. Consequently, the EU effectively turned a blind eye to the Cyprus conflict, preferring to rely on the UN Good Offices. Along the way, numerous 'deadlines' lapsed, but at least a direct confrontation with Ankara was averted.

In short, UN-mediated negotiations have allowed the sides not to make moves that would otherwise be required to normalise relations. The stalemate in Cyprus is now a 'new normal' for observers of the conflict. Although the Turkish side has insinuated a 'plan B' in lieu of a successfully concluded round of talks, it seems that this has been shelved for the time being. But it is only through a change in the status quo that new strategic thinking may induce change, breaking the Nash equilibrium, for better or worse.

Even in the absence of a 'plan B', facts on the ground as well as evolving geopolitics conspire against a settlement. Demographic changes and property development will negate the very intricate balances that the UN parameters entail, making property reinstatement increasingly unlikely. The all or nothing approach has effectively delayed any breakthrough in issues that actually matter to citizens. Meanwhile public opinion polls demonstrate ambivalence regarding federation and power sharing. Younger generations and cohorts will find it difficult to relate to the context in which Makarios and Denktash once agreed to the bizonal, bicommunal model in 1977. Most factors that hold the whole project together are exogenous. A series of UN Security Councils that reject the Turkish Republic of

Northern Cyprus (TRNC) along with Turkey's (flagging) ambition to join the EU remain rationales for a compromise settlement package. However, failure in this round will entice Turkey and the Turkish Cypriot side in particular to question the viability of federalism.

An audit of the negotiations is overdue

The upshot of all this is that should the UN pronounce that the negotiations have come to an inconclusive end, an audit of the entire approach becomes inevitable. While the UN's commitment to reengaging with the sides prevents a further falling out and may have been more blessing than curse during a testing time in the run-up to Cyprus' EU presidency, it can also be argued that this precludes any meaningful steps being taken during the interlude.

The UN has already hinted at this audit, with the Secretary-General's review of the UN's peacekeeping operations in Cyprus (UNFICYP). This has been construed as a move designed to exert coercive pressure on the Greek Cypriot side, since the peacekeeping mission continues to treat the Green Line that divides Cyprus as a ceasefire line rather than an administrative border. However, for the UN to prove convincing, Turkey will also have to demonstrate its will to change the status quo. Withdrawal of some troops would at least give the UN a rationale for not renewing UNFICYP's mandate. In short, negotiations involving Turkey independent of the inter-communal talks could pave the way for normalisation. Whereas the status of Varosha is also complicated by extant UN Security Council Resolutions forbidding its repopulation by Turkey, it is conceivable that a change in status that favoured the rights of (predominantly Greek Cypriot) property owners would at least be tacitly acknowledged by many international actors, if not supported. In other words, UN Resolutions will need to be reinterpreted.

Reinterpreting Security Council Resolutions is complex, since there is no consensus regarding change other than through a negotiated settlement. This means that it is unlikely that the UN would agree to a commission to investigate settlement alternatives. Mistrust between the US and Russia regarding previous episodes, including Kosovo and currently Syria, limit the scope for action.

Any genuine rethinking must be proposed outside the confines of the UN. On the face of it, given Turkey's role in NATO and Cyprus' membership in the EU, there are many overlapping interests among members of either organisation to support a resolution to the

Cyprus conflict. Any multilateral approach would prove beneficial, especially in reducing anxiety regarding security arrangements in a post-settlement Cyprus, regarding the fears expressed by Greek Cypriots in particular. Efforts that include the Turkish Cypriots, in turn, would tend to satisfy need for effective participation in decision making bodies. This in turn would provide for leverage and democratic oversight in the development of institutions in Cyprus.

A comprehensive, federal settlement should not serve as a precondition for cooperation and coordination. Commitments to resolve property disputes, to demilitarisation and to democratic institutions could underpin a process that builds on experience rather than rendering all work legally null and void in the event of a failure to agree on all matters, as is the case in the extant UN process.

Failing this, there is the possibility that Turkey may consider leveraging some of its soft power for diplomatic purposes in support of its Cyprus policies. Thus, an alternative 'plan B' designed to upgrade the TRNC independently of the EU may emerge with unforeseen consequences. While Turkish Cypriot claims to 'remedial self-determination' may fall on deaf ears in Western capitals, Cyprus' division could take on a more geopolitical flavour should any other countries side with Turkey on the matter. In that case, the Cyprus Problem will have solved itself, as international politics evolves away from a rationale for compromise and power sharing.

Conclusion

The conclusion must be that the UN framework insisting on an 'all or nothing' approach is unlikely to yield a positive result. Moreover, the UN Security Council is too divided to resolve differences otherwise. If Cyprus is to be reunified the most viable way is through a piecemeal approach that effectively incorporates Turkey and Cyprus. Otherwise the Cyprus Problem, as we know it, will not be resolved.

References and recommended reading

Asmussen Jan, 'Cyprus: should the UN withdraw?', *Newsletter*, European Centre for Minority Issues, Flensburg, Germany, 2011.
Christou, Spyros, Ahmet Sozen, Erol Kaymak and Alexandros Lordos, *Bridging the Gap in the Inter-communal Negotiations: An island-wide study of public opinion in Cyprus* (Geneva: International Peacebuilding Alliance, 2011).

Heraclides, Alexis, 'The Cyprus Gordian Knot: an intractible ethnic conflict', *Nationalism and Ethnic Politics* 17/2 (2011), pp. 117–39.

Kaymak, Erol, 'If at first you don't succeed, try, try again: (re) designing referenda to ratify a peace treaty in Cyprus', *Nationalism and Ethnic Politics* 18/1 (2012), pp. 88–112.

Ker-Lindsay, James, Hubert Faustmann and Fiona Mullen, *An Island in Europe: The EU and the Transformation of Cyprus* (London: I.B.Tauris, 2011).

Lordos, Alexandros, Erol Kaymak and Nathalie Tocci, *A People's Peace in Cyprus: Testing the Options for a Comprehensive Settlement* (Brussels: Centre for European Policy Studies, 2009).

Varnava, Andrekos, 'Why the latest initiative to reunify Cyprus will fail: the six pillars of the Cyprus "Problem" and the impregnable roof', *The Cyprus Review* 23/1 (2011), pp. 147–54.

16

The Case for a Loose Federation

JAMES KER-LINDSAY

It is a desperately difficult task to identify one specific area that could and should be the focus of efforts to break the deadlock between the two sides. For some, the path to reunification lies in tackling specific issues. For example, many see security, either for the Greek or the Turkish Cypriots, as a fundamental point that needs to be addressed. This was borne out in 2004, when many Greek Cypriot respondents listed this as the main factor shaping their decision to vote against the Annan Plan. Take away the Turkish troops, and the unacceptable guarantee system that allows Turkey to intervene in the affairs of Cyprus, and the Greek Cypriots would be more amenable to a solution. Others focus on process, such as the way in which the UN handles the talks as the problem.

To my mind, the key problem lies in the way in which the end outcome of the process has been presented and debated. In particular, it seems regrettable that the concept of 'loose federation' has come to be seen by Greek Cypriots as a wholly unacceptable model for a settlement. Indeed, the mere mention of the term tends to provoke strongly negative reactions from many ordinary Greek Cypriots. This is unfortunate. In many ways, and being wholly realistic, as much as it would be desirable to see the two communities forge a close cooperative working relationship, it seems obvious that this is not going to happen at this stage. Instead, limiting the points of likely or potential political friction between the two communities represents the most logical aim for any settlement process.

Towards a federal settlement

In some ways, Cyprus has always been a federation. The late Rauf Denktash used to like to say that the 1960 constitution, which gave considerable autonomy to the two communities, was in fact a 'functional federation'. There is a certain degree of truth in the assessment. That said, it was not until 1977 that the two communities formally agreed – in the first High Level Agreement – that any settlement should allow for a bizonal, bicommunal federation; in other words, a more 'traditional' geographic federation.

Despite this apparent agreement, which was reconfirmed in 1979 and has been the basis for settlement efforts ever since, deep divisions have always existed between the two sides over what a federation means in real terms. For a start, the Greek and Turkish Cypriots have deep differences over their understanding of the relationship between the concepts of bizonality and bicommunality. For the Turkish Cypriots, the two must be intrinsically tied to one another. In any settlement there would be one exclusively Turkish Cypriot state and one exclusively Greek Cypriot state. For the Greek Cypriots, the understanding of the relationship has always been rather less fixed. Although they recognise that one state would in all likelihood be predominantly Turkish Cypriot and the other would be mainly inhabited by Greek Cypriots, there was always a deep aversion to some form of constitutionally formalised segregation between the two communities. Thus, at the most basic level, there has always been a deep philosophical difference about the very nature and meaning of a federal settlement in terms of the future relationship between the land and people, or peoples, of Cyprus.

At the same time, the question of just how the institutions of the state would be ordered and managed has also presented difficulties. When the latest UN-sponsored process began, in 2008, there was a widespread view that the structure of a federal state could be readily resolved by tweaking the proposals that had been put forward in the Annan Plan – although no one would refer to the Plan directly. Many of the ideas concerning the nature of the executive, legislature and judiciary were already in place and appeared to have been accepted. Instead, issues such as property and security would be more problematic. However, this was not the case. The shape and nature of the institutions became a source of endless bickering. This exemplifies a fundamental problem that Cyprus faces. Politicians brought up (both personally and politically) in a deeply divided society usually think in 'us and them' terms. The fact that they are also, by the very choice of their career, likely to be naturally combative by nature does not make matters easier. Given that this situation is not likely to lessen after a settlement, it seems logical to argue that the less room given to politicians from the two communities to argue with each other, rather than with ideological opponents within their respective communities, the better.

At the same time, there seems to be good reason to believe that the two communities would actually prefer a situation in which as many key public policy issues as possible – especially those with a clear community dimension, such as education – are decided within their community. While most Greek Cypriots feel deeply aggrieved at the loss of lives and land caused by the Turkish invasion in 1974, they nevertheless also recognise that they now determine their own future. Greek Cypriots are no longer lumbered with what they see, perhaps with a certain degree of justification, as a deeply undemocratic system whereby a minimal Turkish Cypriot majority, 9 per cent plus one of the island's population, could block a decision favoured by the absolute majority of the Greek Cypriots. Of course, in some senses this system was necessary in order to prevent the tyranny of the Greek Cypriots over the Turkish Cypriots. However, it also created situations whereby the Turkish Cypriots were able to block decisions that had no direct effect on them, thereby creating a tyranny of the minority. This no longer happens. Since 1964, the Greek Cypriots have been masters of their own affairs; just as the Turkish Cypriots have been, to a degree, of theirs. Simply put, the Greek Cypriots accept, either tacitly or overtly, that they now have the Greek Cypriot state they originally wanted – even if there has been a high price to pay for it.

The case for a loose federation

While there may be good reasons to pursue a 'looser' type of federation that would minimise the points of friction between the two communities and let them control their own affairs, the problem is that the language of a federal settlement has become deeply politicised. For many Greek Cypriots the term 'loose federation' is anathema. There seem to be several reasons for this. In part, it reflects the wish of most Greek Cypriots to see Cyprus reunited under a unitary state in which the Greek Cypriots would have overall control and the Turkish Cypriots would have minority rights.

Indeed, polls have shown that this is the Greek Cypriots' most favoured solution. To this end, in the process of negotiating a federal settlement, it appears as if many believe that it might be possible to produce something that approximates to a unitary state; albeit within a nominally federal model. Although called a federal state, the new state of affairs would in fact see the Turkish Cypriots given their own 'canton' or autonomous area. Meanwhile, in the federal institutions, lying at the very heart of government and covering as many policy areas as possible, the Greek Cypriots would have the real power. This is unrealistic. There is simply no chance that the Turkish Cypriots would be willing to accept such a settlement. Their mantra has always been 'political equality' in the governance of any future reunified state. Under these circumstances, if the range of central government competences were made as broad as possible, it would not mean that the Greek Cypriots would exert control over the two communities. Instead, it would simply reintroduce Turkish Cypriots into policy areas that Greek Cypriots currently control on their own.

At the same time, the deep hostility to a loose federation also appears to be driven by a feeling that that this would be giving the Turkish Cypriots an unacceptable victory. By accepting a loose federation, many Greek Cypriots feel that they would be effectively legalising and legitimising the division created by the Turkish invasion in 1974. Again, while such a view is certainly understandable, it is also unfortunate. As difficult as it often is to forget past injustices, it is important to remember that the continuation of the status quo entails that the partition simply means the perpetuation of those injustices. By accepting a loose federation, the Greek Cypriots would be able to redress the situation somewhat. At the very least, they would strengthen their hand in other negotiating areas. More power devolved to the Turkish Cypriots could be traded for more land for the Greek Cypriot federal state. (It is universally accepted that any settlement would see the area under Turkish Cypriot control reduced from the current 36 per cent of the island.) This would enable even more refugees to return to their properties and live under Greek Cypriot administration. Moreover, as several reports have shown, there is strong evidence to suggest that a settlement of the Cyprus Problem, in whatever form, could deliver many political, social and economic benefits to both communities.

Fear of (another) secession

Another of the key worries – perhaps even the main worry – that many Greek Cypriots harbour about a loose federation is that the Turkish Cypriots would be able to break away more easily from this model, as opposed to from a 'tight' federation. There is a widespread belief that the Turkish Cypriots are therefore pressing for a loose federation as a means by which to legitimise their entity as a prelude to another attempt at secession; this time with international support. In some ways, such fears are not unreasonable. There are certainly those within the Turkish Cypriot community who have also come to realise that this may well be the best way in which to bring about a wholly legal and legitimate Turkish Cypriot state on the international stage. At the same time, international trends also give little comfort to those who fear such a scenario. In September 2014 the people of Scotland will vote in a referendum on independence. Elsewhere in Europe there are strong separatist tendencies emerging, for example in Catalonia and Flanders. But it is important to be realistic about these 'threats'.

In terms of the first problem, the wish of the Turkish Cypriots to use a settlement to push for a legal act of secession, this can actually be relatively easily tackled. Safeguards can be introduced that would effectively prohibit this. One obvious mechanism would be to outlaw unilateral secession within any new constitution. Another would be to pass a UN Security Council Resolution reaffirming the territorial integrity of the new state and expressly prohibiting any future act of separation. (Of course, this could always be changed if the parties were subsequently to agree to separate.) Moreover, there would be other political safeguards to protect the new state. Apart from the general aversion states tend to have to recognising unilateral acts of secession, few in the international community would want to see a situation in which years had been spent trying to reach a comprehensive settlement only for it to unravel quickly. Moreover, the Turkish Cypriot cause, and the chances of gaining international recognition, would be especially weak if it appeared as if they were the ones trying to bring down the new state. In a purely legal sense, therefore, Greek Cypriot concerns about the intrinsic dangers of a loose federation would appear rather overstated.

The second factor, concerning the wider international environment, is certainly more problematic. In reality, forcing the two communities to live together in an unhappy and fractious union is not an appealing idea. We can see the results of such an approach in cases such as Bosnia and Belgium. Crucially, though, in both cases the argument can be made that forcing a centralisation of power is not the solution. Indeed, it would only serve to increase separatist tendencies. By creating a system that allows the two communities to function as autonomously as possible from the start, and by making full secession as difficult as possible, one would hope that pressure for full secession could be minimised – although it seems highly unlikely that it would disappear entirely. Certainly one has to accept that the pursuit of a loose federation presents risks. However, it can be argued that such risks are no greater, and I would argue that they are in fact considerably lower, than those that would be faced – not only from resentful Turkish Cypriots, but also be disaffected Greek Cypriots – if one tries to force the two communities together inside a 'tight' federation.

Subsidiarity: a new angle on loose federation

Despite the deep-rooted public opposition to the idea of a loose federation, there is good reason to suspect that some are starting to see the benefits of pursuing this option. Even if few will say so openly, the principle of a loose federation is nevertheless creeping into the debate; albeit under different titles. Perhaps the most inventive example of the way in which the issue is being tackled by other means came from Nicos Anastasiades when, during his campaign for the presidency, he raised the notion of incorporating the idea of 'subsidiarity' into any settlement. Traditionally used in European Union contexts, the term merely refers to the principle whereby decisions are taken at the most appropriate level. If a matter is best tackled by central government, then so be it. If it is better dealt with by the federal (communal) states, then that is where the decision should be made. But if it is better addressed at a local level then so be it. This approach obviously provides a very clear rationale for devolving power down to the two communities. Crucially, though, the communal level does not stand against the central level. Instead, it is merely a middle tier in a hierarchy of decision making. This also offers another distinct advantage inasmuch as it could even open the way for Greek Cypriot communities within the Turkish Cypriot community to be self-governing on many day-to-day issues. This could in turn encourage an even greater number of Greek Cypriots to return to villages that will officially remain within the

Turkish Cypriot state than would be the case otherwise. In other words, a settlement based on subsidiarity might actually create the conditions for a settlement that is more closely attuned to Greek Cypriot notions of bizonality and bicommunality.

In view of all this, it is rather ironic, then, that perhaps the greatest obstacle to a loose federation may yet be the European Union itself. EU officials have often said that a reunified Cyprus must speak on a range of issues with a single voice, thereby potentially requiring discussions and agreement on issues that may otherwise best be left to the communities to decide on for themselves. This is something that all the relevant parties, especially the EU, will need to consider carefully in any future negotiation.

Conclusion

Efforts to resolve Cyprus have now been continuing for 50 years. For the past 35 years the goal of the United Nations has been to broker a bizonal, bicommunal federal settlement between the two sides. During this period, the Greek Cypriots have fought to create a strong federation. This is counterproductive. Such a settlement would not only give the politicians ample room to play national politics across a wide range of policy areas, it would also threaten to disrupt the current situation whereby the two communities essentially control their own affairs (albeit with differing degrees of external involvement).

In essence, therefore, the ideal type of second-best solution for the Greek Cypriots would in fact be a loose federation. The problem is that the term 'loose federation' has become so politically loaded that no one dare use it. Indeed, at a conceptual level, hostility to the idea of a loose federation is so deeply ingrained that the mere mention of the fact that anything being proposed is akin to a 'loose federation' is enough to force politicians to retreat from otherwise promising ideas. However, if politicians and people were able to look beyond the emotionally laden language that has emerged around the idea of a loose federation, they would see that this is the model of a settlement that is likely to deliver the greatest benefits. Greek and Turkish Cypriots would see little major change in terms of the encroachment of the other community into their day-to-day lives. Moreover, by limiting the areas where joint agreement is necessary, the space for destabilising political disputes is reduced. At the same time, it would also allow for the return of considerable tracts of territory to Greek Cypriot control, and the return of even more refuges to their homes; a significant reduction in the number Turkish troops, with a view to their eventual departure altogether; and the repatriation of many, though by no means all, Turkish settlers. Meanwhile, there is little reason to fear that the Turkish Cypriots could use this as a stepping-stone towards full, internationally recognised independence. At the very worst, even if it was to become apparent that the solution was not working, and the two sides could agree on some sort of negotiated separation, one could argue that the terms of the divorce would be easier to negotiate following the creation of a loose federation than they are under the present messy situation.

References and recommended reading

Beyatlı, Derya, Katerina Papadopoulou and Erol Kaymak, *Solving the Cyprus Problem: Hopes and Fears* (Nicosia: Interpeace/Cyprus 2015 Initiative, 2011).

Faustmann, Hubert and Andrekos Varnava, *Reunifying Cyprus: The Annan Plan and Beyond* (London: I.B.Tauris, 2011).

International Court of Justice, *Accordance with International Law of the Unilateral Declaration of Independence in Respect of Kosovo*, Advisory Opinion, 22 July 2010.

Ker-Lindsay, James, *The Cyprus Problem: What Everyone Needs to Know* (New York: Oxford University Press, 2011).

——, *The Foreign Policy of Counter Secession: Preventing the Recognition of Contested States* (Oxford: Oxford University Press, 2012).

Mullen, Fiona, Praxoula Antoniadou Kyriacou and Oğuz, Özlem, *The Day After: Commercial Opportunities Following a Solution to the Cyprus Problem* (Nicosia: PRIO Cyprus Centre, 2008).

17

Preconditions and Expectations of a Solution

PASCHALIS KITROMILIDES

The very fact itself that the question 'can Cyprus be solved' continues to be asked is a hopeful sign, particularly welcome at this time of impasses and uncertainties over the future of the island republic. It is equally heartening that a journal concerned with social justice has posed the question. This is especially so because the Cyprus Problem has been, as a rule, considered in terms of power politics or of nationalist conflicts and very often such perspectives tend to slide toward vacuous analyses or sentimentality, which obscure the social substance of the issues involved. Considered from the perspective of social justice the Cyprus Problem might be approached in terms of social criticism and this could enhance not only the understanding of the conflict but especially deepen the self-awareness of the parties involved, primarily the Cypriots, Greek and Turkish themselves.

An ever elusive solution

Since my childhood I have been hearing about the solution of the Cyprus Question. My earliest political memories are associated with the passionate discussions of the solution of the Cyprus Problem in the closing years of British rule. I can still recall the heated discussions of the adults at the time and inflammatory headlines in the local press about the various proposals or plans of solutions, real or imaginary, in circulation 50 years ago – and the problem is still with us, always eliciting debates over scenarios, passions, headlines and rhetoric, having meanwhile caused enormous pain to the people of Cyprus themselves. This protracted history of solutions-to-be can probably explain why I found myself totally convinced two years ago, during a meeting at a kibbutz in Northern Galilee, when a former teacher of mine in America and one of Israel's genuine intellectual leaders today confided in another Cypriot scholar and myself, 'we must accept that there are two problems in world politics today that can have no solution, yours and ours'. The explanation, he continued, was that in both cases, the Cyprus Problem and the Israeli-Palestinian problem, there have been no real motivations for a solution.

That was more or less where my thoughts were left in connection with the prospects of Cyprus until the question posed in this volume forced me to turn my reflection to Cyprus and its prospects once again and rethink the question 'can Cyprus be solved?' To this epigrammatic question there might be two answers: one very brief and straightforward, and a second one more complex and fraught with ifs, conditionals and exercises in creative thinking. Let's begin with the simpler answer.

Cyprus cannot be solved, that is there cannot be a viable and workable solution to the Cyprus Problem for as long as Turkey, the major power in the equation, insists on the terms it has imposed by force in 1974. These terms, geographical and institutional, are unjust and violate fundamental human rights and remain totally unacceptable to the Greek Cypriots. Furthermore, as it turns out almost four decades later, Turkey's actions are repugnant to a majority of the original native Turkish Cypriot community, for whose protection ostensibly Turkey undertook the military invasion in 1974. As a consequence of Turkey's policies of massive military build-up and colonisation, the Turkish Cypriot community appears to be one of the victims of the 1974 invasion, as they have been submerged and increasingly dislocated in their own community and regions by the settlers transferred by Turkey to the island. This is the 'simple' answer to the question: Cyprus cannot be solved for as long as Turkey's strategic motivations and policies remain unchanged and fundamentally divisive.

The second answer is more complex and conditional but I think also more interesting and intellectually challenging. It has to do with the domestic aspects of the Cyprus Problem, to which I have pointed on a number of occasions since 1976 in the hope of bringing a perspective of social criticism – and self-criticism – to bear on the understanding of the problem. In engaging in this project my hope had been to make a small contribution to redeeming Cypriot political thought from its self-blinding tendency to blame everything on foreign schemes and machinations and to see only the responsibilities of others. After 36 years I continue to think that these constraints of political thought remain major obstacles on the road to a solution.

I cannot here go into these issues in any depth. In considering the possibility of a Cyprus solution, nevertheless, I feel that three relevant questions should be placed in the focus of reflection. All three of them constitute, in my judgement, essential preconditions of an eventual solution as fundamental components of Cyprus' political culture. These questions are the following:

The question of leadership

Since the 1950s the Cyprus Question has been handled by a very narrowly-based political leadership in both of the Cypriot ethnic communities. The history of the Cyprus Question since World War II leaves no doubt that the record of this leadership group has been quite dismal. On the Greek Cypriot side, none of the overriding 'national goals' rhetorically articulated by the Greek Cypriot leadership in the successive phases of the problem has been achieved. Consider these objectives: union with Greece through self-determination, unfettered independence and unitary state, a federal sovereign republic and finally, after many concessions and reappraisals, a bizonal bicommunal federation with unitary international personality. This record of failure inevitably leads to the thought that in articulating these goals, Cypriot leaders at best had a poor and unrealistic understanding of international society, but at worst (which unfortunately is not to be excluded), were motivated by self-serving considerations of power and interests rather than by a painful ethic of responsibility. To be fair two important achievements must be recognised in the 50-year history of the Republic of Cyprus: the maintenance of the international status of Cyprus as a sovereign state member of the United Nations and its accession to the European Union at the 2004 enlargement. In terms of achieving a just and stable solution of the Cyprus Problem, however, the record of Cyprus's leadership has been poor. This should lead the Cypriot leaders themselves to some serious soul searching. This concerns also the leadership of the left, who had been excluded from decision making up to the 1959 solution but have been active participants since 1960 and especially since 1963–4 in all decisions on the future of the island and therefore share in the responsibility for handling the Cyprus Question.

If the Greek Cypriot leadership has failed in all the major strategic objectives it has set to itself, the Turkish Cypriot community has, on the contrary, produced the most successful leader in the history of Cyprus, Rauf Denktash. This controversial political figure managed to achieve all the goals he set himself and single-mindedly pursued, primarily the division of Cyprus. His successes, however, have been triumphs for a particular retrogressive and narrowly chauvinistic strand of mainland Turkish nationalism and from the point of view of the interests of Cyprus as a whole these triumphs have been achieved at the expense not only of a Cypriot society looking at a peaceful and just future, but also at the expense of the prosperity and survival of the Turkish Cypriots as a distinct community.

Where does the consideration of the Cyprus Problem from this perspective really leave us? The answer is inescapable: for 'Cyprus to be solved' there is an urgent need for a radical renewal of political personnel and political leadership and their replacement by persons with a better understanding of international society and a livelier awareness of their responsibilities, persons concerned, to remember John Rawls, not just for the outcome of the next election but for the interests for the next generation.

The role of the intellectuals

If political leadership has been on the whole inadequate – with exceptions of course – and unequal to the task of leading Cypriot society to a just solution, the intelligentsia of the insular society in the long years of the evolution of the Cyprus Question has been simply destructive. For anyone familiar with the history of the Cyprus Question since the early twentieth century the destructive role of the intellectuals would be easily recognisable. Greek Cypriot intellectuals, very often under the influence of militant ideologues from mainland Greece, remained unshakably embedded in a provincial nationalism, which nurtured a completely one-dimensional – in the Marcusean sense – and narrow-minded vision for the island's future. Through their rhetoric Cypriot intellectuals contributed decisively to the development of a normative outlook on politics that never weighed seriously the consequences of political positions and actions, never considered alternatives and totally excluded disagreement and dissent as legitimate options in public life. It was this intellectual climate that shaped the 'dialectic of intolerance' that accompanied the successive disasters in the recent history of Cyprus.

This intellectual position appeared weakened after 1974 and its most extreme expressions were certainly discredited in the public conscience on account of their implication in the coup of July 1974. Yet conventional intellectual outlooks on Cyprus's destiny and a normative culture of rhetorical nationalism, which over the years became powerful vested interests, remained influential as a source of normative discourse in the period after 1974. Some of its exponents, whose motivations were never free of calculations of material advantages to themselves, influenced the leadership of the Church in particularly detrimental ways.

More recently, however, it has not been the conventional one-dimensional nationalist outlook that has been most destructive, but a novel intellectual position, espoused by self-appointed critics of nationalism who now populate the cultural life of Nicosia and have been greatly sustained by the politics of patronage so extensively practiced by the leftist government that has ruled Cyprus since 2008. This new outlook represents an equally one-dimensional conceptualisation of history and politics and is informed by very poor scholarship. Its major premise consists in a demonisation of Greek nationalism and the Church, as the main culprits of Cyprus's troubles. It is quite interesting from the point of view of the sociology of knowledge, and occasionally even amusing, to note the many similarities of this 'critical' position to the conventional outlook it seeks to supplant. One source of antinationalist rhetoric in Cyprus is the arguments of leftist scholars from Greece, who are keen to find jobs in the University of Cyprus. This very much recalls the role of mainland Greek nationalist ideologues in early twentieth-century Cyprus. Similar roles are played by scholars of Cypriot origin, born to emigrant families in Britain or Australia, who have a very limited sense of or concern for the deep antinomies of the historical problems of Cyprus and understand nothing of the moral, cultural and intellectual traditions and values of the island society, which they want to refashion on the basis of their ideological preconceptions. This ideological position finds its justification or rather 'legitimation' in a totally understandable and reasonable argument, widely shared in Cyprus, of 'rapprochement' with the Turkish Cypriots through the auto-critique of Greek Cypriot nationalism. The schematic and often aggressive and generally misinformed way the overall position is put forward remains unconvincing in Cypriot society at large. The only substantial political result of the anti-nationalist argument thus boils down to its own undermining as a serious ideological option and the hardening of insecurities and preconceptions on the other side. All this provokes ideological defensiveness that remains inimical to the much needed healing of the traumas of the past and the rethinking of history – without just ignoring it – that might lead to the transition to a new phase in the political culture of Cyprus. Thus it would seem that a more responsible intelligentsia is among the critical factors of a Cyprus solution.

The reeducation of public opinion

What has been said so far about the failure of leadership and the destructive role of the intellectuals may appear to leave very little hope for the reeducation of public opinion, which is a necessary precondition of a workable and just solution. Yet this is an urgent need, which is obvious to every independent and fair-minded observer. Suffice it to recall the indifference of younger generations to the reunification of the island and the adjustments in mentalities and attitudes this would require, in order to appreciate the urgency of this need. It is not easy in this brief set of remarks to articulate the full range of the issues involved in this fundamental component of a Cyprus solution. Some clarifications, nevertheless, might be relevant by way of conclusion to these reflections.

Reeducating public opinion in Cyprus does not mean, and should not be understood as, a project of telling Cypriots who they really are and who they should be. Like every other people, Greek Cypriots and Turkish Cypriots know who they are, have a strong sense of their identity and treasure their history. This must be respected by all those concerned with a solution of the Cyprus Question, including representatives of international organisations and foreign diplomats who too quickly – and naively – rush to take under their wing and support those who, with their behaviour and unthinking and uninformed rhetoric, tend to show disrespect for Cypriot identities and sensitivities.

What Cypriots need to learn is to live with pluralism and to handle with maturity the multiple identities that make up their social reality and symbolic environment. By learning to handle these multiple identities, as Greeks and Turks, as Cypriots, as Europeans, they will also learn to engage in mutual recognition and this will breed respect for each other as fellow citizens. Ultimately, a political culture of ideological generosity, and with it a sense of security, will provide the necessary domestic substratum to a solution. But for all this to come about the Cypriot political class themselves will need to be reeducated first and recognise with honesty and sincerity the ideological transitions that need to be effected for a culture of reunification to replace the culture of division.

Conclusion

Cyprus cannot be solved unless Turkey abandons the strategy of division, and a possible solution will not work unless the insular society learns to live with a political culture that will lead it away from the forms of ideological thinking involved in the dialectic of intolerance toward the practice of the values of fairness and justice and respect for the rights and needs of its members as autonomous individuals.

References and recommended reading

Attalides, Michael (ed.), *Cyprus Reviewed* (Nicosia: Jus Cypri, 1977).
——, *Cyprus: Nationalism and International Politics* (New York; St Martin's Press, 1979).
Christou, George, *The European Union and Enlargement. The Case of Cyprus* (Basingstoke: Palgrave Macmillan, 2004).
Heraclides, Alexis, 'The Cyprus Gordian Knot: an intractable ethnic conflict', *Nationalism and Ethnic Politics* 17/2 (2011), pp. 117–39.
Kalotychos, Vangelis (ed.), *Cyprus and its People* (Boulder, CO: Westview Press, 1998).
Kitromilides, Paschalis M., 'Relevance or irrelevance of nationalism? A perspective from the Eastern Mediterranean', *International Journal of Politics, Culture, and Society* 24 (2011), pp. 57–63.
Stefanidis, Ioannis D., *Isle of Discord. Nationalism, Imperialism and the making of the Cyprus Problem* (London: Hurst, 1999).
Worseley, Peter and Paschalis Kitromilides (eds), *Small States in the Modern World: The Conditions of Survival*, revised edn (Nicosia: Cyprus Sociological Association, 1979).

18

The Rule of Law

KLEARCHOS A. KYRIAKIDES

Viscount Palmerston is said to have remarked that 'only three people... ever really understood the Schleswig-Holstein business'. This was a fiendishly complex diplomatic problem which simmered away in Northern Europe for much of the nineteenth century. Viscount Palmerston, who became the British Prime Minister in 1855, identified the three cognoscenti as being 'the Prince Consort, who is dead, a German professor, who has gone mad, and I, who has forgotten all about it'.

With the above in mind, the primary purpose of this chapter is to outline why, in terms of its bewildering multidimensional complexity, the 'Cyprus Question' has emerged as the 'Schleswig-Holstein business' of the twenty-first century – baffling to diplomats from afar, exasperating to the citizens on the ground and apparently incapable of being resolved.

In a sense, the modern history of the 'Cyprus Question' can be traced back to the annexation of the island of Cyprus by the United Kingdom in 1914, upon the entry of Turkey into the Great War as an Axis power. Under the Treaty of Lausanne 1923, Turkey recognised that annexation. However, the 'Cyprus Question' acquired a complexity to rival Schleswig-Holstein over the next few decades, particularly during the late 1950s, when the Greek Cypriot leadership as well as Greece campaigned for the incorporation of British Colonial Cyprus into Greece, whilst the Turkish Cypriot leadership as well as Turkey called for its partition. As Enoch Powell pointed out from the Conservative back benches of the House of Commons on 19 March 1959, the situation on the then colony was 'complicated by the communal divisions of the island and by the involvement of those communal divisions in an international situation itself of great complexity'.

Powell spoke exactly one month after the conclusion of the Lancaster House Agreement. That Agreement exemplified his point. After all, it was drafted by Greece, Turkey and the UK – with no input by Cypriots – and presented to the Greek Cypriot and Turkish Cypriot leaders as a non-negotiable *fait accompli*. In due course, in August 1960, the Agreement resulted in the establishment of the Republic of Cyprus ('Cyprus') as an independent, unitary sovereign state subject to a bicommunal constitution of astonishing intricacy and subject also to multiple treaty rights in favour of the three 'guaranteeing Powers' namely Greece, Turkey and the UK.

Each of the 'guaranteeing Powers' acquired a right to station military forces in Cyprus. Each also gave a guarantee *inter alia* to 'recognise and guarantee the independence, territorial integrity and security' of Cyprus, while reserving the right to 'take action' there – collectively or individually – if certain circumstances arose. For its part, the UK exclusively reserved additional treaty rights which went considerably further than those obtained by Greece and Turkey. Indeed, the outgoing colonial power retained two British sovereign base areas, together with an array of sites dotted around Cyprus plus an extensive assortment of ancillary rights. In other words, not only did the UK retain bases on the island of Cyprus, but the island resolutely remained as a British base. The island continues to fulfil this role today, as illustrated by the post-2001 British deployment to Afghanistan, which has largely hinged upon RAF Akrotiri in one of the sovereign base areas, not to mention the multiple forms of support quietly provided by Cyprus.

The extraordinary state of affairs described above was enshrined in a 222-page British Parliamentary Command Paper published in July 1960. This embodied one 82-page bicommunal constitution, one three-party treaty, two four-party treaties and several other instruments. These came into force on 16 August 1960, but they continue to lie at the core of the 'Cyprus Question' today.

Evidently enough, Cyprus came into existence in 1960 and continues to subsist today with its sovereignty, independence and territorial integrity severely curtailed under the terms of treaties which were effectively foisted on the citizens of the new republic without any popular mandate. Needless to say, this continues to rankle with many citizens of Cyprus, all the more so in view of the staged passage to full independence of another nearby island which was once under British rule – Malta.

1960–90: the escalation of the 'Cyprus Question'

Notwithstanding the arrangements introduced in 1960, the 'Cyprus Question' did not go away in the decades that followed. According to the *Oxford English Dictionary*, a feature of communalism is 'allegiance to one's own ethnic group rather than to the wider society'. Partly for this very reason, the bicommunal Constitution of 1960 did not make for cross-communal integration. Indeed, the 1960s were characterised by a doomed attempt by President Makarios to achieve constitutional reform, an ensuing constitutional crisis and the decision of the Turkish Cypriot leadership to extricate itself from the constitutional structures of Cyprus. The 1960s were also marked by multiple acts of external interference, the outbreak of inter-communal clashes and the deployment of the United Nations Peacekeeping Force.

Then, in the summer of 1974, the three 'guaranteeing Powers' individually and collectively failed to honour their treaty duty to 'guarantee the independence, territorial integrity and security' of Cyprus. The Greek military junta, which was in power at the time in Athens, engineered an unconstitutional coup d'état in Nicosia. In turn, this offered Turkey a pretext to execute an unlawful military operation in Cyprus which was conducted in two phases. As for the UK, it failed to stop or reverse the consequences of these fateful acts. The ramifications were shattering. In the carefully chosen words of Lord Justice Mummery (with whom Lord Justice Potter and Lord Justice Nourse agreed) in the English Court of Appeal case of *Polly Peck International Plc* [1998]:

> In the summer of 1974 Turkey invaded the island. By 16 August 1974 it had occupied a large area in the North amounting to just over one third of the whole island (the occupied area). Many members of the Greek Cypriot community in the occupied area fled, in fear of armed force, from their homes and businesses to other parts of the island.

A *de facto* exchange of populations followed and Cyprus was *de facto* segregated along racial lines, contrary to international law generally and the International Convention on the Elimination of All Forms of Racial Discrimination 1965 in particular. This unlawful and unethical outcome persists to this day, not least because Turkey does not apply the Convention to the areas of Cyprus occupied by it. All of which brings to mind a telling point made by Dr Martin Luther King Jr, the 1964 Nobel Peace Laureate: 'segregation… ends up relegating persons to the status of things'.

If the Turkish invasion and *de facto* segregation of Cyprus were an affront to the UN Charter, then the occupation and *de facto* partition of Cyprus were – and remain – in clear breach of the Treaty of Guarantee 1960, under which 'Greece, Turkey and the United Kingdom likewise undertake to prohibit, so far as concerns them, any activity aimed at promoting, directly or indirectly, either union of Cyprus with any other State or partition of the Island'. However much Turkey tries to justify its actions taken in 1974, there is no escaping this conclusion.

In view of the manifest illegality of the Turkish invasion and the incompatibility of the occupation with the Treaty of Guarantee, the United Nations Security Council has issued a number of Resolutions. Be that as it may, Turkey has not only perpetuated its military occupation but, since 1974, has committed or turned a blind eye to additional violations of law.

To begin with, as Sir John Killick, a Deputy Under-Secretary of State at the British Foreign Office, reportedly noted on 27 August 1974, within days of the invasion, some of the areas of Cyprus that had been vacated by Greek Cypriots were made subject to 'settlement' by 'certain Turkish mainlanders'. Since 1974, the occupied area of Cyprus has been unlawfully populated by tens of thousands of other citizens of Turkey, the occupying power, in breach of the Fourth Geneva Convention of August 1949; this not only prohibits 'the transfer by the Occupying Power of parts of its own civilian population into the territory it occupies', but treats any such act as a 'grave breach'.

The rule of law is predicated on various principles, including the central notions that nobody is above the law and that court decisions ought to be obeyed. Even so, Turkey has consistently flouted these principles and thereby produced what amounts to a rule of law vacuum in the occupied area of Cyprus that persists to this day. As explained by Lord Justice Richards (with whom Lord Justice Ward and Sir David Keene both agreed) in the English Court of Appeal case of *Yollari* [2010]:

> Following the invasion of the island by Turkish troops in 1974, the island was divided along a 'green line', patrolled by a peace-keeping force, which separated the community in the North from that in the South... On 15 November 1983 the Turkish Cypriot authorities in the North declared an independent state called the Turkish Republic of Northern Cyprus ('the TRNC'). UN Security Council resolution 541 (1983) deplored the declaration and considered it legally invalid, and called upon all states to respect the sovereignty, independence, territorial integrity and non-alignment of the RoC [i.e. Cyprus]. A further resolution, 550 (1984), called upon all states not to recognise the purported state of the TRNC. Neither the United Kingdom nor any other state with the exception of Turkey has recognised the TRNC.

1990–2004: the metamorphosis of the 'Cyprus Question'

During the 1990s, at least four fresh developments exacerbated the complexity of the 'Cyprus Question'; these still hover in the background today. The first was the passage of Resolution 649, which was adopted unanimously on 12 March 1990; under its terms, the UN Security Council:

> Reaffirms, in particular, its... support for the 1977 and 1979 high-level agreements... [and] calls upon the leaders of the two communities to pursue their efforts to reach freely a mutually acceptable solution providing for the establishment of a federation that will be bi-communal as regards the constitutional aspects and bi-zonal as regards the territorial aspects in line with the present resolution and their 1977 and 1979 high-level agreements.

Accordingly, the UN Security Council not only envisaged that the *de facto* partition would be regularised in an arguably unjust way with the consequence that unlawful aggression would be rewarded. More to the point, the resolution presaged a settlement embodying a set of arrangements that could be nothing other than unique, convoluted and hard to reconcile with mainstream European constitutional norms.

A second notable development of the 1990s was triggered in July 1990 when Cyprus submitted an application to join what was then known as the European Economic Community. In June 1993, the European Commission embraced the application. By entertaining the application of Cyprus while simultaneously calling for a 'political settlement of the Cyprus question' so as to 'encourage the development of pluralist democracy', the EU smothered the 'Cyprus Question' with fresh layers of complexity. After all, was it possible to develop Cyprus into a 'pluralist democracy' within the EU while simultaneously transforming that state into a bicommunal, bizonal federation?

A third key development of the 1990s arose following the filing of various cases before the European Court of Human Rights. These included *Loizidou* [1996] and *Cyprus v Turkey* [2001]. These – and others – did more than simply highlight the acts of illegality and violations of human rights committed by Turkey in 1974. These cases were seminal for another reason: they thrust the European Court of Human Rights into the orbit of the 'Cyprus Question'.

A fourth key development of the 1990s was the disintegration of the Soviet Union, the apparent end of the Cold War and the formation of a deep relationship between the Russian Federation and Cyprus. This was exemplified during the 1990s by the acquisition of Russian-made S-300 missiles by Cyprus and by the negotiation of a Double-Taxation Treaty. The formation of such an intimate bilateral relationship produced a shock to the regional balance of power. It also represented a poke in the eyes of both the British and the Turks, all the more so if one remembers that the UK acquired possession of Cyprus in 1878 pursuant to a bilateral treaty that was predicated on a common Anglo-Turkish willingness to contain Russia.

In the event, the S-300 missiles did not arrive in Cyprus – they were parked in Crete – but the Russian commercial infiltration of Cyprus gathered pace. So much so that by 2001 Russia represented the largest source of foreign funds into Cyprus and, conversely, Cyprus acted as the largest source of foreign funds into Russia.

All of which provided part of the elaborate context against which the ill-fated Annan Plan was prepared – in secret and in the absence of any consultation with citizens – before the 'double referendum' which took place in Cyprus in April 2004. By then, the swollen complexity of the 'Cyprus Question' had brought about a settlement package consisting of three proposed constitutions, multiple proposed laws, various proposed amendments to existing treaties and numerous other documents stretching over many hundreds of pages; the 222-page Command Paper of 1960 paled by comparison.

In common with the Constitution of Cyprus 1960, the Annan Plan of 2004 was predicated on a bicommunal set of constitutional arrangements. However, the Plan also sought, via bizonality, to legitimise *ex post facto* the illegal consequences of the Turkish invasion and to ensure that Cyprus became a *sui generis* member of the EU. No less importantly, the Plan effectively sought by means of the 'double referendum' to convey a semblance of electoral legitimacy upon the Lancaster House Agreement and the legal instruments it spawned in 1960.

Thanks to a 'no' vote by 76 per cent of the voters South of the cease-fire line in Cyprus, the Annan Plan was stillborn. Thus, pursuant to various legal instruments, Cyprus acceded to the EU as a *de facto* partitioned member state with EU law suspended over the occupied area pending a settlement of the 'Cyprus Question'. At a stroke, in April 2004, the treaties and other legal instruments of EU law thereby entered the bloodstream of Cyprus untainted by the Annan Plan; at the same time, Cyprus extricated itself from the Non-Aligned Movement.

2004–12: the geographical expansion of the 'Cyprus Question'

Since 2004, Cyprus has found itself ever more integrated into the EU by virtue of various additional factors. As a consequence, the 'Cyprus Question' has also entered a complicated new era, the law of which must be taken into account in the search for a settlement. First of all, the relevance of the rule of law to the 'Cyprus Question' has been elevated still further by virtue of the hallowed status of this principle and the related values of the European legal order, such as the principle of equality. In the words of Article 2 of the Treaty on European Union:

The [European] Union is founded on the values of respect for human dignity, freedom, democracy, equality,

the rule of law and respect for human rights, including
the rights of persons belonging to minorities. Those
values are common to the Member States in a society
in which pluralism, non-discrimination, tolerance, justice, solidarity and equality between women and men
prevail.

It bears emphasising that bicommunalism and bizonality are hard,
if not impossible, to reconcile with the above principles and values.
Even so, these two concepts remain at the heart of the ongoing and
hitherto futile search for a settlement.

Second, the Court of Justice of the EU and the domestic courts
of EU member states have been added to the architecture of the
'Cyprus Question'. This was amply demonstrated, albeit in narrow
circumstances, by the case of *Apostolides* [2008] and [2010] when the
Court of Justice of the EU observed *inter alia* that:

According to national legislation, the real property
rights relating to those areas of the Republic of Cyprus
in which the Government of that Member State does
not exercise effective control ('the Northern area') subsist and remain valid in spite of the invasion of Cypriot
territory in 1974 by the Turkish army and the ensuing
military occupation of part of Cyprus.

More broadly, the entry of the Court of Justice of the EU into
the architecture of the 'Cyprus Question' underlines that one or
more courts may be used to challenge the legality of any settlement
package which is incompatible with the rule of law, the principle of
equality and the other founding values of the EU.

Third, the accession of Cyprus to the EU has not altered the
status of the 'TRNC' as a pariah in the international community.
As such, Turkey retains its status as the occupying power in the
occupied area and EU law remains suspended there. Put another
way, the Turkish Cypriot unilateral declaration of independence
(UDI) of 1983 remains illegal. Indeed, in its advisory opinion of
2010 relating to the UDI made in Kosovo, the International Court
of Justice indicated that the illegality of the Turkish Cypriot UDI in
1983, the UDI in Rhodesia in 1965 and the UDI in Republika Srpska
in 1992:

stemmed not from the unilateral character of these
declarations as such, but from the fact that they were,
or would have been, connected with the unlawful use
of force or other egregious violations of norms of
general international law, in particular those of a per-
emptory character (*jus cogens* [i.e. an overriding principle
of international law which is so fundamental that no
derogation is ever allowed]).

The above has seemingly scuppered any lingering prospect that
Cyprus may be subject to a *de jure* partition.

Fourth, in 2009, the Lisbon Treaty brought into force the
Charter of Fundamental Rights of the EU. This reinforces the
rights set out in the European Convention on Human Rights and
enshrines various rights recognised by the EU. On the basis that
any settlement of the 'Cyprus Question' must be incorporated into
EU law, the Charter limits the room for manoeuvre of those who
are negotiating a settlement. Put another way, the Charter throws a
further spanner into the works of Turkey which officially requires a
bizonal settlement to be predicated on what amount to racially-based
'restrictions on the three freedoms (of movement, settlement and
property)'.

Fifth, the discovery of natural gas by Cyprus in December 2011
has extended the 'Cyprus Question' into the Exclusive Economic
Zone of Cyprus 200 nautical miles from the baselines from which
the breadth of its territorial sea is measured. In all likelihood, the
discovery will result in the further integration of Cyprus into the
energy security apparatus of the EU and of Israel. It may also
spark fresh friction with Turkey, which steadfastly refuses to sign
or ratify the United Nations Convention on the Law of the Sea and
other relevant legal instruments, such as the Rome Statute on the
International Criminal Court.

Sixth, Cyprus has been part of the Eurozone since 2008. Indeed,
in 2012 it effectively joined Greece, Ireland and Portugal as one of
the primary victims of this inherently defective and dysfunctional
project. It remains to be seen as to whether Cyprus emerges from
the mess it finds itself in at the time of writing and, if so, how. In
the meantime, the Eurozone crisis has brought into Cyprus extra
waves of European Union law, while effectively giving the French
and the Germans an *entrée* into the politics and government of

Cyprus. Coincidentally, or otherwise, French and German frigates are becoming ever more regular visitors to the territorial sea and ports of Cyprus.

Seventh, Cyprus is favourably positioned to facilitate the response of the EU to the unfolding 'Arab Spring' which may well evolve into an 'Islamist Winter'. The snag is that Cyprus is becoming precariously encircled by Islamist movements in Egypt, Gaza, Lebanon, Syria and Turkey. Meanwhile, Islamism is penetrating the 'Cyprus Question'. For example, Turkey is increasingly referring to the Turkish Cypriots as 'Muslim Turkish Cypriots' and the occupied area is becoming a magnet for Islamists. Ironically, whereas Turkey was considered a bulwark against Communism during the Cold War, Cyprus ought now to be regarded as a bulwark against Islamism. In these circumstances, what could be more dangerous than to legitimise the Turkification – and, by extension, the Islamisation – of the occupied area of Cyprus by means of legalised bizonality?

Eighth, the accession of Cyprus to the EU and other factors have produced a profound demographic transformation. According to the latest census of 2011, as reflected in the *Demographic Report 2010–11* published by the Statistical Service of Cyprus of Cyprus, the lawful population of Cyprus totals 952,100. This encompasses: the Greek Cypriot community (including Maronites, Armenians and Latins), which numbers 684,000 or 71.8 per cent of the population; the Turkish Cypriot community, which is said to number 90,100 or 9.5 per cent; and foreign residents (i.e. people who are not citizens of the Republic of Cyprus), who number 178,000 or 18.7 per cent. (These figures exclude 160,000 or so 'illegal settlers from Turkey'.) The 'foreign residents' include migrants (from within or beyond the EU) and refugees (from trouble spots such as Syria). In such circumstances, how can anybody seriously continue to assert that Cyprus consists of 'two communities' and that its constitutional future should be built on bicommunalism?

Conclusion

As Enoch Powell perceived in March 1959, the 'Cyprus Question' was already complicated enough in the aftermath of the Lancaster House Agreement. Since then, however, the 'Cyprus Question' has mutated and thereby acquired layer upon layer of additional complexity. Nothing illustrates this better than the geographical realities on the ground today. The island of Cyprus is effectively divided into five slices: the Turkish-occupied Northern area of Cyprus; the Southern area of Cyprus; the UN Buffer Zone along the cease-fire line declared in 1974, which is a no-man's land; the British Sovereign Base Area at Akrotiri on the Southwest coast; and the British Sovereign Base at Dhekelia on the Southeast coast. This carve-up is all the more bizarre if one remembers that the island of Cyprus is not much bigger than Corsica and just a little smaller than Connecticut.

Accordingly, it may be said that the 'Cyprus Question' finds itself caught in a net consisting of what amounts to British imperial threads, neo-Ottoman strands and modern European fibres. Furthermore, the geographical scope of the 'Cyprus Question' now extends into the Exclusive Economic Zone of Cyprus and, beyond, into the remainder of the EU.

Looking to the future, it is difficult to be optimistic for the various reasons pinpointed above. Even so, it is clearly in the interests of the citizens of Cyprus that their 'peace process' should be subjected to a greater degree of transparency, consultation and scrutiny. By the same token, there is clearly merit in learning from the constitutional experiences of those other island-states on the European continent that – in contrast to Cyprus, Ireland and the UK – have not been stained by partition. These are, of course, Malta and Iceland. There are also lessons to be drawn from the constitutional simplicity of the United States Constitution, which was originally four pages long.

When all is said and done, however, there can be no satisfactory settlement to the 'Cyprus Question' unless Turkey embraces the rule of law and until the citizens of Cyprus work out who they are and what they want. Above all, do they wish to remain saddled in perpetuity with the 'offspring' of the Lancaster House Agreement, the Turkish invasion and the subsequent occupation? Do they want their state to become a basket-case bedevilled by bicommunalism and bizonalism, two anachronistic concepts that are well past their sell-by date? Or do they want to live in a genuinely pluralist EU member state that constitutes one multi-ethnic democracy governed by the rule of law, the principle of equality and other related values? Time will tell.

In the meantime, one fears that foreign diplomats will continue to visit Cyprus and trot out the usual mantras which have been heard ad nauseam over the decades. Ironically, similar mantras were uttered by Viscount Palmerston whenever he spoke about Schleswig-Holstein.

In Parliament on 25 August 1848, for example, he 'trusted… that the good sense which he hoped animated all the parties concerned would lead to a satisfactory settlement of the question…' *Plus ça change.*

Cases cited

Apostolides (Area of Freedom, Security & Justice) [2008] EUECJ C-420/07.

Apostolides v Orams & Ors [2010] EWCA Civ 9.

Cyprus v Turkey 25781/94 [2001] ECHR 331.

Kosovo Advisory Opinion, 22 July 2010, ICJ Reports, 2010.

Loizidou v Turkey 15318/89 [1996] ECHR 70.

Polly Peck International Plc v Marangos Hotel Company Ltd [1998] EWCA Civ 789.

R (Yollari & Anor) v Secretary of State for Transport & Anor [2010] EWCA Civ 1093.

References and recommended reading

Auer, Andreas and Vasiliki Triga (eds), *A Constitutional Convention for Cyprus* (Berlin: Wissenschaftlicher, 2009).

Constantinou, Costas M. (guest ed.), *The State of Cyprus: Fifty Years After Independence*, special edition of *The Cyprus Review* 22/2 (Fall 2010).

Coufoudakis, Van and Klearchos A. Kyriakides, *The Case Against the Annan Plan* (London, Lobby for Cyprus, 2004).

Faustmann, Hubert and Nicos Peristianis (eds), *Britain in Cyprus: Colonialism and Post-Colonialism 1878-2006* (Mannheim: Bibliopolis, 2006).

—— and Andrekos Varnava (eds), *Reunifying Cyprus: The Annan Plan and Beyond* (London: I.B.Tauris, 2009).

King, Martin Luther Jr, *Why We Can't Wait* (New York: Signet Classics, 2000).

Kyriakides, Klearchos A., 'The 1960 treaties and the search for security in Cyprus', *Journal of Balkan and Near Eastern Studies* 11/4 (2009), pp. 427–39.

19

How and Why the European Union Still Matters

GEORGE KYRIS

Closing his speech at the opening ceremony of Cyprus Presidency 2012, the President of the European Union Council, Herman van Rompuy, concluded 'As long as Cyprus is divided, in a way, Europe will be divided'. More than just a catchy, sentimental line, these words reflect the uncomfortable reality that Cyprus continues to be for the EU. Unlike the United Nations, the European Union never tried to be a direct mediator in the Cyprus issue. Nevertheless, the EU has played a very important role in the dispute and has affected the way the sides of the Cyprus issue think and act.

Lots of ink has been spilt discussing the role of the European Union in the years leading up to the accession of the island. Less has been said about the EU and the Cyprus issue in the post-accession era. This is largely because many believe there is nothing that Brussels can do after welcoming a divided island into the European family. To an extent, this is true. Yet, the European Union continues to have a few 'weapons' at its disposal that could help the resolution of the long-standing dispute. Although Brussels cannot do a lot to 'push' Greek Cypriots towards resolution, the benefits of greater European integration continue to be a motive for pro-solution attitudes amongst Turkish Cypriots, even if they seem less enthusiastic about the European Union in recent years. Most importantly, (better) EU accession prospects for Turkey can still be a significant motive for Ankara to contribute to a resolution of the Cyprus issue.

Turkey

The case of Turkey is perhaps the most obvious example of a positive EU impact on the resolution of the Cyprus issue. During the process that led to the UN-proposed Annan Plan, Ankara instituted a major change in its previously intransigent tactics and supported reunification. The most important catalyst for this shift of policy was the fact that resolving the Cyprus issue was a condition for Turkey's EU accession, which became a prime goal of Ankara after the election of the Justice and Development Party (AKP) in November 2002.

But in more recent years, and after the failure of the Annan Plan, Turkey's policy and rhetoric towards the Cyprus issue have been less flexible. Statements by Turkish officials underlining the separate existence of Turkish Cypriots have returned to cast shadows over the prospects of resolution based on the agreed formula of a bizonal and bicommunal federation. In policy terms, the perpetually slow progress in inter-communal negotiations on the Cyprus Problem does not allow for a full test of Turkish policy on the matter. But the refusal of the Turkish government to fully implement its trade agreement with the EU and open ports to the Republic of Cyprus does not bring reconciliation closer. Neither does the fact that Turkey has repeatedly opposed Greek Cypriot gas exploration in the seawaters around the island, has increased its military presence in and around the island and is attempting similar energy exploration in the North.

This growing Turkish intransigence is also a result of the EU accession of a divided country. This has had a profound impact on the dynamics of the Cyprus dispute. The failure of the Annan Plan due to the Greek Cypriot rejection and the consequent accession of the (Greek Cypriot-led) Republic of Cyprus into the EU have boosted the confidence of Turkey, which blames Greek Cypriots for lack of cooperation and moves towards less flexible behaviour. Meanwhile, the Greek Cypriot attempts to use their membership of EU, and their consequent power over Turkey's accession process in order to force concessions from Ankara over the Cyprus issue appear to have had exactly the opposite results from those intended.

Most importantly, it is the prospects of EU accession that continue to shape Turkish policy towards the Cyprus issue in the post-Annan era, but this time towards less flexible strategies. Fourteen years after the Helsinki European Council, which saw the inclusion of Turkey in the list of candidates for EU membership, the prospects of the country actually joining the EU are still anything but clear. The Cyprus Problem is a hermetic barrier to accession. However, many Turkish officials believe EU partners are hiding behind the dispute, using it to try to disguise their deep scepticism towards Turkey's integration. The truth is that countries like Germany or France have often voiced their concerns about welcoming Turkey as a member and have instead suggested alternative forms of relations, like a 'privileged partnership' between the two sides. European public debate has also seen a lot of scepticism towards Turkey's accession, not least during the referenda on the notorious constitutional treaty in 2005.

This pervasive reluctance to accept Turkey and the slow pace of accession negotiations have also influenced Turkish attitudes towards the EU. Not only have pro-European sentiments declined amongst the Turkish public, but the leadership is often vocal about the 'insulting', in the words of Chief EU Negotiator Egemen Bağiş, suggestions for a privileged partnership. They have not shied away from expressing their general disappointment over the lack of progress of EU integration. In a climate of mounting Euroscepticism, there is little that the Turkish government can do 'in the name of Europe'. As a result, the faltering accession negotiations do not offer Ankara enough reasons to meet the conditionality of EU entry, especially those clauses that relate to the sensitive Cyprus issue.

So, the role of the EU in the Turkish stance towards Cyprus continues to be important. The power of conditionality is evident not only in the EU-triggered support of reunification during the early (and much more promising) phase of accession but also in terms of the more recent inflexibility and slow-down in EU–Turkey relations. In this regard, the ability of the EU to 'shape' Turkish foreign policy is, and will continue to be, related to its accession: the better the prospects of accession, the stronger the role of the EU. This is, of course, not to say that Turkey does not need to undertake generous reforms in preparation for accession, especially as far as Cyprus is concerned (for example, opening ports to the Republic of Cyprus). However, since the lack of progress in accession negotiations relates to issues beyond the Cyprus Problem (such as the wider scepticism towards Turkey's accession), it is perhaps the EU that should take the first step and address the deadlock in its relations with Turkey. Provided, of course, that the EU is still committed to a full accession of the country. Indeed, in early 2013, the EU called for a 'reboot' of the accession process with Turkey.

The Turkish Cypriots

Turkey was not the only side that the EU has managed to influence. In the period before the accession of Cyprus into the EU, the Turkish Cypriots went through groundbreaking changes. After decades during which the community was dominated by the intransigent leader Rauf Denktas, in the last months of 2003 people moved to vote for political parties that favoured solution. This in turn led to the two-thirds support in favour of the Annan Plan in the April 2004 referendum. The EU played an important role in this change in Turkish Cypriot society and politics.

Reunification was (and is) the only way by which Turkish Cypriots could integrate into the EU. This would have occurred as part of a new, bicommunal state that would replace the Republic of Cyprus in the process of accession. For the Turkish Cypriots, EU entry was not only a ticket to a range of political, economic and social benefits, it was also a way out of their international isolation. By voting against the Annan Plan, only the Greek Cypriot-led Republic would accede to the EU. And yet this is what happened in the end anyway. Even if, legally speaking, the entire island is considered to have joined the EU, the Turkish Cypriots do not formally take part in the Cypriot government or EU affairs. EU law is suspended North of the 'Green Line'.

However, the failure of the reunification process in 2004 did not bring an end to the relevance of the EU to the community. In fact, it has done quite the opposite. In the aftermath of the aborted reunification, the European Council declared its determination to 'put an end to the isolation of the Turkish Cypriot community and to facilitate the reunification of Cyprus by encouraging the economic development of the Turkish Cypriot community'. Indeed, since accession, the EU has helped build trade between Turkish and Greek Cypriots. It has also provided financial and technical assistance for socioeconomic development of the Turkish Cypriot community, and has aided in the community's preparations to implement EU law if and when reunification comes. But the unique political context in Cyprus (such as the lack of recognition of Turkish Cypriot authorities or tensions with the Greek Cypriots) has limited the success of those programmes. In addition, other important measures, such as a trade agreement between the EU and the Turkish Cypriot community, have been opposed by the Greek Cypriots, who have argued that the implementation of such an agreement would mean recognition of the self-declared state in the North. As a result, although now the EU has a much more extensive presence in North Cyprus, the benefits of full EU integration continue to be an incentive for Turkish Cypriots to support a solution of the Cyprus issue that will bring them closer to Europe and the rest of the world. In this sense, the Turkish Cypriot community is the party to the dispute over which the EU maintains the strongest leverage.

This leverage should not be taken for granted, though. One problem that Brussels needs to address here is the decreasing pro-EU feelings amongst Turkish Cypriots. Likewise, it needs to think about the fewer (in comparison to the pre-Annan era) motives for reunification. These attitudes have mainly been caused by the failure of the EU to meet its promises to end the community's isolation in the aftermath of the referendum. It is also a result of the Turkish Cypriot lack of understanding of EU matters. For example, the way in which the EU distributes aid has often frustrated local applicants to grant schemes, who find the process very technical and time-consuming, especially in comparison to the way in which Turkey provides assistance. Therefore, the EU needs to invest on better communication strategies in the North and educate people about the EU, how it works and what opportunities it can offer. Perhaps an even trickier problem for Brussels is to fulfil the promises for more integration with the Turkish Cypriot community. As full members, the Greek Cypriots are able to block EU initiatives.

The Greek Cypriots

The membership of Greek Cypriots is the biggest challenge to an effective role of the EU in the Cyprus dispute. The EU has never provided Greek Cypriots with motives to contribute to resolution. On the contrary, on the eve of the Annan Plan, Greek Cypriots were encouraged to show greater inflexibility due to the impending EU membership. The words of the then president, Tassos Papadopoulos, are very illuminating: 'if people reject the plan by their vote, the Republic of Cyprus will become a full and equal member of the EU'. In the period after accession, the EU still offers Greek Cypriots no motives to contribute to a resolution.

The only impact that the EU has had on Greek Cypriot strategies is that it has somewhat changed the way in which the Republic of

Cyprus has used membership to force Turkey towards concessions. Shortly after joining the EU, the Greek Cypriots tried to tie Turkey's accession to a rather long list of demands. This did not go down well with many EU partners. Eventually, the Greek Cypriots had to adopt a more subtle strategy, even if they still retain their strong opposition to Turkish accession before resolution of the Cyprus issue. Perhaps the most obvious example of the way in which they have toned down their approach can be seen in the 2012 Cypriot EU Presidency. During this period, the Republic of Cyprus made a calculated effort not to include the Cyprus issue in their agenda. This was consciously done following previous criticism that they are a 'one issue country', always trying to link EU affairs to the island's dispute.

A more recent development that could impact on Greek Cypriot positions on the Cyprus issue is the economic crisis, especially in relation to the energy resources around the island. But, on this front, the EU does not seem able to have a major impact on developments. The Greek Cypriots see gas resources in Cyprus as a potentially important element of their economic revival. But Turkey has opposed Greek Cypriot exploration on the ground that Turkish Cypriots should also benefit from any potential energy reserves. Many observers expect that a resolution of the Cyprus issue will remove Turkey's opposition and will also provide other, new opportunities for the economic prosperity of a reunified island. But, in the meantime, and again due to the EU membership of the Republic, the EU lacks appears to lack 'sticks or carrots' that could impact on the position of the Greek Cypriots.

Something that could potentially make Greek Cypriots see the benefits of a solution in a different light would be closer relations between the EU and the Turkish Cypriots and the long-term implications of this for Cyprus and the status of the community in international affairs. The EU, although underlining at every given opportunity that they do not recognise any administration in North Cyprus, is gradually improving its presence in the Turkish Cypriot community and, informally, has considerable interaction with the locals, including meetings with officials from the self-declared state. For example, the EU maintains contact with many representatives of the Turkish Cypriot administration, even if they have to meet in 'neutral' buildings rather than the offices of the self-declared state. This might not have legal implications but it could be a potentially crucial step towards a greater, perhaps accidental, *de facto* political acknowledgement of Turkish Cypriots in international relations and, therefore, bring partition closer. As a result, this could become an indirect pressure on those Greek Cypriots who still prefer reunification to act to save the island from partition. The trap here is that more integration between the EU and the Turkish Cypriots is still politically tricky. It could also lead to the Greek Cypriots becoming even more defensive, and trying to block contacts between the EU and the Turkish Cypriots, thereby further damaging relations between the two communities and setting back solution efforts.

Conclusion

The EU is only one of the many different factors that have shaped the Cyprus Problem in recent years. To a large degree, the EU remains a 'hostage' to the peculiar accession of a divided country. With no link between European integration and the resolution of the Cyprus issue, the EU never provided reasons for the Greek Cypriots to contribute to reunification. On the other hand, both Turkey and the Turkish Cypriots favoured the Annan Plan in order to increase their prospects of EU integration. This antithetical impact that the EU has had on different sides of the dispute highlights one simple but crucial point: the most effective way through which the EU can impact the Cyprus dispute is by tying its resolution to certain rewards, particularly the promise for greater integration.

But the post-accession years are different. Not only are the Greek Cypriots still without EU-related motives for resolution, but now Turkish Cypriots and particularly Turkey are beginning to lose faith in the EU and, consequently, interest in a resolution that will advance their European future. Ultimately, the EU can do little with regard to the Greek Cypriot side and needs to do little in North Cyprus, as the prize of EU accession continues to be a strong motivation for approving resolution, despite less 'Europeanism' among Turkish Cypriots. As a result, what the EU needs to focus on is Turkey's accession. If there is a real desire to facilitate a resolution of the Cyprus Problem, the EU should look back at the experience of the Annan Plan and appreciate the power of credible EU rewards for Turkey. Indeed, the recent interest of the EU in indigenous energy resources might be a new motive for Brussels to resolve the dispute and facilitate the exploitation of energy assets in Cyprus without opposition from Turkish Cypriots or Turkey. At the end of the day, a revival in the Turkish accession process is perhaps the EU's best (if not only) card in this game. And, although a more cooperative Turkish policy towards Cyprus will certainly advance its EU prospects, the EU also needs to take generous steps towards improving relations with Ankara. Perhaps most crucially of all, Brussels needs to make its mind up on whether Turkey is still welcome in the EU or not.

Referemces and recommended reading

Christou, George, *The European Union and Enlargement: The Case of Cyprus* (Basingstoke: Palgrave Macmillan, 2004).

Nugent, Neil, 'EU enlargement and "the Cyprus Problem"', *Journal of Common Market Studies* 38/1 (2000), pp. 131–50.

Ker-Lindsay, James, Hubert Faustmann and Fiona Mullen (eds), *An Island in Europe: The EU and the Transformation of Cyprus* (London: I.B.Tauris, 2011).

Kyris, George, 'Europeanisation beyond the contested state: the EU and the Turkish-Cypriot civil society', *Journal of Common Market Studies* 51/5 (2013), pp. 886–3.

Tocci, Nathalie, *EU Accession Dynamics and Conflict Resolution: Catalysing Peace or Consolidating Partition in Cyprus?* (Aldershot: Ashgate, 2004).

20

Challenging Partition in Five Success Stories

Neophytos Loizides

In the second half of 2012, the Republic of Cyprus held the European Union presidency; a highly prestigious distinction for the Eastern Mediterranean Island. In reality, however, Cyprus' current politics have been an unfortunate parody of its last 4,000 years of turbulent geopolitics. A European but divided Cyprus is occupied in the North by Turkey, forced to welcome the British (sovereign) military bases in the South and, following the sovereign debt crisis, financially indebted to the Germans, Russians and others including the cold-blooded technocrats of the International Monetary Fund (IMF) and the European Central Bank (ECB). Some might be tempted to conclude that there is little hope for Cyprus to recover and, more importantly, to materialise its long-aspired ambition for reunification.

This chapter aims to challenge this logic. Why does it choose to swim against the current? Simply stated, the Cypriot experience itself suggests that those civil and political actors who did so in the past often challenged the logic of partition, arguably with relative success. Cyprus features a number of positive stories in peace mediation that demonstrate how peacemakers in divided societies can choose to take their fate in their own hands and mitigate even the most difficult aspects of their territorial division.

Beyond Cyprus, creative institutions elsewhere in divided societies have sustained power sharing, federalism and reconciliation under conditions that initially seemed prohibitive. Institutional innovation and creative leadership are critical for peace mediations. In Cyprus itself, peacemakers have frequently proved, with little outside help, how societies can choose to reverse even the most difficult aspects of territorial division.

Grassroots reconciliation

In the early 1980s the two mayors of the capital Nicosia resorted to an ad hoc set of arrangements in addressing the city's impeding environmental disaster caused by the absence of a sewer system. Leaving legalistic formalities aside, they agreed to call themselves 'representatives', rather than 'mayors', of the city and managed to upgrade the city's sewer system, thereby taking the first step to Nicosia's 'underground' unification. Shortly after, the two mayors agreed on a 'master plan' for Nicosia based on the framework of a 'town which is going to be united'.

Moreover, the 1990s also saw an intensification of the emergence of grassroots movements to support the reunification of Cyprus, not only across the ethnic divide but also across the traditional left–right division. In the Turkish Cypriot community, left-wing parties began to challenge the hegemonic position of the nationalist right. The Bu Memleket Bizim (This Homeland is Ours) movement brought together these forces and successfully mobilised the Turkish Cypriot community in massive peace rallies in 2002–4. As a result of these mobilisations, the Turkish Republican Party (CTP) and its leader Mehmet Ali Talat gradually came to control almost all important posts in the Turkish Cypriot community by 2005. In April 2003, and in response to the public demand for cooperation, the Turkish Cypriot leader Rauf Denktash lifted his restrictions on travel across the so-called Green Line that had separated the two communities for decades, and allowed members of the two communities to cross into each other's sector for the first time since the island's division in 1974. These crossings took place without any incidences of violence and, in most cases, previous and new owners of disputed properties engaged with one another on amicable terms. The 'Yes' vote by the Turkish Cypriots in the 2004 Annan Plan referendum is by itself another major success. In divided societies it is unprecedented for breakaway communities to support reunification and certainly unimaginable among such secessionist communities as the Abkhaz in Georgia.

Another interesting example concerns voluntary peaceful returns of communities forced from their homes by the violence on the island. For example, we can look at the case of the Maronite residents of Kormakitis. There are around 6,000 Cypriot Maronites in Cyprus, descendants of emigrants from Syria and Lebanon who arrived in the eighth century. All four ancestral Maronite villages, Agia Marina, Asomatos, Karpasia and Kormakitis, are located in the Northern part of the island, with their native populations largely displaced, because of the 1974 *de facto* partition of the island. In 2006, and despite the failure of the peace process, the Maronite leadership managed to convince the Turkish Cypriot side to allow a return to Kormakitis, the largest of the Maronite villages. This mediation is particularly paradoxical as it happened at a time of major disappointment for the Turkish Cypriot with the Greek Cypriot 'no' vote in the referendum two years earlier. More puzzling was the involvement in this mediation of a hardliner, Serdar Denktash. Having been persuaded to support the Maronite cause, Denktash junior was central to an agreement that has improved his international image; his photo now decorates the village coffee shop of Kormakitis while the Maronites themselves have played an increasing role in the rapprochement of the two communities. More importantly, the return of Kormakitians to their ancestral lands in the North could potentially inspire the beginning of the process of reversing forced displacement and its bitter legacy in the island.

An even more interesting case is that of the Committee for Missing Persons (CMP) in Cyprus, an institutionalised bicommunal body responsible for the exhumations of those individuals reported as missing in the inter-communal fighting of the 1960s and early 1970s, as well as in the events of July 1974 and afterwards. Despite the political stalemate in 2004, the CMP has become one of the most successful bicommunal projects since then, having exhumed the remains of 941 missing persons by April 2013. On this issue, other divided societies, such as South Africa, provide an interesting contrast to Cyprus. In both South Africa and Cyprus there have been approximately 2,000 reported cases of missing persons. Yet the Truth and Reconciliation Commission (TRC) in South Africa has managed to officially recognise only 447 individuals as missing, out of which only 66 individuals have been exhumed. In other words, the much-celebrated 'South African model' produced only a tiny portion of exhumations compared to the less known 'Cypriot alternative' where almost half of the missing have been exhumed under conditions of a protracted stalemate.

Countering conventional wisdom, these examples show that challenging the logic of partition is not merely dependent on the external environment but is primarily a society's own choice of actions, rational framing and institutions.

Another unexpected challenger to the partition of the island is the Greek Cypriot right. The decade between 1993 and 2003 saw the centre-right Democratic Rally (DISY) in power within the Greek Cypriot community. A paradox from its very inception in the post-1974 era, the party hosted the moderate centre-right elements alongside former paramilitaries associated with violence against the Turkish Cypriots and the left alike. DISY's decade in government marked the steady transformation of Greek Cypriot politics and the vulnerable Republic of Cyprus was steered towards accession to the European Union. More importantly, it led to the gradual transformation of Democratic Rally itself. In its last years in government, DISY's historic leader Glafkos Clerides negotiated the main parameters for the reunification of Cyprus under the Annan Plan. As the main opposition party, DISY voted in favour of the Plan in the 2004 referendum and since then has steadily advocated a politically-agreed reunification of the island. Reversals of contested partitions have been rare, difficult and politically risky for moderate challengers. Yet DISY has managed to keep a stable support for reunification while maintaining its vote. In 2013, Nikos Anastasiades, the party leader, won the presidential elections.

But Anastasiades' rise to power as a moderate is not unprecedented. Both communities have at times voted for pro-federal politicians or rallied in support of the reunification of the island. A notable example was the impressive Turkish Cypriot rallies of 2002–4. Historically, two-thirds of the Greek Cypriot public has voted for pro-settlement politicians hailing either from the nominally communist AKEL (Progressive Party of the Working People) or the centre-right DISY (Democratic Rally). Yet moderate political forces on the island have failed to articulate a shared agenda on the Cyprus issue. The institutional framework for intra- and inter-community cooperation in the island has been missing. On this issue, institutions inspired by the experience of other divided societies might provide alternative avenues for reconciliation.

A Northern Irish-style executive?

Examples of novel institutional arrangements could be drawn from other divided societies such as Northern Ireland, the Balkans and South Africa to stimulate comparable solutions in Cyprus. For instance, the d'Hondt mechanism in Northern Ireland has the potential to inspire a consensus executive in Cyprus through its main principles of inclusivity, automaticity and proportionality. The Northern Irish d'Hondt system has been described as innovative and effective as it has contributed to broad inclusive coalitions and political stability in the province, particularly since 2007. Inspired by Lijphart's vision of consociationalism, d'Hondt procedure entitles each political party not only to be proportionally represented in the parliament but also to automatically translate its representation into ministerial positions. By inviting all major parties to share power, d'Hondt could skip the most problematic and time-consuming aspect of consociationalism, namely that of forming inter-ethnic majority coalitions. Membership in the executive is automatically determined by electoral strength rather than post-election negotiations, as commonly practiced elsewhere. Combined with ideas already familiar to the Cypriots such as cross-voting (e.g. in a semi-presidential arbitration mechanism), d'Hondt might resolve the current deadlock in the Cyprus peace talks and provide a set of negotiable and durable alternatives in power-sharing.

But the transfer of institutional designs from one setting to another in general, and the d'Hondt innovation in particular, are not without their limitations. Unlike Northern Ireland, which can look to the UK and/or the Republic of Ireland for ad hoc arbitration, such as direct rule from London and Dublin if local arrangements fail, Cyprus cannot yet rely on similar arrangements involving Athens and Ankara. Alternative mechanisms have to be identified if parties fail to reach agreements or if problems arise at different levels of governance within the Cabinet, the parliaments or any sub-unit of the federation. The Annan Plan aimed at resolving such disputes through the arbitration of the constitutional court, a slow process at best.

For these reasons, the suggested formula for the federal executive combines the d'Hondt mechanism – or another comparable divisor – for the cabinet with cross-voting mechanisms for the joint presidency. In other words, the Northern Ireland system could be modified into a semi-presidential one for Cyprus where the two co-presidents would be elected through cross-voting, as agreed by Talat and Christofias in 2009–10. Ideas for cross-voting or weighted-voting have a long history in the island and it is undeniably one of the most innovative proposals produced by the peace community in the past decades. Costa Carras, through the London-based Friends of Cyprus Association, has lobbied for cross-voting since the late 1970s and the fact that the two sides have tentatively agreed on such an arrangement demonstrates the potential for future negotiations.

If properly inspired by Northern Ireland, the executive power would still lie primarily with the Cabinet. However, the two co-presidents will maintain key arbitration powers to deal with certain critical issues, such as matters involving security and cooperation with the United Nations force on the island. However, the most important responsibility of the co-presidents would be to mediate and arbitrate deadlocks at all levels of government. If there are remaining unresolved issues, community vetoes or protracted stalemates elsewhere in the system, a consensus by the two co-presidents would be sufficient to resolve such disputes before they arrived at the constitutional court or another arbitration (for example, EU-related) mechanism. The presidential arbitration mechanism would add another democratic layer of governance to the reunification structure, creating a buffer zone between the executive and constitutional court.

By inviting everyone to join the cabinet, the two communities in Cyprus would avoid the most contentious aspect of consociationalism in divided societies, namely the formation of inter-ethnic majority coalitions. Prolonged deadlocks in forming governments could be particularly problematic, especially at a time of wider economic or political crisis. The absence of formal d'Hondt-style arrangements has left countries in similar situations without elected governments for prolonged periods, as happened in Belgium in 2009–10. Coalitions also increase uncertainty and competition among groups; as suggested in the case of Lebanon, where groups have responded violently to attempts by others to ostracise them politically following negotiations to form a government. By extension, third alternatives might turn significant constituencies against the peace settlement.

There are multiple reasons why a modified d'Hondt method could be more suitable and effective in capitalising on the specific advantages of Cyprus as a federation. First, it is more negotiable and acceptable to all parties, including 'hardliners' who might have a veto role in the imminent negotiations. As Cyprus' own past success stories demonstrate, 'hardliners' can often take the right steps forward if offered the appropriate incentives. It is both legitimate and appropriate to offer those incentives that encourage broader segments of the society to support a reunified Cyprus. The suggested formula would combine wider participation by the Turkish Cypriots political forces maintaining the community's veto but at the same time combined with alternative arbitration mechanisms that foster cooperation. Likewise, it would allow the broader participation of Greek Cypriot parties with the added benefit of enabling co-governance by DISY and AKEL, a feature that could sustain long-term Greek Cypriot moderation.

Conclusion

The ideas presented above would be more suitable and effective in capitalising on past success stories in Cyprus and maintaining its advantages as a future federation. This is only one example of how to ensure functionality and negotiability in a future settlement appealing both to moderates and hardliners in the two communities. Countering conventional wisdom, this chapter and the research cited below provide examples on how civil and political groups have challenged partition in the island. looking at different levels of peace engagement including the divided capital of Nicosia, the Maronite village of Kormakitis, the Bu Memleket Bizim movement, the party politics of the Democratic Rally and negotiated institutions such as the CMP and cross-voting. More specifically, with regard to institutional design, novel ideas could be further explored to address the needs of the displaced persons, external guarantees and decentralised federalism; all of which could constitute the very basis of a comprehensive peace settlement. In a nutshell, there are grounds for optimism in Cyprus based not only on its own past achievements but also the availability of options in contemporary peacemaking.

References and recommended reading

Aronson, D. Jay, 'The strengths and limitations of South Africa's search for Apartheid-era missing persons', *International Journal of Transitional Justice* 5/2 (2011), pp. 262–81.

Ellinas, Antonis A. and Yiannous Katsourides, 'Organizational continuity and electoral endurance: the Communist Party of Cyprus', *West European Politics* (2013, in press).

Ker-Lindsay, James, *The Foreign Policy of Counter Secession: Preventing the Recognition of Contested States* (Oxford: Oxford University Press, 2012).

Kovras, Iosif, 'Explaining prolonged silences in transitional justice: the disappeared in Cyprus and Spain', *Comparative Political Studies* 46/6 (2013), pp. 730–56.

McCrudden, Christopher, John McGarry, Brendan O'Leary and Alex Schwartz, Memorandum for the Northern Ireland Assembly and Executive Review Committee (2013). Available at http://www.niassembly.gov.uk/Documents/Assembly-and-Executive-Review/reviews/review-of-d%27hondt/written-submissions/Joint-memorandum-mccrudden-oleary.pdf (accessed 6 April 2013).

McEvoy, Joanne, *Power-Sharing Executives: Cooperation and Conflict in Northern Ireland, Bosnia and Macedonia* (Philadelphia: University of Pennsylvania Press, forthcoming).

McGarry, John and Brendan O'Leary, 'Power shared after the deaths of thousands', in Rupert Taylor (ed.), *Consociational Theory: McGarry and O'Leary and the Northern Ireland Conflict* (London: Routledge, 2009).

Moore, G. et al., 'Winning peace frames: intra-ethnic outbidding in Northern Ireland and Cyprus', *West European Politics* (2014, in press).

Sandal, Nukhet and Neophytos Loizides, 'The centre-right in peace processes: slow learning or punctuated peace socialization', *Political Studies* 61/2 (2013), pp. 401–21.

Stefanovic, Djordje and Neophytos Loizides, 'The way home: peaceful return of victims of ethnic cleansing', *Human Rights Quarterly* 33/3 (2011), pp. 408–30.

Vural, Yucel, 'Seeking to transform the perceptions of intercommunal relations: The Turkish-Cypriot case (2004–2009)', *Nationalism and Ethnic Politics* 18/4 (2012), pp. 406–30.

21

Security is Key to a Settlement

Robert McDonald

The half-a-century old separation of the Greek and Turkish Cypriot peoples, first in enclaves and now in territories, has its basis in concerns about security. The UN peace process has pursued a constitutional settlement focused on division of territory and political power. This chapter argues that a shift in emphasis is necessary. Prior resolution of security issues would pave the way for a constitutional settlement. This would involve abolition of the historical treaties that give interventionist powers to the tripartite guarantors Britain, Greece and Turkey, leaving resolution of constitutional differences to Cypriots – Greek and Turkish – free of outside influences. There are hard line nationalists in both Greek and Turkish Cypriot camps for whom this would be anathema but there is evidence to suggest that left to their own devices, the indigenous populations would be able to resolve outstanding differences to create a viable confederal state.

The establishment of the Republic of Cyprus in 1960 was anomalous. The island had been a British Crown Colony peopled approximately 82 per cent by Greek Cypriot Orthodox (and other Christian communities) and 18 per cent by Turkish Cypriot Muslims. Half a decade of warfare by communal guerrilla forces (financed and militarily supported by Athens and Ankara) sought to secure the island for their respective motherlands. The colonial compromise of independence under a power-sharing constitution was sought by neither side. Control of the island was not 'won' by the anti-colonial forces; rather, 97 per cent of the territory was ceded to the new Republic by the colonial authorities, who continued to retain 3 per cent of the island in Sovereign Base Areas (SBAs) at Akrotiri and Dhekelia. These are British Overseas Territories responsible directly to the Crown.

The new nation's power-sharing constitution was buttressed by Treaties of Guarantee and Alliance, which contradicted the notion of independence. The Treaty of Guarantee made three foreign powers – Britain, Greece and Turkey – responsible for the independence, defence and territorial integrity of the new nation state and forbade 'either the union of the Republic of Cyprus with any other State or the partition of the Island'. The Treaty of Alliance provided for a tripartite military headquarters to which would be assigned an indeterminate number of UK forces plus 950 Greek and 650 Turkish mainland troops. The treaties proved unworkable, in large measure because of British government unwillingness to exercise the country's guarantor role for fear of compromising interests in the SBAs, the value of which for many years was vital to its overseas defence policy but which today is much diminished.

The Alliance forces were unable to stop Greek/Greek Cypriot instigated violence in 1963, which led to enclavement of the Turkish Cypriots and to the request in 1964 for the United Nations to provide a force that would stand between the warring factions – not making but keeping the peace. The United Nations Force in Cyprus (UNFICYP) remains on the island today, 50 years later. The Guarantee provided in the event of a breach for the three allies to take concerted action to restore constitutional order but also reserved their right of unilateral intervention, 'with the sole aim of re-establishing the state of affairs created by the [independence] Treaty'. This provision was abused by Turkey in 1974 when it responded to a Greek-sponsored coup against the government of the Republic with two massive invasions that partitioned the island into two contiguous territories and forcibly separated its population into two, more-or-less ethnically homogeneous communities. This divided the island rather than restoring its power-sharing constitutional order and today the nation of Cyprus consists of two *de facto* states: the Republic of Cyprus in the South, comprising roughly two-thirds of the territory and some 75 per cent of the population; and, the Turkish Republic of Northern Cyprus (TRNC) in the North, consisting of one-third of the territory and a roughly a quarter of the population, a majority of whom are settlers from the Turkish mainland. The Republic of Cyprus is *de jure* recognised by the international community as the government of the whole island; the TRNC is not recognised by any member state of the United Nations except Turkey, although many countries do business with it and have informal diplomatic relations. UNFICYP controls the demilitarised zone (DMZ) between the two ceasefire lines established upon cessation of hostilities in 1974. The DMZ constitutes approximately 3 per cent of the territory of the island.

The bizonal, bicommunal division of the island has been an established fact for 39 years. Each territory has a complete political, legal, economic and social infrastructure. The only constitutional construct that likely might reunite the island is the creation of a confederation consisting of two constituent states with virtual autonomy in all domestic matters coupled with central government responsible only for those matters that transcend state boundaries and for projection of the country's international personality. To negotiate this will require extensive good will on the part of both communities but it is posited here that it is possible if the Cypriots are left to their own devices, free from the corrosive influence of the foreign guarantors whose pursuit of national interests until now has derailed all efforts at a solution.

Security is the key issue

The core problem remains security. Memories are still fresh among Turkish Cypriots of the atrocities committed in the 1960s that led them to retreat into their defensive enclaves and among Greek Cypriots of the savagery and forced displacement suffered during and after the Turkish invasions to partition the island in 1974. Each community fears for its safety in a re-united Cyprus. Each state maintains conscript armies with air and naval elements, at a severe cost to the standing of its economy. The Greek Cypriot National Guard consists of some 12,000 active troops and 75,000 reservists with a mixture of local and Greek officers and under the overall command of a mainland general. It is supported with heavy and light armour, helicopter gunships and transports, and coastal patrol boats. The Turkish Cypriot Security Force consists of some 5,000 active troops and 26,000 reservists with Turkish mainland officers and a commander who reports nominally to the government of the TRNC. This is supported by the Cyprus Turkish Peace Force, a mainland contingent estimated at 36,000 backed with substantial heavy armour and artillery (something of the order of 450 main battle tanks and 625 artillery pieces). It has support from the Turkish air force and coastguard. These forces stand poised on either side of the DMZ for possible resumption of hostilities. Occasionally there are minor incidents which to date have been successfully defused by UNFICYP.

In a settlement featuring demilitarisation, the indigenous forces would be stood down, their mainland officers withdrawn, and the Turkish occupation troops repatriated. A portion of the domestic contingents might be retained as an unarmed civil guard to deal with natural disasters. (This might also be desirable to help mop up youth unemployment, which is currently alleviated by conscription.) Internal security would be a matter for police forces maintained by the constituent states. They would be issued only with sidearms and non-lethal weaponry (such as water cannons) for crowd control. To prevent violence by nationalist extremists, the possession of shotguns and rifles by private citizens would be banned, at least until such time as peaceable co-existence was deemed by both sides to be secure. If mutually agreed by the two states, a small, elite, national anti-terrorism force might be created to deal with internal emergencies. UNFICYP could continue to have responsibility for securing the DMZ until such time as a constitutional settlement allows the territory to be apportioned to the constituent states.

This leaves the question of external defence. The proposition of this chapter is that during a transitional period – perhaps of two decades or more – it should be a function of the European Union, of which the unified Confederation of Cyprus would be a full member. This would be a major evolutionary step for Common Security and Defence Policy (CSDP) and Europe's effort to create a Synchronised Armed Forces Europe (SAFE). So far joint EU military actions have been undertaken on an ad hoc basis, such as EUFOR, the European Union Force, for Bosnia and Herzegovina. Assumption of responsibility for the external defence of the reunified island member state would require the creation of a Cyprus Standing Defence Force (CSDF), consisting of troops from states of the European Union rotated through the island under a permanent command structure of seconded officers, reporting to the EU High Representative for Foreign Affairs and Security Policy via national government channels. This would imply early EU membership for Turkey. Until such time as it was a full member and thus able to contribute forces, Greek troops would have to be excluded from the CSDF. This might be no bad thing, providing a cooling off period to help expunge the negative historical legacy of both nations' militaries. Eventually, however, Greek and Turkish forces should be incorporated because of their intimate knowledge of Cypriot political culture, custom and languages.

The SBAs should be ceded by the UK to become EU Overseas Territories that would provide a permanent garrison and HQ for the CSDF. The SBAs historically were used to project Western military might in Middle and Near East (at one time aircraft capable of delivering nuclear strikes on Iran were stationed on the island) and as centres for over-the-horizon intelligence gathering. The former role has largely been subsumed by long-range missiles and the latter by satellites, making the bases largely vestigial except as communications relay centres. Akrotiri is on the South coast (with British HQ currently established in the Episkopi cantonment) and Dhekelia is in the Southeast east of the island abutting the DMZ. Both have air and sea access. If needs be, this could be expanded by designating areas of nearby Limassol and Famagusta as CSDF naval bases and Nicosia airport, now in the DMZ, as a heavy-lift airfield. The role of the CSDF would be solely the external defence of the new Cyprus confederation.

This raises the question of where would threats emanate from? Greece and Turkey: both are prime candidates but not if they eventually were parties to the CSDF as SAFE contributors; the Middle East (Israel, Jordan, Lebanon, Palestine and Syria): historically there was the possibility of overspill from the Arab–Israeli wars but today Israel is concerned with consolidation of existing territories and development of its offshore hydrocarbon resources, which requires cooperation with Cyprus. Syria is too distracted with its internal civil war while Jordan and Lebanon display no tendency for expansion outside national boundaries; North Africa (Egypt and Libya): both nations are coping with the aftermath of the Arab Spring and seeking to rebuild their economies by delineating and developing their Exclusive Economic Zones. External aggression is unlikely in the medium- to long-term future; the USA and Russia: Cold War confrontation between the US and the Soviet Union, as they vied to project their influence in the Mediterranean region through their Sixth Fleet and the Fifth Eskadra, was indirectly the cause of much of Cyprus' instability. Russia cultivated the Greek Cypriot dominated non-aligned government and the US promoted territorial division in the name of Turkish Cypriot rights. The end of the Cold War has emolliated, albeit not eliminated, this confrontation and it is highly unlikely that either power would be prepared to confront an EU force.

Creating a CSDF would be a major step towards European integration and would bind Cyprus, Greece and Turkey more closely to the European centre. It could be part funded through reallocation of the large volume of national funds now spent on internal military formations. International funding currently allotted to UNFICYP – some $55m a year – might also be used to help finance this process. Over time, it is posited, sufficient amity could be restored to allow creation of a national defence force evolved under the guidance of the CSDF.

With external security guaranteed by a disinterested third party and the self-interested national concerns of Greece, Turkey and the UK removed from the settlement equation, the process of securing a constitutional compromise would be left to the Cypriots, who would give priority to national over community interests. In the first instance the confederal constitution would have to acknowledge the separation of peoples but it would be imperative that it not create any impediments to a gradual process of reintegration over the long term. It is for the Cypriots to decide the ultimate formula but below are some suggestions for consideration.

Conclusion

United Nations efforts to reunite Greek and Turkish Cypriots have focused on a constitutional settlement based on power sharing between the two communities. The efforts have been confounded by the guarantor powers – Greece, Turkey and the UK – each pursuing their own strategic interests. What is necessary is a new approach with a primary focus on security that will eliminate the coercive influence of the motherlands and the former colonial power. The island should be demilitarised, including withdrawal of the Turkish occupation troops and dissolution of the Greek National Guard and Turkish Cypriot Security Force. External security can be provided by an EU Cyprus Standing Defence Force until such time as the two communities can arrive at a constitutional accommodation and create their own joint defence establishment. The likeliest constitutional formula would be a bizonal, bicommunal confederal state. This would consist of a relatively circumscribed, presidential central government with responsibility for international affairs and national matters with cross-border implications plus two largely-autonomous state-governments drawn from local legislatures and responsible for most community matters. A property swap funded with international aid would initially resolve territorial issues. State governments must abjure all barriers to freedom of movement and settlement in order to promote gradual integration over the long term.

References and recommended Reading

Attalides, Michael A. (ed.), *Cyprus Reviewed* (Nicosia: New Cyprus Association, 1977).

Clerides, Glafkos, *My Deposition*, 4 vols (Nicosia: Alithia, 1989–91).

Dodd, C.H. (ed.), *The Political, Social and Economic Development of Northern Cyprus* (Huntingdon: Eothen Press, 1993).

Denktash, Rauf, *The Cyprus Triangle* (Nicosia: K. Rustem & Brother, 1988).

Hoffmeister, Frank, *Legal Aspects of the Cyprus Problem: Annan Plan and EU Accession* (Leiden: Martinus Nijhoff, 2010).

International Crisis Group, *Cyprus: Bridging the Property Divide*, 2010.

Ker-Lindsay, James, *EU Accession and UN Peacemaking in Cyprus* (Basingstoke: Palgrave Macmillan, 2005).

Kyle, Keith, *Cyprus* (London: Minority Rights Group, 1984).

McDonald, Robert, *The Problem of Cyprus*, Adelphi Paper 234, International Institute for Strategic Studies, Winter 1988/89.

Mullen, Fiona, Ozlem Oguz and Praxoula Antoniadou-Kyriacou, *The Day After (I and II)* (Nicosia: International Peace Research Institute, 2008 and 2009).

Palley, Claire, *An International Relations Debacle: The UN Secretary General's Mission of Good Offices in Cyprus 1999–2004* (Oxford: Hart, 2005).

Patrick, Richard A., *Political Geography and the Cyprus Conflict: 1963–71* (Waterloo: University of Waterloo, 1976).

Stephens, Robert, *Cyprus: A Place of Arms* (London: Pall Mall Press, 1966).

22

Historical Legacies of the Dispute

Husam Mohamad

The Mediterranean island of Cyprus, located about 70 miles South of the Turkish coast and 250 miles east of Rhodes and Greece's mainland, has a population of nearly 80 per cent Greeks and 20 per cent Turks. Over the course of its history, Cyprus has been ruled by many powers, notably the Phoenicians, the Romans, the Byzantines, the Ottomans and the British. After Britain decided to end its military occupation of the island, which lasted from 1878 to 1960, the Greek Cypriot community initiated the *enosis* movement that viewed Cyprus as an integral part of Greece. Greek Cypriot calls for *enosis* enticed the Turkish Cypriot community, backed by Turkey, to promote the concept of *taksim* (partition) of the island along ethnic lines. Greek Cypriots had also considered their *enosis* with Greece as consistent with their historically dominant ethnic and the religious status in the island. Turkish Cypriots however, believe that *enosis* does not only undermine their own claims, including the right to self-determination in Cyprus, but also deepens the larger Greco–Turkish rivalry in the region. Given the heated claims and counterclaims between the two communities, the 1960 London–Zurich Agreement determined that Greece, Turkey and the UK would remain Cyprus's guarantor powers following Cyprus's independence. The three countries were expected to determine the future of the island and its inhabitants.

However, the inability and/or unwillingness of the guarantor powers to fulfil the aspirations of Cypriots have not only intensified internal tensions among Cypriots, but have also increased the pressures on Greece and Turkey, along with complicating their already complicated relations within the NATO alliance. The Cyprus issue would also, mainly in the 1990s, play a significant role in the dismissal of Turkey's application to the European Union (EU). Greece's objection to the inclusion of Turkey in the EU became less visible compared to other European powers, namely France and Germany, in much of the past decade.

The staging of a right-wing Greek sponsored coup in Cyprus in 1974 triggered the Turkish invasion and subsequent occupation of the Northern part of the island. Just as the Greek Cypriot attacks against the Turkish minority resulted in deaths and destruction in Turkish towns and villages, the Turkish invasion of Cyprus also caused deaths and displacements among Greek Cypriots. Ever since Cyprus was separated along ethnic lines (the North–South divide) following the Turkish invasion, the Greek Cypriots have managed to internationalise the dispute and receive worldwide recognition. Along with lacking international legitimacy and recognition, the Turkish Cypriot community suffered from the imposition of severe economic and travel embargos that gradually subjected them to a growing dependency on Turkey and isolation from the rest of the world. For the next three decades, Turkish Cypriots became economically, politically and culturally more reliant on Turkey. Many Turkish labourers, viewed as settlers, also managed to inhabit the island. The sizable increase of Turkish immigration and land purchasing has, in recent years, become one of the most important contentious issues that widened the divide between the Turkish Cypriot and Greek Cypriot communities in the island.

The Cyprus dispute in historical context

Greece and Turkey have repeatedly expressed conflicting claims justifying their involvements in the Cyprus dispute. Greece flatly opposed the Turkish invasion and occupation of the island, considering it illegal. Turkey, however, insisted that its offensive against Cyprus was a necessary act intended to counter Greece's interferences in the island, which endangered the physical well-being of the Turkish Cypriot minority. Those who have visited or lived on either side of the island will quickly become aware of the degree of linkage that exists between Cypriots and their so-called motherlands. Observers of the Cyprus conflict cannot also overlook or underestimate the depth of the emotional dimension and human drama that continues to undermine the prospect for a lasting peaceful settlement between the two sides. Although Turkey's invasion of the island has been widely condemned by the world community, the geopolitical location of Cyprus in relation to Turkey's mainland will continue to compel Turkey to maintain a military presence, perhaps similar to the British military bases, over parts of the island. On the other hand, with the exception of the ethnic dimension of the Cyprus question, the island lacks similar strategic value for Greece. Although the Greek and Turkish Cypriot communities share similar cultural and social backgrounds, their lengthy divide, since 1974, has widened the gap between them and highlighted their differences. Over the course of their conflict, however, Greek and Turkish Cypriot pursuit of both official and unofficial diplomatic contacts with each other, which were often held at the UN Buffer Zone that divide the two communities along ethnic and geographic lines, represents one of the few examples of hope and optimism about the future of the island and its people.

Regional and international mediation efforts to resolve the Cyprus conflict remain unable to bridge the gap between the two conflicting parties. The Turkish Cypriot side has always expressed interest in a federal solution to the Cyprus conflict. This position treats the two communities within the framework of an equal partnership in a unified Cyprus. The Greek Cypriot side, however, tends to favour the establishment of a unitary state by which the Turkish Cypriots would be granted an ethnic minority status that is legally protected from potential discrimination exercised by the Greek Cypriot majority. The Turkish Cypriots have rejected such offers and expressed fear and scepticism that their minority status could, once again, be hindered by the Greek Cypriots. With Turkey's approval, the Turkish Cypriot leaders decided to declare, in 1983, the formation of their own independent state, which became known as the Turkish Republic of Northern Cyprus (TRNC). Although the TRNC has enjoyed internal sovereignty, it failed to generate any meaningful international recognition. The internationalisation of the Cyprus conflict, and the legitimatisation of the Republic of Cyprus in the South, have further increased tensions between Turkey and Greece and strained relations within their NATO alliance.

The Cyprus dispute, which arose mainly out of ethnic and political challenges facing the two local Cypriot communities, has increasingly become reflective of a mounting rivalry between Greece and Turkey. Throughout much of the Cold War era, Cyprus was viewed as geopolitically and strategically vital for the NATO alliance. The UK particularly treated Cyprus as geographically significant for the pursuit of its regional goals, and has thus maintained two military bases and an early warning radar system on the island. While trying to contain Soviet expansionism in the region, the US also managed to become involved in efforts to stabilise the island as a step towards improving relations between Turkey and Greece. Over the course of the Cold War period, the US's main concern was centred on containment of Soviet communism, which was often maintained by the establishment of military and political alliances in the region. Moreover, the UN has also invested major political and economic resources in its attempts to resolve the Cyprus conflict. The 1977 High Level Agreement, and subsequent efforts directed at Greek and Turkish Cypriot leaders, shifted attention more towards establishing a non-aligned, bicommunal and federal state in Cyprus. Cypriots across the dividing lines also pursued what became known as the UN confidence-building measures that were held directly and quite often between community activists and ordinary people from both sides of the island. This unofficial diplomatic track has been utilised as a tool, highlighting the human dimension of the conflict. Although their efforts may have helped build confidence between both sides, the current political realities on the island remained unchanged due to interference from outside powers, notably Greece and Turkey.

Until 2003, access across the island's UN Buffer Zones isolating Cyprus's two communities from each other was heavily restricted. By early 2004, however, the two communities were allowed to cross those lines, and in April 2004, a referendum was carried out on both sides of the Island to determine Cypriots' views of a new UN plan that aimed at reuniting Cyprus prior to its inclusion into the European Union. The referendum was rejected by three-quarters of the Greek Cypriot side, while two-thirds of the Turkish Cypriots approved the plan. Consequently, the Republic of Cyprus, excluding Turkish Cypriots, was granted membership of the EU on 1 May 2004. The failed UN plan aimed at reuniting Cyprus on the basis of a Swiss-style federation that recognises the political equality of both sides. Had the plan been approved, other adjustments were also expected to be addressed, especially those relating to disputes concerning the reduction of the Turkish military forces from 35,000 to 6,000 soldiers, the resettling the refugees on both sides in their original towns, along with increasing the power of the UN forces in order to supervise the implementation of the plan. Greek Cypriots also demanded the return of most or all Turkish immigrants who settled in the island since the start of the Turkish invasion in 1974. Given how close the two communities came to resolving their differences, it is essential, therefore, that any future solution to the Cyprus conflict would have to include in it both the official and unofficial diplomatic routes and components.

Although Cyprus continues to be an elusive conflict, one of the ways for resolving it might perhaps rest on the United States, which can, as a mediator, exert equal influence on both Turkey and Greece. In the meantime, however, and given the UN's failure to resolve the Cyprus issue, Turkey feels relieved that it supported the 2004 UN plan, and thus avoided criticisms that were often raised by the EU members. In any future settlement, the Greek Cypriot community should perhaps be given more assurances about the need to remove Turkish military presence, along with addressing Turkish nationals residing on the island, prior to conducting similar referendums concerning the future of the island and its people. The future of the Turkish Cypriots will likely continue to be dependent on decisions and policies made by Ankara than by anywhere else. This is also understandable given the amount of support and backing that Turkey has invested in Cyprus since the start of the conflict between the two Cypriot communities. Turkey's application to join the EU was expected to be taken more seriously after Turkish leaders had shown readiness to abandon their occupation of Northern Cyprus. Other outstanding differences between Turkey and the EU must also be resolved before Turkey can become an EU member. The Cyprus issue may have already proved not to be the main, or a major, factor that has historically obstructed Turkey's inclusion into the EU.

Conclusion

Thus far, diplomacy, both at its official and unofficial levels, has largely failed to resolve the outstanding issues between the two Cypriot communities on one hand, and those regarding Greece and Turkey on the other. Unofficial diplomatic routes may perhaps, at this point in time, need to be considered more seriously as a means to bring the two Cypriot communities closer to each other. In terms of its symbolic effects, unofficial diplomacy can bring about positive effects on official diplomatic negotiations that usually respond to demands raised by ordinary people on both sides.

Challenges to unofficial diplomacy may, however, still derive from hard-core nationalists inhabiting the island, who have often expressed strong alliances with their motherlands. Such nationalists generally believe that their conflict with each other may never be resolved peacefully because of their usual all-or-nothing narratives of their conflict with each other. Moderates on both sides, however, may come to assume that when the large majority of ordinary Cypriots involved in unofficial diplomatic contacts begin to believe that the conditions in Cyprus are ripe enough for a solution, the official diplomatic route of negotiations should then be resumed in ways that must be reflective of the wishes of the majority of the population on the island. Obviously in the 2004 referendum, the majority of the Greek Cypriot community did not believe that such conditions were ripe enough for ending the Cyprus conflict or for reuniting the two Cypriot communities on the island. Finally, placing the Cyprus conflict in relation to other deeply-rooted conflicts in the region, notably the Israeli–Palestinian conflict, may provide ample inspiration for Cypriots on both sides of the conflict to realise that their situation is much less severe when compared to other settings.

This chapter has tried to reflect on the historical legacies of an unending conflict between Cyprus's Greek and Turkish communities which, in part, has been escalated by Turkish and Greek interventions in the island. On various occasions, Greece and Turkey have been, and remain, involved in obstructing ample opportunities aimed at resolving the Cyprus dispute. It is therefore crucial that unofficial diplomacy be utilised to appeal to the human dimension of the tragedy that has shaped the modern history of Cyprus and its people. Along with that, it is also essential for official diplomacy to follow by, among other things, seeking forcible third-party mediators that enforce a package deal/s on the two sides of the conflict. Although success is never guaranteed in either official or unofficial diplomatic routes, it is possible to envision that the Cyprus conflict could one day become a thing of the past.

References and recommended reading

Bolukbasi, Suha, 'The Cyprus dispute and the United Nations: peaceful non-settlement between 1954 and 1996', *International Journal of Middle East Studies* 30/3 (August 1998), pp. 387–410.

Bryant, Rebecca and Yiannis Papadakis (eds), *Cyprus and the Politics of Memory: History, Community and Conflict* (London: I.B.Tauris, 2012).

Calotychos, Vengelis (ed.), *Cyprus and its People: Nation, Identity and Experience in Unimaginable Community, 1955–1997* (Boulder, CO: Westview Press, 1998).

Dodd, Clement, *The History and Politics of the Cyprus Conflict* (Basingstoke: Palgrave Macmillan, 2010).

Joseph, Joseph S., *Cyprus: Ethnic Conflict and International Politics: From Independence to the Threshold of the European Union* (New York, St Martin's Press, 1997).

Rotberg, Robert, 'The Cyprus crucible: the importance of good timing', *Harvard International Review* 25/3 (Fall 2003), pp. 70–5.

Volkan, Vamık D., Joseph Montville and Demetrios Julius (eds), *The Psychodynamics of International Relationships*, vol. II: *Unofficial Diplomacy at Work* (Lexington, MA: Lexington Books, 1991).

Yilmaz, Muzaffer, 'The Cyprus conflict and the question of identity', *Review of International Law and Politics* 1/4 (2005), pp. 74–90.

23

Conceptual Obstacles to a Settlement

MICHAEL MORAN

There are two, essentially conceptual, difficulties that have always stood in the way of attempts to resolve the unhappy state of affairs in Cyprus. The first is that there is no agreement among all the parties concerned about what the 'Cyprus Problem' is. Consequently it is hard to see how the issue could be resolved. For without agreement about what a problem is, one could hardly expect to know what would count as its solution. It might be said that actually everyone is in perfect agreement about what is needed in Cyprus: the unification of the divided island. As we shall see, however, glib remedy obscures more than it illuminates.

The second conceptual difficulty springs from the international community's very different treatment of the two Cypriot communities since UN Security Council Resolution 186 of 4 March 1964. This was the moment when the by then all-Greek Cypriot administration of Archbishop Makarios was first officially referred to as 'the government of Cyprus'. Initially, this administration was internationally understood to be a temporary *de facto* one, to be treated as such until the conflict in Cyprus could be resolved and the Turkish Cypriot vice-president, MPs and three ministers could return to the government. But this reinstatement never happened. And by the late 1960s, for complex political reasons, including President Makarios' intimidating relations with the Non-Aligned Movement as well as with the Soviet Union, the international community found it convenient to treat the purely Greek Cypriot administration as if it were indeed the *de jure* government of the whole island, a view universally shared today, except by the Turkish Cypriots and Turkey.

Specifically, then, this second conceptual difficulty is how to reconcile the following two things: on the one hand, the UN's apparent belief that there is nothing wrong with the present all-Greek government of Cyprus – that it is so unproblematic as, for example, to have been able to negotiate EU membership for the whole of Cyprus and, on the other hand, the efforts the UN has been making, for almost 50 years now, to replace that Greek Cypriot administration with a very different one, an administration that would, once more, be shared with the Turkish Cypriots. Quite apart from what is said in the 1960 Cyprus constitution, mustn't there be at least *some* doubt about the adequacy, appropriateness, even some would say the legitimacy, of a Cyprus government which the UN itself has been trying so very hard to change for so long?

The conceptual difficulties spelt out

My first conceptual point will need most elaboration. This is my claim that there is no agreement about what the trouble in Cyprus is, and hence little hope of a mutually recognisable solution emerging among those for whom the future of the island is important. These interested parties include not only the Cypriots themselves but, in addition, at least the three original 'guarantor powers', Britain, Greece and Turkey; the UN; the EU; and both the US and Russia.

Since 1974 Greek Cypriot leaders have seen the problem as one of 'invasion and occupation' of an essentially Greek island by a large alien power, Turkey, for no good reason. Indeed, they often speak of 'Turkish expansionism' as the cause of Turkey's otherwise inexplicable behaviour. What they want, as a solution to this problem, caused in their view by Turkey, is the abolition of the current division of the island, the removal of the Turkish Army from Cyprus, the return of their homes, property and businesses in the North, and ideally a reversion to things roughly the way they were before the 1974 invasion. As a concession to their Turkish compatriots, however, the Greeks would happily grant an appropriately small role (certainly smaller than they had in 1960) to this Islamic minority in the present, allegedly perfectly legitimate, Hellenic government of Cyprus. This is, at any rate, what the Greek Cypriots would ideally like to happen: a form of reunification indeed; but one involving the assimilation of the Turks into the existing Greek Republic.

The Turkish Cypriot view is, needless to say, not only quite different from, but also utterly incompatible with, these Greek perceptions. For the Turks, the Cyprus Problem emerged quite forcefully not in 1974 but in 1963. This was when Archbishop Makarios attempted to change the Cyprus constitution in such a way as seriously to limit the power and role of the Turkish Cypriots in the running of the country. This the Turkish side sees as a first stage in the premeditated Greek Cypriot strategy of taking over the island for themselves, an aspiration quite contrary to both the letter and the spirit of the 1960 Accords.

Moreover, the Turkish Cypriots maintain that Turkey had a perfectly legitimate reason for (as they would prefer to put it) 'intervening' in Cyprus in 1974. In fact, Turkey had *two* legitimate reasons. The first was to prevent *enosis*, i.e., Cyprus becoming politically part of Greece, something the Greek Cypriots, aided and abetted by the military junta in Greece, had just declared (again in plain violation of the 1960 Accords). These were circumstances that gave Turkey every right to 'take action', as the 1960 Treaty of Guarantee stated. Moreover, between 1964 and 1974 the Turkish Cypriots had been excluded from the government of Cyprus and had managed to survive in very reduced circumstances, with no political representation in their own country. Their exclusion from the government was the second move, the Turkish Cypriots maintain, in the Greek plan to take control of the island, a sequence of events the international community seemed prepared to tolerate. But if Cyprus became part of Greece there was no telling what would become of the Turkish Cypriots. So the second reason the Turkish Army came was to prevent any further deterioration in their condition, quite possibly their actual extermination by fanatical Greek nationalists, inflamed by the prospect of *enosis*. And in the Turkish/Turkish Cypriot view, the eventual division of the island in 1974 was necessary because it soon became clear that, in the subsequent negotiations for a settlement, no agreement with the Greeks could be reached about appropriate power sharing. Given all these circumstances, Turkey took it upon itself to divide the island and thus put an end to further Greek provocations. Now, while the Turkish side doesn't readily admit this, the act of division, as distinct from the original intervention, was surely also a contravention of the 1960 Accords.

So while the Greek Cypriots still stick to their mantra about 'invasion and occupation', for the Turkish Cypriots today the Cyprus Problem revolves essentially around the fact that, since 1964, the Greek Cypriots have illegitimately taken over the title of the government of Cyprus, showing no convincing sign of being prepared to relinquish that title and form an acceptable federation with their Turkish compatriots. Despite nearly 50 years of UN-sponsored negotiations, one aim of which has been precisely to create, once more, some such joint government, the Greek Cypriots leadership has consistently resisted such an outcome and done everything they can to assert their own hegemony in Cyprus. We may discern here a peculiar kind of equilibrium, a natural 'resolution of forces', as it were, *both* doubtless inconsistent with the 1960 Accords: the Greeks have the government of the Cyprus Republic for themselves; but the Turks now possess one third of the island over which that government has no control.

Faced with their isolated situation, in 1983 the Turkish Cypriots declared the existence of their own state in the North of the island, the 'Turkish Republic of Northern Cyprus' (TRNC). This has been recognised as an independent state only by Turkey. Having now lived under their own administration in the North for almost 40 years – and having spent the previous ten years as an unrepresented minority in a Greek state – for the Turkish Cypriots themselves the best outcome might well be having the TRNC internationally recognised. For various reasons this doesn't seem likely to happen. Nevertheless, the Turks would instead, I think, be quite happy to accept some kind of confederation with a Greek state in the South. They would wish also to reduce their dependence on Turkey, both financially and militarily. And a suitable confederation with their Greek compatriots would be compatible with a single citizenship, and a 'single international personality', as the UN parameters for a solution stipulate. But for the Turkish side it would be important that the new Republic of Cyprus be not simply a continuation of the present wholly Greek-run Republic. For them a *new* partner-Republic would need to be created, a 'virgin birth', as some observers have called it.

Needless to say, the so-called Annan Plan of 2002–4, produced after much hard work by various members of the international community, largely met these criteria and was accepted by the Turkish side. But the Greek Cypriots overwhelmingly rejected it. And their reasons for this rejection were quite compatible with Turkish apprehensions about the Greeks' determination to hang on to power in Cyprus rather than to share it. In a TV address on 7 April 2004 the then Cyprus president, Tassos Papadopoulos, made it perfectly clear that he thought Cyprus should remain essentially Greek. 'Taking up my duties I was given a recognised state', he said. 'I am not going to give back "a community" without any say internationally and in search of a guardian... I urge you to defend the Republic of Cyprus, saying NO to its abolition.'

In a way one can hardly blame a president for wishing to prevent the 'abolition' of his country. At the time I asked Rauf Denktash, the former Turkish Cypriot leader, what he thought of Papadopoulos' statement. 'If I were in his shoes I would say exactly the same thing!', Denktash replied, rather to my surprise. This just goes to show how 'compromise' is not something that easily occurs to Cypriot leaders. And if one studies the texts of the many negotiations between the two Cypriot sides, under the auspices of the UN, one is left with the distinct impression that the aim of *compromise* has been at best a secondary consideration. Essentially, the two sides have used the UN forum to reinforce their own incompatible positions: the Greeks always reaffirming their posture as the legitimate Cyprus government; the Turks always insisting that, in these and in any other negotiations, they cannot be seen as a political minority in a Greek state. Paradoxically, the UN has, in effect, endorsed *both* of these positions.

Divergent roles of the international players

Since the failure of the Annan Plan, the UN and the EU appear to have accepted the Greek Cypriot reminder that the international community has no right to try to *impose* a solution to the 'internal' problems of a sovereign state. Everybody knows, of course, that, whatever it may be conceived to be, the 'Cyprus Problem' is by no means a purely internal one. Recently there has been talk about the possibility of organising an international conference on Cyprus. So what about the other interested parties *outside* Cyprus? Are they poised to help? Two of the guarantor powers, Greece and Turkey, agree in all essentials with their respective communities on the island and hence have traditionally had little scope for agreement with each other. It is possible, however, that the current dramatic contrast in the conditions of the two countries may have some positive effect in Cyprus.

Turkey has many internal problems, yet it has not been very adversely affected by the current European financial crisis. Despite European misgivings about official handling of the recent unrest in Turkey, and about Turkey's human rights record more generally, the governing AK Party, led by Prime Minister Erdoğan, has achieved things that would have been inconceivable ten years ago: most notably, their remarkable reduction of the political power of the Turkish Army. Difficult though it will be, finding a solution in Cyprus is important for Turkey's EU membership bid. Since Turkey cannot accept the current all-Greek government of Cyprus as legitimate, the EU cannot admit Turkey to a club one of whose existing members Turkey doesn't recognise.

Greece is at the present time in a state of turmoil. Solving the Cyprus Problem is hardly likely to be an immediate priority. With the recent danger of a collapse in the Eurozone – seen by many as partly due to Greek laxity in financial accounting – which was averted by the EU's imposition of draconian measures on the Greek economy, social instability in Greece is likely to continue. In May 2012, the Greek electorate's show of marked dissatisfaction with both the leading PASOK (Pan-Hellenic Socialist Movement) and New Democracy parties could usher in a long period of fragile, and less internationally cooperative, coalition governments. While quite this degree of volatility hasn't been experienced in Greek Cyprus, the situation there is also worrying. The two main Greek Cypriot banks were heavily exposed to Greek mainland bonds when these lost most of their value, and the Greek part of the island has consequently been shut out of international debt markets for more than a year. With considerable reluctance, the Cyprus government has had to accept a bailout deal with its Euro area partners and the IMF. To receive a €10 billion loan in March 2013, savers in the country's two largest banks were forced to take huge losses on deposits over €100,000. The bank's shareholders suffered even greater losses. Further harsh measures are likely for 2014 if Cyprus is to continue to meet all bailout targets set for it. The economy in the South is projected to shrink by a cumulative 13 per cent over this next year and a half. Unemployment has already reached 17 per cent. There is, however, one bright light at the end of this dark tunnel: the discovery of large deposits of hydrocarbons in the seas around Cyprus. Here, surely, is a genuine prospect both for economic recovery for the South and for their seeking early rapprochement with the North and with

Turkey. For a pipeline to Turkey is the obvious way to export these valuable resources to Europe. Alas, to date there is no sign that the Greeks intend to seize this opportunity.

Britain is the odd man out among the Cyprus guarantors. Its main concern has been to retain at least one strategic military base on the island to serve the interests of NATO in a region where the West has few friends. This is a region where it is important to retain oil supplies; to keep a satellite eye on Russia; to discourage real or imagined 'rogue states' from fomenting terrorism and, especially, to prevent them developing nuclear arms. Britain therefore has never minded too much what new arrangements emerge in Cyprus provided there is stability, so that its bases and other military installations can function. It is important too, of course, that the two regional powers, Greece and Turkey, remain at peace with each other and suitably aligned to the West. Needless to say, it has always been among unofficial Greek Cypriot desires to have the British presence on what they regard (despite the Treaty of Establishment) as their sovereign territory removed. This is why British governments have attempted to placate the Greek Cypriots by regularly assuring them that they will never recognise an independent Turkish state in Cyprus.

It is worth noting that, in a recent 'Memorandum of Understanding', the two countries reiterated 'their commitment to their respective obligations under the Treaties signed in 1960'. This last assertion must seem quite bizarre to anyone knowledgeable about Cyprus. It exemplifies how, as so often in international relations, it becomes necessary to be economical with the truth in order to cover up a fudge – in this instance, the pragmatic decision eventually made by Britain and others in the late 1960s not to question the legality of a wholly Greek government in Cyprus. For haven't both signatories to this Memorandum manifestly *failed* to fulfil their obligations under the 1960 Treaties: the Greeks by taking over and endeavouring to retain the government of Cyprus; the British by letting them do so?

As regards American perceptions, it seems safe to say that the White House sees things in Cyprus in much the same way as Britain does, except that the US is particularly keen to retain good relations with Turkey, which it tries to envisage as an essentially Western-orientated, democratic country providing a model for other less amenable Islamic states in the region. And of course the US has a number of military bases in Turkey and has always helped Turkey to equip and update the second largest army in NATO. Turkey agreed in September 2011 to allow the installation of the early warning radar system, a crucial part of NATO's nuclear missile defence project, on Turkish soil. All this could mean that the US might show some sympathy with the Turkish conception of the Cyprus Problem. On the other hand, there is still a powerful Greek lobby and an even more powerful Jewish lobby in America, Turkey's current *contretemps* with Israel and the US's still seemingly ambivalent relations with Iran, none of which can be altogether reassuring to US diplomats.

The Greek Cypriots have often bought arms from Russia, most memorably the S-300 missiles that they attempted to install near Paphos in 1998. Generally speaking, since 1964 Russia has supported the Greek Cypriot position at the UN Security Council. There is of course an important connection between them via Orthodox Christianity which is still taken seriously by a majority of Greek Cypriots and by an increasing number of Russians, since the collapse of the Soviet Union in 1991. Politically more important than this spiritual liaison, however, is the existence of significant Russian financial activities in Greek Cyprus, including the not entirely transparent operations of at least half-a-dozen Russian banks and various offshore facilities. In December 2011 Russia agreed to loan €2.5 billion to Greek Cyprus on very favourable terms. We have to conclude, I think, that Russia will have difficulty in supporting the Turkish Cypriots' call for a dismantling of the present Cyprus Republic.

Conclusion

Could an international conference about the island help? It must certainly be more useful than simply continuing the predictably futile exchanges between the two Cypriot communities alone. But the obstacles to a positive outcome remain quite considerable. Apart from all the complexities to which I have briefly alluded, two things need preliminary attention: an agreement has to be reached about what the 'Cyprus Problem' is; and the international community must acknowledge that it can't both regard the present Cyprus government as entirely unproblematic while, at the same time, seeking fundamentally to change it.

References and recommended reading

Diez, Thomas and Nathalie Tocci, *Cyprus: Conflict at the Crossroads* (Manchester: Manchester University Press, 2009).

Dodd, Clement, *The History and Politics of the Cyprus Conflict* (London: Palgrave Macmillan, 2010).

Ker-Lindsay, James, *The Cyprus Problem: What Everyone Needs to Know* (Oxford: Oxford University Press, 2011).

Moran, Michael, *Britain and the 1960 Cyprus Accords: A Study in Pragmatism* (Istanbul: Istanbul Kültür University, 2009).

——, *Cyprus: A European Anomaly* (Istanbul: Istanbul Kültür University, 2010).

Tocci, Nathalie, *EU Accession Dynamics: Catalysing Peace or Consolidating Partition in Cyprus* (Aldershot: Ashgate, 2004).

24

One Final Chance for Federalism

Mustafa Ergün Olgun

With the rise of 'self-determination' movements, the collapse of colonialism and more recently the fall of the Berlin Wall, the UN and lately the EU turned to two main remedies in order to manage competing nationalisms, or deep-rooted identity-related conflict that degenerated into violence and war. The first of these is the multinational federal remedy. This is the model used in the bicommunal partnership Republic of Cyprus, the Federation of Rhodesia and Nyasaland and the Federation of Bosnia and Herzegovina. The second approach has been to recognise separate statehood. This can be seen in India, Pakistan, Croatia, Slovenia, Macedonia and Kosovo. The choice between these two alternatives largely depended on the extent of violence, the perceived possibility of reconciliation and the prevailing interests of key international players.

Multinational federal model

The multinational federal model became one of the options because it offered various advantages. For example, while mononational or national federations aspire to national homogeneity, multinational federations aim to unite people who seek the advantages of a common political unit, but differ markedly in descent, language and culture. Multinational federations provide for their constituent peoples to preserve their identity and collective political equality while they allow their citizens to have dual or multiple loyalties, such as a patriotic attachment to the federation and a nationalist attachment to their community/regional homeland. Such federations provide for both shared and self-government, in other words, both union and autonomy, and are built on balance of power/maximum symmetry principles. Moreover, in accordance with the political equality of its constituent peoples/parts, such federations are 'covenantal' – the authority and competences of each government is derived from the covenant/foundation agreement. The federal government cannot unilaterally alter the horizontal division of powers: constitutional change affecting the division of competencies and other main articles of the constitution requires consent from both tiers of government. Neither the federal nor the constituent states' governments are constitutionally subordinate to the other, while each has sovereign powers derived from the foundation agreement and constitution rather than from another level of government. Another point to consider is that such federations are not majoritarian and have inclusive executive power-sharing arrangements in the federal tier of government; institutionalise proportional principles of representation and allocation of public posts and resources; and have mechanisms, such as the separation of powers, bills of rights, monetary institutions and courts, that are insulated from the immediate power of a federal governing majority. Decision making at the federal tier is built around a consensus mechanism.

Based on their competences, both the federal and constituent state governmental units are empowered to deal directly with the citizens in the exercise of its legislative, executive and taxing powers, and each is directly elected by its citizens.

Reasons why federations fail or succeed

Research by O'Leary (2003) on the reasons why federations fail and/ or succeed indicate that the following conditions need to be in place for the successful establishment and functioning of a multinational federation. In terms of the creation of the federation, there must be strong mutual need and overlapping interests on the part of the constituent peoples/units for a federal partnership to be formed and to be sustained. As such, the federation must be a voluntary pact. It should not be regarded as a UN or outside imposition. Moreover, a foundational act of cooperation is more likely to promote future traditions of accommodation. Following on from this, the federation must be ratified by its respective and prospective units through separate simultaneous referenda in their own unit to endorse any freely negotiated constitution.

Constructive relations based on equal status and mutual recognition must be built between the constituent peoples. Although they vary extensively, a multinational federation should be democratic, with the full repertoire of liberal democratic institutions, including competitive elections, freedom for political parties and interest groups to mobilise, a constitution with the rule of law, human rights protections and a free media. In terms of institutions, it would usually involve a bicameral legislature and a federal supreme court, charged with upholding the constitution and umpiring differences between the governmental tiers. Furthermore, in addition to significant constitutional checks and balances, there must be an effective last resort guarantee mechanism, such as the guarantee system of the 1960 partnership Republic of Cyprus, which would inhibit future efforts to hijack or centralise the federation. Robust and adequate agreements have to be built over the sharing of natural resources. There is need to watch out for superior financial and political resources of one tier, usually the federal, which would allow it to weaken the other tier's capacities.

Research by Duchachek (1988), Milne (1981) and Kymlicka (1998) on bicommunal federations and on whether federalism is a viable alternative to secession indicates, however, that competition for power in bicommunal settings tends to end up in tension and one ethnic group's assumption of hegemony – something common to Cyprus since 1963. Kymlincka's conclusion is that it is wrong to assume that federalism provides a 'tried and true' formula for successful and enduring accommodation of national differences. Even in the cases of established federations like Belgium and Canada, federalism has proven to be highly fragile, prone to constant risks of secession.

Case of Cyprus

Despite the 1977 and 1979 High Level Agreements – which established bicommunality, political equality and bizonality as the founding pillars of an eventual federal settlement in Cyprus – and decades of negotiations, a strong majority of Greek Cypriot society has failed to internalise the fundamental requirements of bicommunal federalism. Public opinion surveys amongst Greek Cypriots consistently reveal that a large majority still prefer a unitary state run by Greek Cypriots in which Turkish Cypriots are granted minority rights. In North Cyprus, Turkish Cypriots are very sensitive about their identity and collective political equality. Especially because of the persistent desire of Greek Cypriot society to dominate the island, the majority have sought refuge in a two-state solution. In addition to the absence of trust and interdependence, particularly after the violent separation of 1963, there is no strong sense of mutual/overlapping interests. In fact Greek Cypriot society at large looks upon Turkish Cypriots as a liability and not an asset with which to jointly form a federal partnership. Rebecca Bryant (2004) observed that in the Cyprus case 'freedom' was defined ethnically; freedom for a particular group, at the expense of the other. This continues to this day. The newly elected Greek Cypriot President, Nicos Anastasiades, who in 2004 supported Annan Plan, now says that he wants negotiations to start from a new basis and refuses to accept the convergences that were facilitated by the Special Cyprus Representative of the UN Secretary-General during the most recent 2008–12 negotiations.

Following the rejection of the UN Comprehensive Settlement Plan (Annan Plan) by the Greek Cypriots, in 2004, Kofi Annan, the then-UN Secretary-General, stated in his good-offices mission report to the Security Council (28 May 2004) that, 'I would hope they [members of the Security Council] can give a strong lead to all States to cooperate both bilaterally and in international bodies to eliminate unnecessary restrictions and barriers that have the effect of isolating the Turkish Cypriots and impeding their development'. A study by Deweiks et al. (2012) emphasises that,

> in highly unequal federations, both relatively developed and underdeveloped regions are indeed more likely to be involved in secessionist conflict than regions close to the country average. In addition, we provide evidence that exclusion from central state power as well as ethnic groups' access to regional institutions are associated with an increased risk for secessionist conflict.

Yet, despite the recommendations of the UN Secretary-General, and credible research findings regarding conflict in federations, the isolation of the Turkish Cypriot people is unfortunately continuing and the political and economic inequality is still being preserved while the international community ironically says that it sees no solution other than a bicommunal, bizonal federal settlement based on political equality – an objective the realisation of which is made impossible by the very actions of the UN, the EU and other actors of the international community.

All this is happening at a time when Greek Cypriot South Cyprus is in the midst of a deep financial and economic crisis and urgently needs new economic activity niches to compensate for what it has lost following the collapse of its international banking sector. Exploitation of the recently discovered hydrocarbons in the disputed seas around Cyprus, the construction sector (for the needed reconstruction after a political settlement), tourism and agriculture are probably the four main sectors that in the short and medium term offer opportunities. But the unilateral exploitation of hydrocarbons could turn into a curse if the political problem in Cyprus is not resolved. Furthermore, tourism and agriculture in South Cyprus can only make a substantial increase if the Greek Cypriot South can have access to the huge Turkish market and irrigation water from Turkey. A pipeline is under construction and Turkish water will reach North Cyprus in 2014. However, these opportunities are subject to Greek Cypriots first making up with Turkish Cypriots. Sadly, even all of these glaring benefits have not been sufficient to incentivise the Greek Cypriots to cooperate and share power with Turkish Cypriots. All Greek Cypriot leaders, including Mr Anastasiades, claim that there is no link between hydrocarbons exploitation and the Cyprus negotiating process. As they see it, the exploitation of hydrocarbons is a sovereign right of the Greek Cypriot Republic of Cyprus. This is a hegemonic posture that highlights how far removed they are from a power-sharing deal. The Greek Cypriots have rejected both separation (the 1983 declaration of independence of the TRNC) and reunification (the 2004 UN federal partnership plan) and are forgetting that, under the terms of the 1960 settlement, until a new agreement on the state of affairs is reached both communities are co-owners of all of the natural resources and that neither side can legitimately claim authority or jurisdiction over the other.

The Greek Cypriot controlled Republic of Cyprus may have de facto international recognition, but they also have a democratic/ domestic legitimacy gap. Its government is functioning in violation of the constitution of the bicommunal Republic of Cyprus that it claims it represents. The politically equal Turkish Cypriot community has not given its consent to the Greek Cypriot Republic of Cyprus to represent them and persistently object to the claims of the Greek Cypriot side that they do so. The argument of 'necessity', never convincing, has long expired; especially as Turkish Cypriot MPs were refused their right to return to the Legislative Assembly in 1965, as stipulated under the 1960 Constitution. Without any doubt, the unjustified international status granted to the Greek Cypriot government is the primary factor that makes power sharing and a federal partnership in Cyprus impossible; much to the shame of the European Union, which admitted the Greek Cypriot Republic of Cyprus as a member with the claim that it represents the whole island despite its constitutional and democratic deficiencies.

Kudret Özersay, a former Turkish Cypriot negotiator, has argued that all relevant peaceful means, both in terms of 'process and content' and with leaders from all of the leading parties, have been tried and exhausted within the limits of the existing UN basis for a federal solution. He suggests that if Cyprus could be released, after 36 years of futile negotiations, from being the hostage of one single settlement model it is possible that both sides would find alternative arrangements that would suit their needs and aspirations better.

Recognition of statehood model

Let us now turn back to the second prescription, recognition of separate statehood, in managing competing nationalisms/deep-rooted identity-related conflict and violence. In the case of the former Federal Republic of Yugoslavia, the Badinter Commission established that the state had failed in its purpose of establishment and had thus become defunct. This is exactly what had happened to the bicommunal Republic of Cyprus in 1963. However, in the case of Yugoslavia, and in view of the escalating violence/war, the European Union used recognition as the creative and proactive conflict management tool to end the conflict. This led to the recognition of Slovenia, Croatia and Macedonia. In Cyprus this has not happened. The Turkish Cypriot people have been deprived of the right to exercise their political equality since 1963 and have been under economic, social and even sporting restrictions imposed by their former partners. They therefore decided to establish the Turkish Republic of Northern Cyprus (TRNC), not as an act of secession but in exercise of their separate right to determine their own future – a right that was recognised as far back as 1958 by the then colonial British government. In line with the Montevideo Treaty, which sets out the requirements for state recognition, the TRNC possesses a permanent population, a defined territory, a government and capacity to enter into relations with other states.

In its establishment phase, Burgess (2007) defines failure in the context of a federation as the 'perennial failure of negotiations to produce a constitutional partnership'. Negotiations to establish a bicommunal and bizonal federal partnership in Cyprus have been going on without a result since 1977 – a perennial failure. After 36 years of failed partnership negotiations, criteria other than violence should be used to invoke the use of the proactive recognition option for the Turkish Cypriot state. Turkish Cypriots should not be punished for not resorting to violence in the face of the perennial failure of the federal partnership negotiations and for being kept 'statusless' since 1963. The Turkish Cypriots have been marginalised and prevented from exercising their constitutional rights. They have also been subjected to embargoes. Meanwhile, the unchangeable provisions of the 1960 Constitution were unilaterally changed. It therefore needs to be asked whether the federal solution prescribed for Cyprus was indeed a realistic choice. Or was it a normative choice that has proved to be unfeasible? Since federalism has failed, the time has come for the international community, particularly the UN, to prepare the ground for the discussion of other options for settlement. One such option could be the civilised divorce model, as was utilised by the former Czechoslovakia.

How a resolution may be catalysed

Contacts are already under way to initiate another UN-managed negotiation process to reach a federal settlement. It must be made clear at the outset, however, that this is a final effort. Furthermore, the bicommunal federation to be negotiated, while religiously respecting the agreed principles of political equality and bizonality, must proactively also benefit from the experiences of both successful and failed multinational federations. This will be vital for its sustainability. A quick fix will not work.

In the meantime, a number of other steps need to be taken. Two Joint High Level Ad Hoc Committees should immediately be set up: (a) to work on and develop modalities for working together on the hydrocarbons issue; and (b) to work on and develop a meaty win-win economic recovery/cooperation package that will address the urgent economic and financial needs of both sides. At the same time, international actors need to take practical steps towards minimising political and economic inequalities between the two politically equal/ constituent communities. Such steps should include: a cessation of statements that the Greek Cypriot Government of Cyprus has the sole sovereign right in its EEZ to explore and exploit hydrocarbons, as these statements only help distance the two communities from a possible cooperative deal and are divisive; concrete steps to ease the economic, social and political restrictions imposed on North Cyprus in order to minimise inequalities; relinquishing the expectation or assumption that it is a major unilateral goodwill move by the Turkish Cypriot/Turkish side that will trigger or facilitate transformation on the Greek Cypriot side – both sides must equally and as strongly feel the need to change the status quo because of mutual hurt; refraining from being part of, or supporting, any move that will imply or lead to the subordination of either one of the communities to the will of the other; actively supporting revitalised efforts to settle the Cyprus issue while upholding the significance of respect for the political equality and the equal status of the two inherently constitutive communities; and incentivising the two sides to capitalise on this last chance and benefit from the virtues of cooperation and partnership. In this regard it is imperative that a strong message is also sent out by all that if no agreement is reached yet again, the floor will inevitably be opened for the discussion of alternative options for settlement in order to break the stalemate.

In line with the above, the Turkish Cypriot side and Turkey have given a strong message that they are prepared to give a final chance to the negotiation of a comprehensive federal settlement, within a set time frame, based on the agreed parameters of political equality and bizonality. If this should not be possible because of the urgent need to address the financial and economic crises in South Cyprus, the Turkish side is prepared to negotiate a win-win economic cooperation package that will address the pressing economic issues of the two communities and also facilitate cooperation over hydrocarbons. However, if the Greek Cypriot side wants to go it alone and wants to be the sole owner of the offshore resources in South Cyprus, then it should declare this openly so that a velvet divorce can be negotiated. In the event that they continue to drag their feet regarding a final settlement and refuse to form a Joint Ad Hoc Committee on the hydrocarbons issue, then Turkey and the Turkish Cypriots should be willing to take a range of measures of their own. These should include speeding up hydrocarbon exploration and exploitation on land and sea in all the areas licensed to TPAO; taking steps to convince international companies not to engage in activities in the claimed/disputed EEZ of South Cyprus; actively explore overlapping interests particularly with the USA, Israel, Egypt and Lebanon as regards the delineation and exploitation of hydrocarbon resources and further improve cooperative ties with these countries; actively seek the further enhancement of the status of the TRNC in international bodies; explore the possibility and possible virtues of challenging the UN at the International Court of Justice for recognising the solely Greek Cypriot government as the government of the 1960 bicommunal Republic of Cyprus; be firm about the immediate formation of a Joint Ad Hoc Committee on the hydrocarbons issue and about a time frame at the forthcoming talks and refuse to sit at the table if agreement is not reached on these key points; and, finally, refuse to sit at the negotiating table in future unless the legitimacy of the TRNC is recognised and the inhuman trade and travel restrictions imposed on its sea and airports are lifted.

As pointed out by NATO Secretary-General Anders Fogh Rasmussen, unilateral action regarding hydrocarbon exploration and exploitation before agreement between the two politically equal co-owners of Cyprus could destabilise the island and the region. It is time for all stakeholders and key international players who have an interest in regional stability and energy/trade security to start thinking outside the box before the region is drawn further into the curse that the exploitation of hydrocarbons tends to breed.

Conclusion

The UN system has for too long been stuck with one preconceived model for settlement. The latest convergence paper of the Secretary-Generals' Special Cyprus Representative is simply aimed at narrowing the gap between the longstanding positions of the two sides within that preconceived model – a model that has over the last 36 years proved to be unfeasible. In my opinion, instead of obsessively repeating that there is no alternative to a federal settlement in Cyprus, the UN would do better if it focused more on broadening the options for settlement. In trying to force the federal model, the efforts of the UN are risking or preparing the ground for compromises from the essential requisites of successful bicommunal federalism – another failure strategy that will not yield sustainable results.

Bahcheli (2000) argues that federalism has little chance of success in view of the deep mistrust between the Greek and Turkish Cypriots. This being the case, the merits of a negotiated two-state solution deserve serious consideration.

Consequently, thinking outside the box can open up new avenues and options which can give new vitality to the negotiation process and better serve the economic, security and political interests of both communities, the interests of guarantor powers Turkey, Greece and the UK, as well as the interests of the EU.

References and recommended reading

Bahcheli, Tozun, 'Searching for a Cyprus settlement: considering options for creating a federation, a confederation, or two independent states', *Publius: The Journal of Federalism* 30/1–2 (Winter/Spring 2000), pp. 203–16.

Burgess, Michael D., 'Success and failure in federation: comparative perspectives', paper presented at the Festschrift for Ronald L. Watts in Queen's University, Kingston, Ontario, Canada, 1–2 October 2007.

Caplan, Richard, *Europe and the Recognition of New States in Yugoslavia* (Oxford: Clarendon Press, 2005).

Deiwiks, Christa, Lars-Erik Cederman and Kristian Skrede Gleditsch, 'Inequality and conflict in federations', *Journal of Peace Research*, Peace Research Institute Oslo 49/2 (2012), pp. 289–304.

Dodd, Clement, *The History and Politics of the Cyprus Conflict* (Basingstoke: Palgrave Macmillan, 2010).

Duchachek, Ivo D., 'Dyadic federations and confederations', *Publius: The Journal of Federalism* 18/2 (Spring 1988), pp. 5–31.

Franck, Thomas M., *Why Federations Fail: An Inquiry into the Requisites for Successful Federalism* (London: University of London Press, 1968).

International Conference on Federalism, *Federalism in a Changing World: Learning from Each Other*, Conference Reader, St Gallen, Switzerland, 2002.

Kymlicka, Will, 'Is federalism a viable alternative to secession?', in Percey B. Lehning (ed.), *Theories of Secession* (London and New York: Routledge, 1998).

Milne, R.S., *Politics in Ethnically Bipolar States* (Vancouver: University of British Columbia Press, 1981).

Necatigil, Zaim M., *The Cyprus Question and the Turkish Position in International Law*, 2nd edn (Oxford: Oxford University Press, 1998).

O'Leary, Brendan, 'Multi-national federalism, federacy, power sharing and the Kurds of Iraq', text to accompany keynote to the conference *Multi-Nationalism, Power-Sharing and the Kurds in a New Iraq*, Cafritz Foundation Conference Center, George Washington University, 12 September 2003.

Özersay, Kudret, 'Exhaustion and time of change', *Peace Review: A Journal of Social Justice* 24/4 (2012), pp. 406–13.

Stephen, Temitope Obasaju, 'Self declaration or self determination: a comparative of Kosovo and the Turkish Republic of Northern Cyprus', School of Law, University of East London, 30 May 2012.

25

Chronicle of a Failure Foretold?

Yiannis Papadakis

Since then you have listened to complicated details, bewildering statistics, interminable statements, articles of the constitution, the grievous wrongs committed by the other side, and the Cyprus problem has become elusive, cloudy, and intimidating.

In the decades during which it has resisted efforts at settlement, the Cyprus problem has become overlain with legalistic abstractions and artificial labels, which are more and more difficult to disentangle and which would appear increasingly removed from the actual needs of both communities.

Speaking 35 years apart, these two different commentators, one a humourist, the other a UN Secretary-General, agree on the fundamental elusiveness and confusion that characterise the Cyprus Problem. George Mikes wrote his comments in the chapter on Cyprus which was included in his 1964 book on Greece, *Eureka! Rummaging in Greece*. The back cover teasingly explained how delighted Greek Cypriots were bound to be by this literary inclusion. Given their unfulfilled desire for political inclusion within the state of Greece, they were at least now included within Mikes' book on Greece. The second quote is by Kofi Annan, UN Secretary-General, in his 22 June 1999 report on Cyprus. What if the confusion both point out is not an inadvertent feature of the problem, but an inherent structural one? What if it arises out of the very process itself, with the UN also implicated? Furthermore, as I argue, confusion in the form of legalistic abstractions and artificial labels may actually serve the needs of the communities *as they perceive them*, who are thus actively involved in creating it.

It all boils down to another simple observation Mikes made in 1964: 'A UN debate is imminent and both sides are on their best behaviour.' All three sides, I would add. I argue here that a solution in the form currently negotiated (bizonal, bicommunal federation with political equality) is unlikely because neither side wants this, while the UN process involves all parties (including the UN itself) in the theatrics of negotiating for this position in order not to be blamed for the failure of the negotiations. While both sides may support federation in official public pronouncements, this remains on the level of rhetoric without any signs of a serious active desire to bring it forth, and lacking general public endorsement. Performative aspects of politics where social actors may not mean what they say or say what they mean have been noted in works like the classic study of the Roman Empire by Shadi Bartsch, *Actors in the Audience: Theatricality and Doublespeak from Nero to Hadrian*, David Runciman's wide-ranging overview on *Political Hypocrisy*, arguing that hypocrisy is an inescapable (though not necessarily always negative) aspect of political life and anthropological studies like Clifford Geertz's *Negara: The Theatre State in 19th Century Bali*, which focused on ritualistic aspects of politics. While the aim here is not to accuse the three involved parties, I argue that they are complicit in this joint performance and that, following Runciman, if one can distinguish between less and more harmful forms of hypocrisy, this belongs to the latter. This is so because, in my view, there may well be, for the first time, significant majorities in the two sides that agree on what is a jointly acceptable solution (not a federation), yet this cannot be publicly acknowledged and discussed.

The major focus here is the Greek Cypriot community and why federation may no longer be the desired political solution for the majority. The Turkish Cypriot side, despite its positive vote for the Annan Plan, has been consistent in the insistence (of a fairly significant majority with the occasional exception of the Turkish Cypriot left) on partition or confederation; in short, living apart and independent of each other to the greatest extent. The Greek Cypriot side has continuously insisted on reunification in a federation with a strong central government. But is this what most Greek Cypriots really desire today? I believe not.

On the one hand, Greek Cypriots officially proclaim their unwavering desire for federation with as powerful as possible central (i.e. federal) government, instead of a polity with two more autonomous constituent states. On the other hand, they are very afraid of the possible influence that the Turkish Cypriot community may have over their own affairs. This, to me, is the fundamental contradiction in Greek Cypriot political thought. The more powerful the central government, the more say each community has on the affairs of the other community – thus the more authority Turkish Cypriots will have on the affairs of Greek Cypriots. In my view, the greatest Greek Cypriot fear currently is losing their autonomy through power sharing by entering into any system of joint decision making with Turkish Cypriots.

Why is power sharing such a deep Greek Cypriot fear? The first thing to note is that this, i.e. choosing not to share power, can well be a reasoned political option. Greek Cypriots may make a choice that they prefer to live in a self-governed polity. This, however, entails certain costs and political outcomes which are rarely openly discussed. Secondly, the Turkish Cypriot community is to a great extent unknown to Greek Cypriots. The two communities have lived apart since 1963, that is for half a century, and this came about as a result of the violent ethnic conflict that erupted in 1963, creating widespread animosity. Thirdly, all Greek Cypriot political leaderships and political parties present Turkish Cypriots as lacking an autonomous political will; they are just 'puppets of Ankara' while 'the key to the solution is in Ankara', as the two mantras shared by all Greek Cypriot political parties go. The argument that should a solution take place these worries could be alleviated appears a highly hypothetical one, and cannot reverse deeply embedded fears in place for decades. The presence of tens of thousands of Turkish settlers and immigrants, many of whom will stay in the case of a solution, increases the fears that ultimately Turkey will 'remain in control'. The lack of trust towards Turkish Cypriots is vividly illustrated by the fact that 90 per cent of Greek Cypriots expressed mistrust towards Mehmet Ali Talat, the left-wing Turkish Cypriot leader (Cyprus 2015 survey). Yet, it is difficult to imagine a more compromising Turkish Cypriot leader who could also have wide appeal within his community. A counter-argument to the above is the often-expressed Greek Cypriot view that 'we had no problems in the past and lived in peaceful coexistence with Turkish Cypriots', a view which entails the erasure from Greek Cypriot social memory of the inter-ethnic violence that took place during the 1960s, a point which I will come back to later.

Federation as an unjust solution: Greek Cypriot views

There are two reasons why a political arrangement of joint decision making based on 'political equality' appears as unjust to Greek Cypriots. First, it is felt to deviate from what appears as the 'natural' form of democracy (one person, one vote), which is the political system they know of, have lived with and are accustomed to. 'What now, are we asked to accept the equality of the 18 per cent with the 80 per cent?' is the often-heard objection towards any discussion of political equality. The counter-argument that simple majority rule can lead to the oppression of minorities is hardly heard, or indeed understood, given the lack of any such public discussion. Even if the Republic of Cyprus has been part of the EU for many years, a political arrangement whereby the Republic of Cyprus amounting to only 0.18 per cent population-wise has veto powers on highly significant political decisions, this experience is not taken into account.

A deeper reason why arguments like the ones presented above are not even taken into consideration lies in the perception of many Greek Cypriots that Cyprus has historically been a purely Greek island. According to this logic, prevalent in history schoolbooks and everyday political rhetoric, if Cyprus has historically been just Greek, then the presence of Turkish Cypriots is viewed as a historical injustice, a result of the Ottoman occupation of the island. Turkish Cypriots are thus regarded as 'remains of foreign conquerors', leading to the question, why those who should not be in Cyprus in the first place should have any rights at all. Politicians of all parties and speakers in the media constantly, consistently and daily employ the term 'Cypriot' as equivalent to 'Greek Cypriot', thus implying that Turkish Cypriots are not Cypriots and do not belong to Cyprus. This practice also permeates Greek Cypriot school history textbooks.

Treating Turkish Cypriots as outsiders is a strong indication of the absence of a common civic consciousness upon which the reunification of Cyprus could be based. The term 'reunification' has a specific content for most Greek Cypriots, meaning 'return of our refugees, reclaiming our homes, towns and villages' which has lacked any reference to Turkish Cypriots. 'Reunification' for many Greek

Cypriots expressed a vague state of affairs where Greek Cypriots returned to their homes and Turkish Cypriots to theirs, and things could go on as in the past. The notion of things going on 'as in the past' was equally vague – can Greek Cypriots now accept a state of affairs like the 1960 Republic of Cyprus, which gave significant veto powers to the Turkish Cypriot vice-president? The realisation that 'reunification' has a specific political content (bizonal, bicommunal federation with political equality) has emerged with the various detailed plan-proposals presented since 2002, and this was a traumatic realisation for many Greek Cypriots. It can plausibly be argued that to a significant extent Greek Cypriots literally did not want to hear and know what 'reunification' could mean in practice and in detail, which is why no Greek Cypriot government dared inform the populace of the meaning of 'bizonal, bicommunal federation with political equality' for 33 years since 1974, with the exception of the publication of a meagre pamphlet by the previous AKEL-led government.

How about 'past peaceful coexistence' then, another mantra of Greek Cypriot political rhetoric? The only period within living memory when this may have applied are the three short years between 1960–63, and this only for those beyond, say, currently their mid-60s or older, i.e. those old enough to remember. When Greek Cypriots argue that 'we lived in past peaceful coexistence with Turkish Cypriots' what they actually mean is that they wish to live in a 'reunified' Cyprus, with the meaning of 'reunification' previously discussed. 'If we lived well together in the past, then this means that we can also live well in the future, so the island should be reunified', is how the argument is presented by projecting from an idealised past.

Is 'reunification' still desirable?

It is difficult today to ascertain the conditions for any realistic form of reunification, whether on a level of civic consciousness, a political arrangement or even in the more mundane geographical sense of populations mixing which any form of return to previous homes would imply. For the young to middle-aged Greek Cypriots, 'return' to a place they do not know or remember is too abstract an idea, while for the elders who have made the South their home for almost 40 years it would imply another painful displacement, away from friends, children and relatives since the previous communities cannot possibly be recreated. In the most extensive recent poll, 73 per cent of Greek Cypriots said they would not return under Turkish

Cypriot administration (Cyprus 2015). Surveys indicate that young Greek Cypriots are the most negative group when it comes to return even under Greek Cypriot administration, an understandable stance given that the other side and its people are totally unknown and have mostly been presented as evil or threatening. The same group appears as the most negative to any notion of reunification for the same reasons. If the youth represent the future, the portents clearly are not positive.

Here I argue the possibility that certain fundamental political desires of a large section of Greek Cypriots are not publicly expressed, and that it may be not be easy to document them through large-scale questionnaire-based surveys, though some indications have recently been emerging. Greek Cypriots have been struggling against the partitionist goals of Turkish Cypriot leader Rauf Denktash for decades. To his proposed partition or confederation, Greek Cypriot leaderships replied with centralised federation, a reaction that has become almost instinctual, hence perhaps the continuing Greek Cypriot call for reunification. Since 2002, Greek Cypriots have come face to face with what 'bizonal, bicommunal federation with political equality…' means in practice, yet for reasons already explained it does not have widespread legitimacy, while this cannot be publicly discussed either, though in my experience it often is, privately. Moreover, with the 2003 opening of the checkpoints, elderly Greek Cypriots realised that 'return' (upon which the notion of 'reunification' is based) can no longer be possible under Turkish Cypriot administration. They would be too intimidated to live in relative isolation in these now different places, while their children, and younger people in general, show no interest in returning to 'homes' they have never known. Since 1974, Greek Cypriots have argued for 'all refugees to return to their homes', which made sense in the first years, but they may simply not desire this any longer, something once again difficult to publicly acknowledge. In my view, these factors seem to make it difficult for Greek Cypriots to acknowledge *even to themselves* that a centralised federation is not what they want.

Conclusion

The previous analysis can explain the negative vote cast by most Greek Cypriots in 2004 for the federal solution proposed in the jointly negotiated, UN-finalised Annan Plan. Greek Cypriots had international recognition, they had secured EU entry (which also meant a highly significant feeling of safety vis-à-vis Turkey), and lived in the wealthiest state of the 2004 new EU enlargement group. Any change involving power sharing within a virtually alien federal framework was plausibly regarded by most as taking too big a *risk*. Turkish Cypriots, on the other hand, even if they would prefer partition or confederation, accepted the federalist polity proposed by the Annan Plan, since lacking international recognition, living in political and economic isolation and experiencing (relative to Greek Cypriots) lower economic standards, they felt it could be a risk worth taking, especially since this also meant they would become part of the EU with the securities this could ostensibly provide to smaller communities and the wealth it promised. In any case, federation, as the word's etymology indicates, requires *fides*, namely trust, something still lacking. A federal state's success in operating adequately is based on the arduous art of *compromise*, a value that must be wholeheartedly espoused, yet one with a negative ring on both sides.

The research by Eiki Berg and Raul Toomla based on a large-scale survey conducted in 2009 lends credence the scenario outlined above: 'those [Greek Cypriots] most strongly identifying themselves with the Republic of Cyprus, and approving the regime legitimacy of the Greek Cypriot government, are actually for *status quo* and not for the reunification of the country which makes the return to the partnership state mission impossible' (2013: 1). A recent (2012) survey by the Cyprus 2015 group on how people on the two sides might vote on a proposed federal solution also supports the argument presented here:

> In both communities the 'trending towards a no' category is ascendant as the formerly undecided move toward voting 'no' in a future referendum. The trend among Greek Cypriots is most clear where a majority (51 per cent) now declare that they are likely to vote 'no' should a referendum be held. Meanwhile, 'yes' votes (18 per cent) are at the lowest level since tracking began. (See Ahmet Sozen's presentation, 2012).

The most recent opinion poll by CyBC (the Greek Cypriot state TV channel) presented on 17 October 2012, documents for the first time as far as I am aware, a Greek Cypriot majority against reunification. To the question whether 'the two communities, Greek Cypriots and

Turkish Cypriots, should live together or apart', 55 per cent of Greek Cypriots polled replied that the two communities should live apart, 40 per cent that they should live together and 5 per cent that they do not know.

In my view, the solution that many Greek Cypriots would now prefer is a polity that would allow the two communities to live to the greatest extent autonomously, more apart rather than mixed, and this could be acceptable provided there were significant territorial adjustments and compensations for the properties lost. All surveys indicate this kind of arrangement to be the preferred choice of most Turkish Cypriots.

Paradoxically, then, it is possible that significant majorities on both sides may for the first time ever converge, yet both sides keep on negotiating for an ostensible federal solution, both unwilling to ask for a change in the framework for negotiations in order not to be blamed for their failure, with the UN complicit in this process, locked into its own mandates as determined by the Security Council. The difficulty all parties have in operationalising this convergence could be the current tragedy of Cyprus.

Postscript, August 2013: the recent discovery of potentially large hydrocarbon reserves in the coast off the Southern side of the island and the devastating economic crisis that has hit the Greek Cypriot-controlled Republic of Cyprus, along with many other EU states, could have significant geo-political implications. It is too early, however, to ascertain whether these could enhance the possibilities of a solution to the Cyprus Problem.

References and recommended reading

Berg, Eiki and Raul Toomla, 'Mission impossible in Cyprus? Legitimate return to the partnership state revisited', *Nationalities Papers* 41/2 (2013), pp. 276–92.

Cyprus 2015 (survey). Available at http://www.cyprus2015.org/.

Papadakis, Yiannis, *Echoes from the Dead Zone: Across the Cyprus Divide* (London: I.B.Tauris, 2005).

——, 'History education in divided Cyprus: A comparison of Greek Cypriot and Turkish Cypriot schoolbooks on the "History of Cyprus"', PRIO Cyprus Center Report 2/2008.

Sözen, Ahmet, 'Heading towards the defining moment in Cyprus: public opinion vs realities on the ground', *Insight Turkey* 14/1 (2012), pp. 109–29.

——, presentation on http://vimeo.com/45893566.

26

A Constitutional Law Perspective

Nikos Skoutaris

Before I provide a constitutional law perspective on whether a solution of the Cyprus issue is feasible, let me briefly consider a definition of the term 'solution'. At times it has been rather provocatively suggested that the Cyprus issue was solved in 1974 or that 'no solution is a solution'. For the purposes of this chapter, a solution entails any settlement – comprehensive or not – of the age-old dispute that both ethno-religious communities would democratically accept. In that sense, a solution could also denote extreme options such as secession or the unification of the island as a unitary state with a central government for the whole island. Obviously both prospects are totally unconceivable and largely unacceptable in the current political setting. Potentially, however, they could be considered in the future as possible solutions if both communities democratically opt for them. What is definitely not a solution is the current stalemate that has led the European Court of Human Rights to characterise Northern Cyprus as a vacuum in the European public order.

So, for this chapter, 'solution' means any settlement that would be democratically accepted by both Greek Cypriots and Turkish Cypriots and would address this 'vacuum' in the European public order. In that sense, the Cyprus issue can be solved as long as both communities reach an agreement about the political and constitutional future of the island. Of course, this sounds like a truism. And largely it is. At the same time, it points to the fact that the answer to such an existential question is, and should be, first and foremost decided by the communities themselves. They are the ones that will always share the island in one way or the other.

However, the communities have failed so far to reach an agreement, despite the fact that they set the basic parameters of the solution since the High Level Agreements of 1977 and 1979. Even when, in 2004, the UN presented them with a comprehensive settlement plan based on those parameters, the Greek Cypriot community overwhelmingly rejected it. Of course, the fact that the two communities have not managed to reach the long-awaited settlement, although they have agreed on the basic parameters, for the last 35 years is rather unsurprising for students of conflicts. One just needs to consider the case of Northern Ireland. However, one has to wonder whether, after almost four decades of negotiations, it is time not only to discuss the precise context of the agreed parameters but whether those parameters can indeed lead to a mutually acceptable solution. In other words, it may be time to challenge the conventional wisdom according to which the Cyprus issue may only be solved along the lines of a 'bizonal, bicommunal federation'.

The purpose of the present contribution, however, is far more modest. Rather than provide an alternative to the 'bizonal, bicommunal federation', the aim is to briefly describe whether it is feasible from a constitutional law point of view to have a 'bizonal bicommunal federation' in Cyprus. It will do so by focusing on what such an institutional structure might look like and by referring to similar paradigms in Europe. The reason for choosing this more modest aim is not dictated just by the fact that the UN and the ethno-linguistic segments have reconfirmed time and again the known basic parameters. It is, rather, necessitated by the fact that recent surveys, such as one conducted by Cyprus 2015, seem to suggest that despite the many years of fruitless negotiations, the framework of the 'bizonal, bicommunal federation' is considered an acceptable compromise by both communities. In other words, a 'bizonal, bicommunal federation' might be seen as the only realistic middle ground where the conflicting political aspirations of the different segments of this divided society might meet. To achieve its aim, the chapter describes how the principles of bizonality and bicommunality might be applied in a future reunified state and refers to similar structures in Europe. Overall the chapter concludes that a future solution based on such a constitutional framework is feasible from a constitutional point of view.

Bicommunality

Concerning bicommunality, the idea has always been that this principle will shape the constitutional aspects of a reunified Cyprus. This conforms to the constitutional history of the island. The 1960 constitution was based on bicommunality. To this extent, it is worth recalling that the Constitution provided for an independent and sovereign Republic with a presidential regime; the president being Greek and the vice-president being Turkish. The Cabinet had to consist of seven Greek ministers designated by the president and three Turkish ministers designated by the vice-president. A seven-to-three ratio was also to be put in place regarding the composition of the single-chamber legislature. The Constitution also guaranteed a great deal of autonomy for the two ethnic segments by setting up two separately elected communal chambers with exclusive legislative powers over religious, educational, cultural and personal status matters. Additionally, several other constitutional provisions were designed to safeguard the bicommunal nature of the state. For example, Article 173 provided for the establishment of separate municipal councils in the five largest towns of the island. At the same time, while the public service had to be composed in accordance with the aforementioned seven-to-three ratio, a six-to-four ratio was set for the army and the police.

However, it is not only the constitutional history of the island that provides a hint of how bicommunality might be applied in a reunified Cyprus. Within the European constitutional landscape, there are a number of paradigms where bicommunalism has been applied in one way or another. For instance, the Belgian constitution contains a formal requirement that the executive includes representatives of the main linguistic groups. According to the Constitution, '[with] the possible exception of the Prime Minister, the Council of Ministers [cabinet] includes as many French-speaking as Dutch-speaking members'.

Similarly, in Northern Ireland, the posts of the First Minister and Deputy are tied together by the Northern Ireland Act 1998. According to this, 'the largest political party of the largest political designation shall nominate... the First Minister' while 'the largest political party of the second largest political designation shall nominate... the deputy First Minister'. More interestingly, the ministers are not chosen by this dyarchy. Instead, the Northern Ireland Act provides that the ministerial posts are allocated to all of those parties with significant representation in the Assembly. The number of posts to which each party is entitled is determined according to the d'Hondt method of proportional representation. The actual posts are chosen by the parties in the order that the seats were awarded, ensuring the effective political representation of both communities in the executive. More importantly, bicommunalism is deeply enshrined with regard to the legislature and the administration in the constitutional structure of Northern Ireland.

More broadly, the effective participation of different ethno-linguistic or religious segments in the institutions of a given divided society is secured in a number of constitutions of multinational states. The 'magic formula' of the Swiss executive, the tripartite Bosnian presidency and the consociational characteristics of the South Tyrolean arrangement are just some of the different models used to provide 'shared rule' in societies comprised of different ethnic, religious or linguistic groups. It is therefore rather unsurprising that the Annan Plan suggested a model that was inspired by the Swiss arrangement and that the current bicommunal negotiations seem to opt for a 'rotating presidency'.

In sum, a solution that based on bicommunality is feasible from a constitutional law point of view, not only because the constitutional history of the island is very much influenced by the application of this principle, but also because, within the European constitutional space, there are numerous examples where the effective participation of different segments in the state institutions is constitutionally secured.

Bizonality

The existence of a number of states, including EU member states such as Belgium, that have opted for an institutional structure that secures the effective participation of different groups proves beyond reasonable doubt that a settlement that based on bicommunality is feasible from a constitutional point of view. With regard to bizonality, however, the situation is less straightforward.

According to the UN, the bizonality of the reunified federal Cyprus would be reflected 'in the fact that each federated state would be administered by one community which would be guaranteed a clear majority of the population and of land ownership in its area' (Report of the Secretary-General of 8 March 1990, S/1990/21183, Annex I, para. 20). This means that the future constitutional arrangement would entail that the sub-state level would be comprised of two constituent entities/states: one Greek Cypriot and one Turkish Cypriot. In each, the respective community will enjoy a clear majority not only of the population but also of land ownership. More importantly, such arrangements should be guaranteed.

Evidently, the exact definition of the crucial term 'clear majority' should be settled during the negotiations of the interested parties. What is particularly interesting, however, from a constitutional law point of view, is how such arrangement may be guaranteed. It is worth recalling at this moment that the 1960 constitution provided for the fact that the basic Articles of the Constitution that had been incorporated from the Zurich Agreement could not be amended. This means that in the constitutional tradition of Cyprus there has been an important precedent of a constitutional guarantee securing the power-sharing arrangement.

More broadly again, provisions securing important features of a given constitutional arrangement are not uncommon within the European constitutional landscape. For instance, Article 79(3) of the German Basic Law provides that the principles contained in Articles 1–20 may never be amended. Similarly, in France, the republican principle may not be modified according to Article 89(5) of the Constitution. In that sense, it is not hard to imagine a provision guaranteeing bizonality in the constitution of the future reunified Cyprus.

However, what is less common within the European public order is to find another constitution guaranteeing a 'clear majority' of population and land ownership of an ethno-linguistic group over a certain territory. Even in the case of Belgium, where territoriality is an important characteristic of the federal arrangement, the constitution does not guarantee the majority of population of any community over any territory. This is very apparent if one looks more closely at the changing demographics of Brussels and the surrounding area. However, a form of bizonality (or trizonality if one takes into account the German-speaking community that accounts for less than 1 per cent of the population) is de facto applied in Belgium in the sense that it is virtually impossible for a French-speaking Belgian residing in Flanders to vote for a French-speaking party or send their children to a French-speaking school and vice versa. The closest one gets to an arrangement that secures both the demographics and the land ownership of a certain territory is the case of the Swedish-speaking Åland islands in Finland. The Act on the Autonomy of the Åland regulates both the right to domicile but also the right to buy property in Åland *erga omnes*. Notwithstanding, one has to recognise that the constitutional guarantee of 'clear majority' in population and ownership is rather uncommon in the European constitutional landscape.

More importantly, however, the introduction of such a constitutional guarantee poses limits to the application of EU law in a reunified Cyprus. In particular, the guarantee of 'clear majority' in population and land ownership necessitates certain restrictions on the free movement of persons and capital. This was known to the drafters of the Annan Plan, which contained such restrictions, given that it was also based on bizonality. Such incompatibilities could be summarised in three different aspects. First of all, there were the restrictions on the right of non-residents in the constituent states to purchase immovable property. Secondly, restrictions were envisaged on the right of Cypriot citizens to reside in a constituent state in which they do not hold internal constituent state citizenship status. Thirdly, restrictions were proposed on the right not only of Greek and Turkish nationals but also of Union citizens to reside in Cyprus after the comprehensive settlement takes place in order to maintain the demographic ratio between permanent residents speaking either Greek or Turkish as their mother tongue. More to the point, these restrictions could not be substantially altered. It is for this reason that Protocol No. 10 on Cyprus to the Act of Accession 2003 contained a special provision allowing such territorial exceptions to the application of EU law in case the two communities were to accept the UN plan.

More generally, and with regard to the accommodation of such restrictions within the Union legal order, it should be recalled that the member states are the 'masters of the Treaties' and, as such, they enjoy an almost unfettered autonomy to amend EU law. So, despite functioning as a European constitution, the treaties are still subject to the intergovernmental method of treaty-making and the will of member states to accommodate specific economic interests has not, so far, been subject to legal limitations. In the past, the member states have occasionally restricted EU law, even permanently as in the case of the Danish prohibition on secondary residences in the Maastricht Treaty, or with the special regime for the Åland islands. In that sense, one could imagine that they could amend EU law in order to accommodate the tensions between a settlement that would be based on bizonality and the application of EU law. In fact, the treaties provide that the Union should 'respect the equality of Member States before the Treaties as well as their national identities, inherent in their fundamental structures, political and constitutional...' So, as a number of legal commentators have argued, there is a legal obligation on the part of the EU to respect the constitutional identity of the Member States. In that sense, the EU should accommodate the tensions that would occur from a new Cypriot constitutional identity that was based on bizonality among other things, as long as the settlement was in conformity with the founding principles of the EU as enshrined in Article 2 of the Treaty of the EU.

Conclusion

It is often said that the Cyprus issue entails a conflict between 50,000 Turkish soldiers in the North and 50,000 Greek Cypriot lawyers in the South. Despite its exaggerated manner, this common joke among students of the Cyprus dispute accurately depicts the transition of the conflict from warfare to 'lawfare' and the fact that this conflict has been one of the most judicialised disputes in the world. In that sense, and given that the parties to the conflict have showed a tendency to use every forum as yet another arena for their political battle, as a platform from which to seek international and local endorsement of their political arguments, it is important to examine whether a settlement based on a bicommunal, bizonal federation is feasible from a constitutional point of view.

This chapter has shown that bicommunality is part of the constitutional history of the island and that within the European constitutional landscape, there are a number of cases where the participatory rights of different ethnic, religious and linguistic groups to the state institutions are protected. At the same time, and despite the fact that the constitutional guarantee of 'clear majority' in population and land ownership is less common, the EU may accommodate an arrangement that is based on bizonality not least because of its legal obligation to respect the constitutional identity of its Member States. In that sense, although law cannot solve *per se* this predominantly political problem, it can definitely facilitate its actors to design a more efficient institutional structure of a member of the

EU constitutional order of states. In other words, if the communities decide to solve the problem, law will not stand in their way.

References and recommended reading

Bell, Christine, *On the Law of Peace: Peace Agreements and the Lex Pacificatoria* (Oxford: Oxford University Press, 2008).

Cyprus 2015, 'Research and Dialogue for a Sustainable Future'. Available at www.cyprus2015.org.

Hoffmeister, Frank, *Legal Aspects of the Cyprus Problem: Annan Plan and EU Accession* (Leiden: Martinus Nijhoff, 2006).

Kymlicka, Will and Bashir, Bashir (eds), *The Politics of Reconciliation in Multicultural Societies* (Oxford: Oxford University Press, 2008).

Laulhé Shaelou, Stephanie, 'Market freedoms, EU fundamental rights and public order: views from Cyprus', *Yearbook of European Law* 30 (2011), pp. 298–357.

Skoutaris, Nikos, *The Cyprus Issue: The Four Freedoms in a Member State under Siege* (Oxford: Hart Publishing, 2011).

Tierney, Stephen, *Constitutional Law and National Pluralism* (Oxford: Oxford University Press, 2004).

27

Updating Our Thinking on Cyprus

Mary Southcott

Settling the 'Cyprus Problem', as it is known, requires not only acknowledging the past. It must also be based on being honest about the present. It is about recognising the vested interest of the actors involved. It is not so much about thinking out of the box as updating one's nomenclature and concepts; moving away from the 1950s and into the twenty-first century.

Rethinking concepts of justice and a settlement

The first changes that need to take place concern the way people on the island think about a peaceful coexistence. Fifty years ago Martin Luther King said, 'true peace is more than the absence of war; it is the presence of justice'. In the context of Cyprus, those who do not want a solution are willing to settle for negative peace – where there is an absence of armed conflict between the communities or between Cyprus and Turkey – or say that Cyprus was solved in 1974. And yet, both communities continue to see themselves as victims and demand justice. In the case of some Greek Cypriots, this justice is centred on the three freedoms: movement, settlement and right to property. For some Turkish Cypriots, justice is about the recognition of the 'Turkish Republic of Northern Cyprus'.

Neither community seems to think about justice from a wider perspective. Justice in Cyprus is more likely to be achieved if approached from the perspective of John Rawls' (1971) veil of ignorance. According to this model, any future settlement would be created by the people of Cyprus with no reference to their current identity; a Greek- or Turkish-speaking Cypriot, a Maronite, an Armenian or a Latin, perhaps an asylum seeker or guest worker from Eastern Europe, Sri Lanka or the Philippines, or even a settler from Turkey. Rather, they would focus on building a solution that would protect them if they happened not to be from a dominant group. Through his approach, any constitutional system put in place would be based on trying to protect minorities in society, whoever they might be.

However, as we are reminded by Amartya Sen, democracy goes beyond structures. It depends on people (2009). Sen might have joined the ranks of people for whom a perfect settlement is elusive and for any settlement to work the key is political will. He would also caution against thinking about justice in absolute terms. You cannot see whether or not social justice has been achieved. Nor should it be the case that justice, like freedom, for one should impinge on the 'other'. Without empathy and acknowledgement of the other's loss, pain or injustice there is little hope of moving on.

The second key change that is needed relates to the way in which Cypriots understand the concepts of solution and settlement. A solution is like an ending. It is a goal or an achievement. In contrast, a settlement is like a marriage. It moves beyond the 'happily ever after' moment. It needs to be worked on and to evolve. In the case of Cyprus, perhaps we need to seek a settlement, and not a solution.

The new politics for a settlement

In addition to the way they think about the nature of a settlement, Cypriots need to update the way they approach the process of reaching a settlement. The political culture needs to change. This especially applies to the political parties. Over the past 50 years, the ability to put things together before elections drove people apart has been noticeably absent. Nationalism is an easy card to play in elections, where you speak to your own rather than address the vital 'other' audience. The absence of a non-nationalist right-wing party in the North, and the divisions between the right and left non-nationalists in the South, has helped to push a settlement further and further away. Overtures between the two largest parties in the South, AKEL and DISY, may herald a new politics in Cyprus where they are able to cooperate on the 'national issue' while suspending their battles on other issues, where they know that they will never agree.

Tied to this, politics must also move beyond political parties. The idea of direct democracy and referendums is that the people should own the process of a settlement. There has been, during the recent post 2008 discussions much emphasis on a Cypriot owned process. However the reality is that people have not been involved and the idea that nothing is decided until everything is decided has kept people in the dark. Until the 2013 leaking of the document by Alexander Downer, no one knew that anything had been agreed. The appointment of Representatives Osman Ertuğ and Andreas Mavroyiannis may change the alienating non-communication from the Leaders after each meeting. Involvement and understanding needs to precede the referendum campaigns. Concepts such as rotating presidencies, federal areas and cross voting need to be understood so that people recognise what they mean and, more importantly, what they don't mean. Constitutional conventions which have proved so useful in the UK, particularly in Scotland, can be used to bring civil society together. Certainly some public discussion and examination of issues, examining of equivalent processes in other countries, needs to happen.

But it needs to go further than this. Working together and separately, Cypriots also need to show political will and individual leadership. It cannot simply be left to leaders. If you look at what is happening in Cyprus, there is evidence that whenever Cypriots have the chance to work together they build friendships and get on with the task; leaving the propaganda at the door. And yet, somehow, the overall approach to the Cyprus conflict is stuck in the 1950s. In the 1950s, and even 1960s, human and women's rights were not on the agenda. Such a lot of development has taken place elsewhere in human rights, anti-racism, disability awareness and women's involvement in politics. Lack of progress on a solution has led to a 'fossilisation' of politics on the island. The almost complete absence of women in the peace negotiations leaves a crucial dimension out of everyone's lives. Whereas men are the decision makers in politics and the media, women are in charge of nurturing, families and emotional responses. Heart and head are best in union. Adversarial cultures can be replaced by seeking and building another Rawls' concept – 'overlapping consensus'.

Moreover, diversity rather than dichotomies can be recognised. In the Cyprus context, it is also important to recognise the role of 'civic nationalism'. Until 1974, most Cypriots lived in villages and identified with their locality, whether Christian or Muslim. Now Cypriots are on a spectrum of self-identification from Greek to Greek Cypriot to Cypriot to Turkish Cypriot to Turkish with Maronites, Armenians, Latins and Roma choosing to add Cypriot to their own identity. Cypriots can be Greek or Turkish culturally and linguistically, but a state has citizens. There is room for a civic nationalism. This would relate to geography, love of the island and a patriotism that does not exclude the other, but embraces equality before the law and freedom of expression. In addition to political equality between Greek and Turkish Cypriot entities of Cyprus, all individuals who qualify to vote in their lifetime would be equal citizens.

These are just some of the changes that need to occur. There are many more. For example, here are 13 points that Cypriots might like to consider:

1) accentuate the positive, eliminate the negative and end megaphone diplomacy, particularly by public information offices;

2) realise that it is more than the opening of the Green Line, the internet and the media that have created new means of communication, meaning people cannot again be artificially separated;

3) build empathy by putting themselves in the shoes of the other rather than perpetuating a blame culture;

4) remember that they have more in common with each other than points of difference (what Freud termed 'the narcissism of small differences');

5) understand that the language barrier is not insurmountable if investment is made in simultaneous interpreters, in bi- or trilingual media, in the translation of books and poetry from one language to the other and into English;

6) build capacity between people who know and like each other, starting with young people, as in the Cyprus Friendship Partnership, their families, their friends, in technical committees, as in the Stelios Awards and Green Line trade;

7) encourage cooperation between the Greek and Turkish Cypriot mayors, municipalities and people in Nicosia, Kyrenia and Famagusta, whether on sewage or culture or opening up Varosha;

8)   challenge myths and acknowledge inconvenient truths, leading
     to common workbooks and removing the 'ammunition' used by
     politicians and others, and perhaps even reconciliation;
9)   recognise the evolution from multiculturalism in the Byzantium
     and the Ottoman Empires to national state nationalism and
     now back to diversity and multiculturalism;
10) introduce rules for the conduct of referendums and give
     ownership by involving people in the process; 'not nothing is
     decided until everything is decided', but involving the people
     with the discussants;
11) remember that equality does not mean sameness and self-
     identification can change depending on where you are, and your
     geography, culture and language;
12) accept that subsidiarity can be a useful model for Cyprus;
     devolution can work to bring decisions nearer to the people
     they affect;
13) adopt neutral or diplomatic language which respects and
     includes the other without granting recognition where it does
     not exist.

A changed geopolitical environment

While it is important to recognise the changes that need to take place
in terms of attitudes on the island, it is also important to consider
how the wider external factors relating to a settlement have changed
in the 50 years since the Republic of Cyprus broke down and came
under Greek Cypriot administration. Of course, the benefits of a
settlement are not the same for all actors and their vested interests
in the status quo all differ. But it should not be assumed that these
vested interests have remained the same over half a century. Not
only have the dynamics within the communities changed, but the
vested interests of the wider geopolitical actors have undergone
a transformation. Does the partition that divided the island and
safeguarded the Sovereign Base Areas during the Cold War still have
the same logic? Could it be that gas and oil off Cyprus and the need
for water on it mean a settlement makes sense to a wider community
and an internal audience?

In the case of the Turkish Cypriots, communication technology
has changed the ability to assemble people on 'the street'. Outside
Cyprus, no coverage was given to the Turkish Cypriot demonstrations,
including against Turkey, in 2011; at the same time as Tahrir Square

was topping the agenda of the Western media. When Turkish Cypriots make the same points about the quality of democracy in Turkey and the autocratic decisions of Mr Erdoğan as the Gezi Park demonstrators, they receive no recognition. Ever-increasing decision making from Turkey and its Ambassador, the Turkification and Islamification of the North (there is an extensive AKP directed programme of mosque building and the teaching of the Qur'an in schools is challenging the largely secular nature of the Turkish Cypriot community), the economic dependence on Turkey and the selling off of Turkish Cypriot assets to the private sector have consolidated support for reunification among Turkish Cypriots. Meanwhile, the demographic changes in the North of the island, infringing as they do on Geneva Conventions, make it difficult to define the wishes of Turkish Cypriots. Indeed, many fear the eventual extinction of their community without a settlement.

For their part, Greek Cypriots changing circumstances have served to introduce a number of incentives to reach a settlement. For a start, the recent bailout by the European Union and the economic situation, which has caused real hardship, also provides an incentive to gain the peace dividend. The economics of the South mirror the results of Turkey's decisions in the North, affecting jobs particularly in the public sector and privatisation of government assets. At the same time, a settlement would mean that the gradual Turkification and Islamification in the North could be checked. This is crucial if Greek Cypriots wish to continue dealing with Turkish Cypriots rather than Turkey after a settlement. Then there is the possibility of reopening Famagusta. The town can be reunited and the ghost town reconstructed. This could also bring sizeable economic benefits. Finally, the exploration in Cyprus' exclusive economic zone for gas and oil has given a settlement a new imperative. However, without a settlement this will lead to problems because of Turkey's objections.

Ankara and Athens also stand to benefit. Turkey, despite noises to the contrary, still wants to be a member of the EU; especially as the Middle East becomes more incendiary and uncertain. Turkey has a lot to gain potentially from a deal in terms of international and regional kudos, the ability to redeploy troops to more problematic areas like the border with Syria and potentially a reduction in expensive subsidies to Northern Cyprus. If nothing else, a settlement would give Turkey a cleaner image in international forums. In order to take this forward, the Turkish government needs to implement the Ankara Protocol, signed in July 2005, by which they agreed to open ports to Republic of Cyprus traffic. They can do this without recognising the Republic of Cyprus, especially as the ports were in fact open until 1987. For Greece, a settlement would bring to a close a difficult chapter in its modern history and potentially open the way for a full normalisation of relations with Turkey. Britain, the third guarantor, along with Greece and Turkey, also has a vested interest in a settlement. It will help the relationship with the Republic of Cyprus, its own Sovereign Bases, its Cypriot diaspora, its own energy situation and its historic responsibility after its divide and rule colonial experience.

Various external actors also stand to gain from a settlement. The European Union will benefit by not having a divided country in their membership. The decision to allow Cyprus into the Union without a solution was not a mistake. It would have worked as a strategy had Denktash not said 'no' in March 2003. However, since Cyprus joined the EU, the situation on the island has been aggravated by, and become an aggravation for, the Union. Different EU funding streams aggravate the division on the island. Meanwhile, the Acquis only covers the South, not the North, of the island. A settlement would also help deal with Turkey's accession. Also, the USA needs to recover from the Cold War thinking that led it to support the Acheson Plan – basically partition – and help create stability for the exploitation by US companies of the gas and oil in the region. A settlement could help safeguard Israel by having a secular state of Cyprus close by. This means the major powers may well see it as being in their interest to end partition.

Conclusion

Cypriots have not lost hope of a settlement but have lost belief that one is possible. If Cyprus stays stuck in the past without updating the thinking there is much to be lost. Already things have deteriorated since 2004. Had the Annan Plan been accepted to be put to referendum in 2003 the Greek Cypriots might have accepted this version. That was prevented by Mr Denktash and Tahsin Ertuğruloğlu. By the time of the actual referendums in April 2004, Turkey could afford to publicly back the 'Yes' knowing that the Greek Cypriots were going to say 'No'. Each plan as it emerges offers less to both Greek and Turkish Cypriots. More and more Cypriots who lived together and did not experience the violence of the past – or knew it was not typical of the other community – are now aging if they have not already died. The 40 years of separate development is built upon as every year passes. The opportunity cost of not solving what is called the Cyprus Problem, distorted and defined into a conflict between two entities, means that everyone else has to take sides between Greek and Turkish Cypriots.

You can take Cypriots out of Cyprus but you cannot take Cyprus out of Cypriots. Each and every one loves their country, its environment, its food. The status quo is not stationary. It is working against the people in Cyprus. It is in the interests of everyone concerned for a Cyprus settlement to be agreed. The point now is to move away from outdated concepts, not values, draw on experience of other places, speak of the expectation and possibility of change and never to lose hope. A settlement is possible if the current tide is taken at the flood and leads on to fortune.

References and recommended reading

Friends of Cyprus, Reports (1974–2013), http://www.peace-cyprus. org/FOC/.

Georghiou, Costas, *British Colonial Architecture in Cyprus 1878–1960* (Nicosia: En Tipis Publications, 2013).

Hitchens, Christopher, *The Trial of Henry Kissinger* (New York: Verso, 2001).

Koumi, Andy, *The Cypriot* (London: Dexter Haven Publishing, 2006).

Packard, Martin, *Getting it Wrong: Fragments from a Cyprus Diary 1964* (Bloomington, IN: AuthorHouse, 2008).

John Rawls, *A Theory of Justice* (Cambridge, MA: Belknap Press, 1971).

Sen, Amartya, *The Idea of Justice* (London: Allen Lane, 2009).

Sterne, Laurence, *The Wrong Horse: The Politics of Intervention and the Failure of American Diplomacy* (New York: Times Books, 1977).

Uludağ, Sevgül, *Oysters with the Missing Pearls: Untold Stories about Missing Persons, Mass Graves and Memories from the Past of Cyprus* (Nicosia: İkme Bilban, 2007).

28

Blending Idealism with Pragmatism

Ahmet Sözen

Yes, the Cyprus Problem *can* be solved. And, what needs to be emphasised in my opinion is that it *should* be solved. So, in that regard, I am not an 'impartial' Cyprus Problem scholar, but rather a biased and strongly opinionated one who has been championing the idea of solving the Cyprus Problem through a federal model since the early 1990s. However, solving the Cyprus Problem through a federal model is not just a blind choice, but a deliberate choice which is a hybrid product of my 'idealism' and 'pragmatism', which might seem contradictory on a superficial level. However, I argue that the two can coexist perfectly if considered on a deeper level.

My idealism comes from my deep personal ideological conviction (choice) that Cyprus is a multi-ethnic society which should be governed by a progressive consociational model based on power sharing by the two communities, as well as the minorities of the island (Maronites, Latins and Armenians), rather than succumb to the dominant paradigm of the nation state. The obsession of the two Cypriot communities with being part of their own respective nation states – Greece (*enosis*) for Greek Cypriots and Turkey (*taksim*) for Turkish Cypriots – was the main reason why the 1960 Republic of Cyprus, a bicommunal consociational model, failed. The failure of the state, and the continued insistence on the nation state by the respective communities led to inter-ethnic violence and huge human suffering. This is what we should avoid in the future. That is why we need to use our idealism to design the future in a consociational model where there will be peaceful coexistence of communities with different ethnic and religious identities.

My pragmatism comes from a purely cool-headed, rational and scientific evaluation that I made a long time ago. In this calculation/evaluation, federation seems like the only alternative solution model for the Cyprus Problem, compared to others that have been proposed, such as two states, one unitary state, confederation and status quo. Leaders of the two conflicting sides in Cyprus long ago decided that if the two negotiating leaders reach a comprehensive settlement in the Cyprus peace negotiations this will be put to simultaneous separate referenda for the approval of the Greek and Turkish Cypriots. So, on a very practical level and for purely instrumental purposes, the opinions and positions of common people on the substantive issues of the Cyprus Problem are very important. Simply, without the approval of the people on the ground, a comprehensive settlement of the Cyprus Problem is impossible. The role of the common people is also important after a settlement is reached, for implementation. Without sincere endorsement of the settlement by regular people, the solution of the problem will not be durable. If we are to solve the Cyprus Problem through negotiations after which there will be approval of the settlement through referenda, then a bizonal, bicommunal federation is the only solution model (alternative) that has the chance of being accepted by the people on the ground on both sides of the UN divide (see Cyprus 2015 poll results).

Bizonal bicommunal federation

Island-wide public opinion polls conducted by the Cyprus 2015 Initiative during the period from 2009–12 clearly show that bizonal, bicommunal federation is the only solution model with a chance of being endorsed by the majority of both Greek Cypriots and Turkish Cypriots. In both communities bizonal, bicommunal federation is the second choice/preference, coming after the 'two-state' solution as the first preference of Turkish Cypriots and the 'unitary-state' solution as the first preference of Greek Cypriots. Other possible solution models, such as 'confederation', 'continuation of the status quo', 'Hatayisation of North Cyprus', 'Taiwanisation of North Cyprus' and 'Kosovoisation of North Cyprus' (Sozen 2012) were all rejected by either one or both communities. Bizonal, bicommunal federation is rejected entirely by only 19 per cent of Greek Cypriots and 24 per cent of Turkish Cypriots. The remainder finds it either 'absolutely essential', 'desirable', 'satisfactory' or 'tolerable if necessary' (Cyprus 2015 poll results). Hence, bizonal, bicommunal federation is the solution that would make both sides of the conflict only 'slightly unhappy'. Neither side will be able to get 100 per cent or maximalist demands satisfied since federation is its second preference. Nonetheless, through a bizonal, bicommunal federation both sides would be able to satisfy an important part of their demands.

Agreement and peace

The intercommunal negotiations started in 1968. Under the aegis of the United Nations (UN) Secretary-General, the Mission of Good Offices has continued on and off – sometimes with a few years of non-existent negotiation intervals – until the present time. As a result of these negotiations the UN was able to produce draft framework agreements such as Cuellar's 'Draft Framework Agreement' in the mid-1980s and Boutros-Ghali's 'Set of Ideas' in the first half of the 1990s. However, these draft framework agreements were rejected by either one or the other side. In 2004, for the first time the UN was able to produce a comprehensive settlement – known as the Annan Plan – which was put to simultaneous, separate referenda for the two communities. That, too, was rejected in referendum by an overwhelming Greek Cypriot majority (76 per cent), though it was supported by a good majority (65 per cent) of the Turkish Cypriots as an 'agreement' – a settlement plan – that would have started a new 'state of affairs' and a new relationship between the two communities – a kind of 'renewed partnership'. However, this is hardly the end of the road. What is also missing in the Cyprus issue is 'peace' – a state of intercommunal harmony where there is no violent conflict as well as no fear of future violent conflict in the minds of people. That 'peace' needs to be consciously and tactfully constructed on the future 'agreement' reached.

It is a plain truth that an 'agreement' itself is not going to bring peace to Cyprus. There are a lot of lessons that the two communities can learn from the experience of the post-agreement era of the 1960 Republic of Cyprus as to what to do and what not to do in order to preserve the state as well as the intercommunal harmony. Today the two communities need to go through a real reconciliation process in the pre- and post-agreement era which should be built into both the peace negotiations as well as the comprehensive agreement itself.

Roadmap for comprehensive settlement and beyond

The goal here should be twofold: (1) reaching comprehensive settlement; and (2) establishing real peace in Cyprus. The focus of the two Cypriot leaders who have been the chief negotiators for their respective communities should be on reaching this twofold goal and they should not get bogged down by the infinite number of the details of the Cyprus issue.

First of all, in terms of reaching a comprehensive settlement, here the leaders (first track) should have determination and courage. In other words, by definition they should be able to lead their respective communities, rather than follow public opinion. There are many examples of conflict situations where public opinion moved towards concessions on sensitive conflict issues in response to bold leadership. In addition, the leaders should work closely with both local and foreign technical experts and make them a routine part of the peace negotiations. That way more alternatives would be produced to resolve the disputed and deadlocked issues in the negotiations as opposed to the process whereby the leaders try to solve these issues with their full political baggage and multiple red-lines on the negotiated issues. Through technical experts, the peace negotiations would be much more technical and hence much less politicised. This would give the leaders flexibility and more room to manoeuvre. In addition, once the tedious and cumbersome details were taken care of by the technical experts, the leaders could stay focused on the goal of reaching comprehensive settlement and not get lost in the details – unlike most of the Cypriot leaders in the past.

A comprehensive settlement should be seen as the starting point – sort of *sine qua non* – of establishing the real peace in Cyprus. However, official peace negotiations, while focused on reaching comprehensive settlement, should be fortified by the implementation of concrete confidence building measures (CBMs) between the two communities that would expose common people to the experience of real intercommunal cooperation. Here, for example, a package deal including several CBMs could work wonders to unlock many issues in the Cyprus dispute. Imagine that the two sides agreed on the following package of CBMs:

(a)	Establishing a joint teachers' commission to remove elements of historical animosity and hatred from all schools curricula and adopt a new philosophy that emphasises intercommunal coexistence and harmony.

(b) Opening of the fenced area of Varosha under UN administration as a free zone between the two communities where the original inhabitants would be able to go back to their properties. This would mean that a considerable number of Greek Cypriot displaced persons would be able to go back to their properties without waiting for the comprehensive solution. This would dramatically ameliorate the environment of lack of trust in Cyprus and strengthen the hands of the leaders to take steps in the peace negotiations. This is because the fenced area of Varosha has become one of the most symbolic and therefore emotional aspects of the conflict since its first appearance on the 1979 High Level Agreements between the two leaders (Article 5). In addition, opening the fenced area of Varosha would, in a way, mean rebuilding of the 'ghost city'. This would result in billions of Euros-worth of new business opportunities for the two communities as well as cooperation between the Greek Cypriot and Turkish Cypriot business sectors.

(c) Opening of the Ercan Airport under UN administration (but under the effective operation of Turkish Cypriot administration) for direct international cargo and passenger traffic (as a suggestion, Ercan Airport could be named 'Nicosia Airport Terminal B'). This would help remove some of the isolation of the Turkish Cypriots and restore their trust in the international institutions, which has deteriorated dramatically since the 2004 referenda.

(d) Opening of the port of Famagusta under nominal EU or UN administration (but under the effective operation of Turkish Cypriot administration) for direct trade with the EU. Similarly, in addition to lifting some of the isolation of Turkish Cypriots, direct trade through the port of Famagusta, especially in relation to the rebuilding of adjacent Varosha, would mean huge new business opportunities for both communities.

(e) Turkey opening its ports to the vessels carrying the 'Republic of Cyprus (RoC)' flag, while RoC lifts its opposition on opening and closing of EU accession chapters with Turkey. Turkey being more closely anchored to the EU would simply be more flexible and more conciliatory on the Cyprus issue.

(f) Turkey withdrawing a symbolic number of its troops (5,000–
10,000) from Cyprus as a goodwill gesture. This action would
give out the signal that Turkey's new relationship with the island
will be less security-oriented.

(g) Starting unofficial talks between Greek Cypriot, Turkish
Cypriot, Turkish and Greek representatives – at the beginning
through second-track diplomacy – regarding the future use
of the natural resources (in other words, hydrocarbons) in
the Mediterranean. The financial output from the natural
resources could be used as a source to pay some of the costs
of peacebuilding and reconciliation processes in future Cyprus.
In addition, cooperation on extraction of the natural resources
could spill over to create regional stability and prosperity in the
Eastern Mediterranean.

The implementation of such concrete CBMs, such as (a)–(d)
above, is important because successful cooperation experiences
would send out the message that intercommunal cooperation really
works even in the absence of comprehensive settlement, and hence
mutually beneficial intercommunal cooperation is the order of the
day in a comprehensive settlement. In other words, power sharing
intercommunally, which can roughly be translated as running a
federation, is possible in Cyprus. Such CBMs, combined with more
regional ones such as (e)–(g) above, would greatly improve the peace
negotiations' atmosphere and shorten the period for reaching a
comprehensive settlement.

At this stage, the first track (the leaderships) should also cooperate
and work closely with multiple tracks within the civil society. For a
truly comprehensive settlement the leaders need the participation
of all the relevant stakeholders in various different tracks, be it the
media, the hard-core peace activists, the academicians or the trade
unions and so forth. Ultimately, the prerequisite of a successful
referendum result is ownership of the comprehensive settlement –
the actual solution plan – by relevant stakeholders in multiple tracks
within society.

As for establishing real peace in Cyprus, the second element,
the active participation of stakeholders in multiple tracks into the
peace process, should not be seen as a one-shot attempt with the
instrumental purpose of only reaching a comprehensive settlement.
On the contrary, the comprehensive settlement should have built-

in mechanisms that would necessitate the continuation of active participation of relevant stakeholders into the post-settlement peacebuilding and reconciliation processes in Cyprus. Hence, here there is need for perpetual multi-track cooperation and coordination in the post-settlement peacebuilding and reconciliation processes. In layperson's terms, the leadership and relevant stakeholders in multiple tracks within the society should work together in the post-settlement peacebuilding and reconciliation processes to make sure that Cyprus is a place where conflicts are resolved through non-violent means and that it becomes a place of intercommunal harmony and remains as such forever.

Exposure of people to such values as consociationalism, cosmopolitan democracy, pluralism and multiculturalism which should have started in the peacebuilding and reconciliation processes during peace negotiations should be institutionalised within the future federation in the post-settlement era. Comprehensive revision of the history textbooks in particular and the overall education curricula in general through the abovementioned values should be the starting point. The comprehensive settlement should also have a built-in mechanism through which monitoring the education curricula at all levels and future revisions are carried out by an independent intercommunal body. That body should also play an instrumental role in designing programmes on the state-run TV and radio channels where these values are disseminated.

Conclusion

It is now an established fact that as a solution model for Cyprus a bizonal, bicommunal federation is not the first preference of either Greek Cypriots or Turkish Cypriots. Island-wide public opinion results have repeatedly shown that it is the second preference of both communities (see Sözen et al. 2010). However, what is more important to note is that according to the same poll results bizonal, bicommunal federation is the only solution model that has the chance among other possible solution models to pass from a referenda similar to the one in 2004.

There are, however, other benefits of establishing a bizonal, bicommunal federation in Cyprus. For a start, and simply put, establishing a federation in Cyprus would set an important example of a model of power sharing and consociationalism in a multi-ethnic society for other cases of unresolved ethnic conflict. Secondly, the establishment of a federation would help break the dominant paradigm of 'nation state' in a 'unitary state' format in Cyprus. I refer to the initial establishment of a Cyprus federation as 'Belgianisation' (Sözen 2012) of Cyprus. What I mean by Belgianisation is to have a difficult(-to-run) federation, where sometimes two communities' reaching a consensus and making a decision would be almost impossible. Nonetheless, just like the Flemish (Belgians) and the Walloons (Belgians), the Turkish and Greek Cypriots would learn not to resort to violence in cases of deadlock in the running of the state. So, this federation would initially be a 'rational business partnership' and not a 'love marriage', which might evolve into something more positive in the future. The mere establishment of the Cyprus federation – a solution to the Cyprus conflict – would make regional cooperation and stability possible, with the inclusion of Turkey and Greece in the mix, and in return foster the settlement of the Aegean-related conflict issues between Turkey and Greece. Finally, the establishment of a federation would provide the legitimate platform to resolve the long-lasting challenging property issue as well as ending the approaching crisis on the exploitation of hydrocarbons in the Eastern Mediterranean. If the federation was long lasting, the property issue would be resolved in a couple of years. Similarly, hydrocarbons would be non-issue, since any decision on them would be under the competence of the federal government, which would be jointly run by Turkish and Greek Cypriots. In the event that the two communities came to realise that the federation could not continue – what I call the 'Czechoslovakiaisation' of Cyprus – then the communities could divide and distribute their respective shares in the federation in a peaceful way and each could go its own way. In other words, the experience of living in a federal state would provide the ground for negotiating a civilised divorce should both sides deem it appropriate, which it is not possible today due predominantly to the lack of a meaningful and legitimate platform for communication and cooperation between the two sides.

References and recommended reading

Cyprus 2015 polls. Available at Cyprus2015.org.

Hannay, David, *Cyprus: The Search for a Solution* (London: I.B.Tauris, 2005).

Ker-Lindsay, James, *The Cyprus Problem: What Everyone Needs to Know* (Oxford: Oxford University Press, 2011).

Michael, Michalis Stavrou, *Resolving the Cyprus Conflict: Negotiating History* (Basingstoke: Palgrave Macmillan, 2009).

Sözen, Ahmet, 'Heading towards the defining moment in Cyprus: public opinion vs realities on the ground', *Insight Turkey* 14/1 (2012), pp. 109–29.

——, Alexandros Lordos, Erol Kaymak and Spyros Christou, 'Next steps in the peace talks: an island-wide study of public opinion in Cyprus', (2010). Available at Cyprus2015.org.

29

The Role of 'Invaluable Assets'

ZENON STAVRINIDES

Can the Cyprus Problem, which has been festering in Cypriot society for most of the lifetime of most Greek and Turkish Cypriots now alive, ever be resolved? The answer that immediately suggests itself is simple: it all depends! If the agreed basis of the solution – a bicommunal, bizonal federation – and the character of the UN-sponsored intercommunal negotiations aimed at achieving it stay as they have been for nearly 40 years, and if there are no drastic changes in the beliefs, attitudes, desires and calculations underlying the demands and inhibitions of the Greek and Turkish Cypriot leaders, then a negotiated solution to the Cyprus Problem will remain blocked in the foreseeable future. If, on the other hand, there are substantial changes in the basis of the solution and the factors determining the thinking of the negotiating parties, then it is possible that the dispute can be resolved to the satisfaction of the majority of Greek and Turkish Cypriots, as well as the Turkish government which controls and directs the Turkish Cypriot leadership. In that case a new era could begin on the island and its relations with Turkey, Greece and the European Union.

In this chapter, I will identify and examine one fundamental factor that has effectively blocked the achievement of a solution, despite a dozen or so rounds of negotiations held since 1977. Put bluntly, the factor – in fact a dual factor – is that (1) each party seeks a solution which will secure for it a range of benefits to which it believes it has a right, but have been usurped by the opponent by violence or stealth. Consequently, (2) when one party realises that its opponent

is not willing to offer more than a little of what it has usurped, but
nevertheless it makes proposals designed to acquire or share control
of a number of that party's most valuable assets, it is bound to reject
the proposals out of hand. The result is the undramatic stalemate
which has kept Cyprus divided into two mono-ethnic entities facing
each other in unfriendliness: the internationally recognised Republic
of Cyprus run and controlled by the Greek Cypriots, and the Turkish
Republic of Northern Cyprus (TRNC), run by the Turkish Cypriots
under the tutelage and control of Turkey.

Despite the huge human, political and material losses sustained
by the Turkish Cypriot community in 1963–4 and 1974 and by the
Greek Cypriot community in 1974, whose full or partial recovery
is integral to their divergent conceptions of a 'just solution',
neither community is desperately insecure or bereft of all political
resources. Each community has possession or control of a number
of significant political, economic and social assets that it perceives as
essential to its own distinctive identity, vitality, security and welfare.
Both communities have drawn up 'red lines', separating the matters
they are reluctantly willing to negotiate from those invaluable assets
they steadfastly refuse to hand over or share. This fact inevitably
places severe limits on the give-and-take process and blocks any
serious progress to a solution. In the nature of the case, what is
an invaluable asset for one community is regarded by the other
community as something to which it has a just claim. The idea will
become clearer once we consider the Greek Cypriot invaluable assets
(GInvAss for short), and then the Turkish Cypriot (and ultimately
Turkish) invaluable assets (TInvAss).

Invaluable assets of the Greek Cypriot community

For the Greek Cypriot community the principal GInvAss are the
following:

GInvAss 1: Greek Cypriots run and control the Republic of Cyprus
(RoC), to the exclusion of Turkish Cypriots. The Republic is a modern
state, older than several of the new states set up in decolonised
countries, which boasts a high Human Development Index. It is a
member state of the UN, the Council of Europe, the EU and many
other international organisations. Further, it has political, diplomatic
and economic relations with many other states and organisations,
and has the ability to argue for its interests in the international

arena and forge alliances with other countries. Most Greek Cypriot politicians have made their careers by occupying positions of power and authority in the RoC, and speaking and acting in support of its interests. These politicians would not be happy to share their control of the RoC with the Turkish Cypriot community – for all the vague reference to 'political equality' contained in UN resolutions – much less to see the RoC dissolved and replaced by an entirely new two-state system of governance with an doubtful future. Greek Cypriots know, of course, that no solution is possible which does not include the participation of Turkish Cypriot politicians and officials in a federal polity, but they want the federation to come about as a result of suitable amendments to the existing constitution of the RoC in order to safeguard the continuing existence of the RoC and their control over it. Their reasoning is that if the federation is set up and subsequently falls to pieces, they can protect their security and welfare interests by holding fast to the RoC. To put it another way, they want to be able, if the worst came to the worst, *to minimise the maximum loss they will sustain* (in the terminology of game theory, to 'minimax').

GInvAss 2: until the financial crisis that broke out in 2009 Greek Cypriots had had a thriving economy based mainly on tourism and legal and financial services. The current crisis has brought levels of unemployment and poverty that the younger generation had never known – but all is not lost! Explorations have been carried out in the sea off Cyprus's Southern shores within its exclusive economic zone (EEZ) by reputable foreign companies under contract to the RoC which indicate the presence of large deposits of hydrocarbons, comprising mainly natural gas and smaller amounts of liquid oil. The Turkish government has been incensed by the initiatives of the Cyprus government, and has made menacing noises, issued threats and sent its air force and navy to harass engineers and workers on offshore platforms. However, Greek Cypriots, for all their anxieties about Turkey's intentions, have not buckled under. The RoC has concluded agreements with Greece, Egypt, Lebanon and Israel for the demarcation of their respective EEZs, and approached companies from the United States, France and other powerful countries to tender for contracts to extract natural gas and to invest in the construction of a liquefied natural gas terminal in Cyprus. The Cyprus government has made it clear that after the conclusion of a negotiated settlement and the establishment of a federation, the revenues from natural gas and oil will be used for the benefit of both communities – but not before.

The linkage between *GInvAss 1* and *GInvAss 2* is clear. There is a deep conviction among Greek Cypriots that the protection of their legitimate political, economic and security interests is connected with, and indeed presupposes the maintenance of, the RoC and its continued ability to pursue freely diplomatic, economic, commercial and financial goals in the international arena. If Turkey is ever able to dissolve the Republic or extinguish its international credibility, Greek Cypriots will become hostages to the will of Ankara.

GInvAss 3: the RoC became a full member of the European Union on 1 May 2004. The Greek Cypriots believed, and the Turks feared, that the Republic could use its enhanced diplomatic clout to persuade the EU to extract substantial concessions from Turkey in return for starting its own accession negotiations with the EU. The EU has not applied any serious pressure on Turkey, but nevertheless Greek Cypriots have succeeded in creating a tenuous linkage between Turkey's progress in its accession negotiations and progress towards a Cyprus settlement. If this linkage did not exist, Europe would have heard even less about the Cyprus Problem. Many Greek Cypriots, however, are worried about Turkish Cypriots demands that, as part of a settlement package, the EU should agree to a number of long-term derogations from aspects of the *acquis communautaire* which are thought to favour the rights and liberties of Greek Cypriots in the North.

Invaluable assets of the Turkish Cypriot community

When Turkish Cypriots reflect on their present unsatisfactory social and economic conditions and compare them with their deprivations and humiliations in the pre-1974 period, they appreciate things are much better now because they have acquired a number of invaluable assets which they are determined not to give up in the negotiations, no matter what is offered to them in exchange. The principal Turkish Cypriot (and ultimately Turkish) invaluable assets (TInvAss) are as follows:

TInvAss 1: the Turkish Cypriots have a continuous stretch of territory in the Northern part of Cyprus containing ports and airports which is, in some sense, 'theirs', an economically viable and militarily defensible 'homeland' for their community and also a large group of Turkish settlers. The community is determined never to go back to being a set of Turkish urban neighbourhoods, villages and hamlets spread all over Cyprus, which could pass for a small minority in a Greek island. For the Turkish Cypriots there will always be a Northern Cyprus, and any Greek Cypriots who may be allowed to live among them will have to be a small minority which would be unable to exercise any serious influence on its institutions, including its economy.

TInvAss 2: the TRNC is an organised state, though not one which is independent. The European Court of Human Rights described the TRNC as 'a subordinate local administration of Turkey operating in Northern Cyprus', but nevertheless Turkish Cypriots believe in it as it is able to maintain public order, organise utilities, social and health services, schools and universities and so on. The state has a president who is generally respected by the people and who represents the community effectively to the UN, foreign officials, the Organisation for Islamic Cooperation and so on. It has a parliament and a legal system, courts, police and a conscript army. If there is going to be a settlement in the form of a bicommunal, bizonal federation, Turkish Cypriots believe that (in the vague expression they are fond of using) 'it must be based on present realities'; that is, the TRNC must be, in effect, one of the founding states of the Cyprus federal republic. The continued existence of the TRNC constitutes a mark of their distinctive collective personality, and their history of struggle and achievement.

TInvAss 3: the TRNC has not been economically self-supporting, and so it cannot survive without substantial economic assistance from Turkey. Nevertheless, the natural beauty and resources of Northern Cyprus, together with its dynamic and enterprising population, encourages Turkish Cypriots to hope in the future development of a strong economy based on tourism, agriculture, higher education and natural gas which will be under their own firm control, and invulnerable to any Greek Cypriot pressures.

TInvAss 4: the Turkish Cypriots are entirely safe in the TRNC as it is protected by Turkish armed forces and the Turkish Cypriot conscript army. The military situation provides an absolutely credible deterrence against any attempts by Greek Cypriots to 'liberate' the North. The Turkish Cypriot community, and indeed Turkey, want to retain the vital asset of continued Turkish security guarantees and probably an effective military presence to protect the community and its institutions. If a federation is established in future and subsequently breaks up, Turkish Cypriots may stand to lose many advantages, but they are not willing to risk losing lives and a secure Turkish Cypriot 'homeland' in the North. This is their own version of the policy *to minimise the maximum losses they could suffer under a worst-case scenario* (to 'minimax').

Clashing demands and invaluable assets

The various GInvAss and TInvAss identified above, in so far as they are held to be non-negotiable by the respective communities, clearly block a successful outcome in the negotiations. The more assets one side considers non-negotiable, the fewer benefits it is able to deliver to the other side in order to take back the benefits it itself demands. The clash between one side's crucially important demands and the other side's invaluable assets can be made clear by means of the following tables.

Crucial GC demands	Clash with TInvAss
Repatriation of all or most Turkish settlers and the return of Greek Cypriot (GC) refugees, together with their descendents, to their homes and properties. Freedom of movement, residence and property ownership for all GCs, and unrestricted political rights for those who wish to live in the North.	*TInvAss 1*: a continuous stretch of economically viable and defensible territory completely dominated and administered by a compact and coherent Turkish Cypriot (TC) community (and the Turkish settlers who will remain).

Crucial GC demands	Clash with TInvAss
The bicommunal, bizonal federation will come about as a result of amendments to the constitution of the RoC. The TRNC will not be given any retrospective authority as a state equal in status to the RoC.	*TInvAss 2*: TRNC must be one of the two founding states of the projected bicommunal, bizonal federation.
The terms of the settlement should secure the unity of the territory, society, people, economy and institutions of the federation.	*TInvAss 3*: a potentially thriving economy in the North which is controlled by the TC community (and Turkey), and able to withstand any pressures from the larger and wealthier GC community.
Any new settlement should provide for the withdrawal of all Turkish troops. It should also exclude any Turkish security guarantees, and *a fortiori* any unilateral right of intervention by any power.	*TInvAss 4*: the maintenance of Turkish security guarantees, and probably the actual presence of Turkish deterrent troops.

Crucial TC demands	Clash with GInvAss
Political equality between the two communities and constituent states of the federation, rotating presidency, effective participation of TC officials in federal bodies.	*GInvAss 1*: Maintenance of the RoC and exercise by GC officials of control or preponderant influence in all federal bodies.
A substantial slice of the natural resources of the island, and joint control of the Cyprus Central Bank.	*GInvAss 2*: The control of a potentially thriving economy capable of supporting high living standards and social welfare programmes.

Crucial TC demands	Clash with GInvAss
Derogations from the *acquis* and the establishment of policies which will be supportive of Turkey's efforts to join the EU.	*GInvAss 3*: EU membership which gives the RoC a basis from which to demand democratic freedoms all over the island, and to exercise influence in the EU, including influence on the conditions for Turkish accession.

As long as each of the two communities seeks to achieve, through uncoerced negotiations, what it regards as a 'just settlement' embodying its legitimate demands which, however, clash with what the other community regards as its own vital and invaluable assets, it is hard to see how these negotiations can lead to a successful outcome. The two communities recognise that the negotiations have long reached a stalemate which is most unlikely to be broken. Yet Greek and Turkish Cypriots do not go out into the streets in mass demonstrations to demand their respective leaders to make more generous concessions to the other community for the sake of a compromise settlement.

Adjusting to the blocked negotiations

Given that the two communities realise that they cannot obtain sufficient concessions from each other to open up the prospects for what each regards as a 'just solution', and they are unwilling to give up their own invaluable assets, are there any alternatives to the cementing of the impasse? Will there be a war? Neither of the parties to the Cyprus dispute has considered war to achieve its objectives and neither seriously believes the other party will wage war to force a settlement. Will the parties agree to go to a binding arbitration? This is out of the question as the Greek Cypriot community fear the repetition of the UN Plan of 2004, when the then UN Secretary-General Kofi Annan used his discretion to fill the gaps in the incomplete draft agreement, and produced what most Greek Cypriots regarded as an unfair document. Perhaps an international conference, as has been suggested from time to time? This, however, has no chance of success if the two communities do not reach agreement on all the main 'internal' issues. So, if the negotiations remain blocked, what does the future hold for the communities?

The chances are that the communities will simply stop thinking about the blockage of any real progress in the negotiations and adopt the attitude of silent acceptance of the longstanding division, without admitting that this is what they are actually doing. The two communities may get to develop a Stoic indifference to their situation – in fact this is beginning to happen. Beyond this indifference, they may develop a kind of positive attitude to the situation. Former President Tassos Papadopoulos, whose government orchestrated to No vote to the UN Plan in April 2004 among Greek Cypriots, probably spoke for the majority of his people when he said that the existing state of affairs was 'the second best' to a viable solution. Although Greek Cypriots claim that their motherland is 'semi-occupied', the fact is that they all live (with the exception of a few hundred compatriots left in the North) in the 'free' part of Cyprus, and they enjoy the liberties and protection of their own free state, an imperfect liberal democracy run by themselves for themselves. Their personal and collective experiences, work and politics, hopes and aspirations, relationships and projects are by now shaped by and adapted to the post-1974 environment. For the Turkish Cypriots, too, the present situation is 'the second best' to full international recognition of the TRNC with all the implied benefits as their daily experiences, customary practices, political loyalties, expectations and aspirations are fashioned by the 'present realities' in the North.

Conclusion

Even if they do not say so, Greek and Turkish Cypriots accept their *destiny* to live their own lives in their own part of a divided Cyprus, and they experience a sense of perverse contentment and self-respect for having withstood in dignity their deprivations and frustrations, and refused the superficial attractions of an 'unjust' solution. Once you accept a state of affairs as your community's destiny, you may get to see it as something necessary in the prevailing historical circumstances, something that puts your community's inner strengths to the test, something that steels your will and character. Your destiny is even something to love because it has been absorbed into your collective personality and selfhood. This is what Stoic philosophers called *amor fati*, the love of one's destiny. It may be apposite to cite an aphorism by Nietzsche from his book *Gay Science*:

'I want to learn more and more to see as beautiful what is necessary in things; then I shall be one of those who make things beautiful. *Amor fati*: let that be my love henceforth! I do not want to wage war against what is ugly. I do not want to accuse; I do not even want to accuse those who accuse'(page 223).

However, the last sentence of the aphorism does not apply to Greek and Turkish Cypriot politicians, officials, journalists and other opinion leaders since they have long been expert players in what the UN Secretary-General Ban Ki-moon has called 'the blame game'. Both sides accuse the other of practising injustice and cruelty and demonstrating ill will in the negotiations. There is some pleasure to be had in accusing your opponent of injustice, because that makes you feel that you yourself represent justice in as much as you articulate the self-understanding of your unjustly suffering people who refuse to break down or abandon their just claims. Arguably, the public assertion of just claims and criticisms of one's opponents strengthens the cohesion of one's community and gives purpose to the politicians' rhetoric of defiance.

Many politicians and officials in the RoC and TRNC expend energy in devising and pursuing 'strategies' to undermine the institutions and restrict the international actions of the other. The strategies of both governments are pretty ineffective, in that they do not have any significant impact on the way the other community plans and lives out its life; it simply confirms in the community's collective consciousness the untrustworthiness and ill will of its opponents. Most ordinary Greek and Turkish Cypriots have reached a point where they see no advantage in deviating from their chosen courses of action, which is to turn their backs on their opponents and pursue their own social and economic advancement. Each community's combined assets, goals, political resources and diplomatic capabilities are more or less balanced by the other community's combined assets, resources and capabilities. A kind of static equilibrium has been reached between the two communities – not unlike a Nash Equilibrium – which the communities have come to accept on the quiet as the state of the non-violent non-solution of the Cyprus Problem. In all probability, the Cyprus Problem will remain unsolved in the indefinite future, but this fact and its consequences will be absorbed by degrees into the social cultures, self-images and customary practices of the two communities.

References and recommended reading

Ker-Lindsay, James, *The Cyprus Problem: What Everyone Needs to Know* (Oxford: Oxford University Press, 2011).

Moore, Gavin, 'Federalism and the "one-person one-vote principle": political accommodation in Cyprus and the Annan Plan', *Federal Governance* 8/2 (2011), pp. 29–41.

Morelli, Vincent, *Cyprus: Reunification Proving Elusive* (Washington, DC: Congressional Research Service, 2013).

Nietzsche, Friedrich Wilhelm, The Gay Science (New York: Random House, 1974).

Stavrinides, Zenon, *The Underlying Assumptions, Structure and Prospects of the Negotiating Process for a Cyprus Settlement*, Proceedings of the Sixth International Congress on Cyprus Studies held at the Eastern Mediterranean University, 24–26 October 2007, Famagusta (Cyprus: EMU Publications, 2008).

——, 'Dementia Cypria: on the social psychological environment of the intercommunal negotiations', *The Cyprus Review* 21/1 (Spring 2009), pp. 175–86.

——, 'Cyprus negotiations: searching for a federal settlement in a divided society', in Arshi Khan and Kushal Pal (eds), *Federalism, Democracy and Conflict Resolution* (Basingstoke: Palgrave Macmillan, 2012).

30

A Viable Peace Process Already Exists

BIRTE VOGEL AND OLIVER RICHMOND

Like several UN Special Representatives before him, Alvaro de Soto thought that the only thing the Turkish Cypriot President Denktash feared more than a bad agreement was a good one. Both sides' local political, economic and partly cultural elites may have shared this opinion. For more than 50 years the conflict's dynamics, debates about territory, sovereignty and identity, have survived despite international peacekeeping, UN mediation, EU governance reform and civil society investment. The 'so-called' high-level negotiations have so far failed to achieve any notable progress towards a breakthrough (it seems that anything which represents political agency in Cyprus is prefixed by terms like 'so-called' or 'pseudo'). Yet there has long been a *de facto* peace process amongst Cyprus' so-called intercommunal, bicommunal, peace-orientated civil society movements, which have developed in a variety of different forms and strands over the years and in the background.

Political elites have, for reasons of justice or nationalism, often resisted external attempts to promote a settlement or change the parameters of political debate about what peace and justice entails. Because of the lack of progress some analysts have argued supporting civil society would offer a complementary component for a sustainable solution. But what if large sections of civil society resist an internationally acceptable settlement resting on a bizonal, bicommunal federation, with territorial adjustments and compensation? What if they ally with their ethno-nationalist leaders using arguments that draw on substantiable claims of ethnic cleansing against one side, or deviations from international law against the other? Unsurprisingly, in an environment where political elites tend to popularise nationalism, most of Cypriot civil society indeed is ethno-nationalist. Paradoxically it also supports international law, democracy and human rights. For this reason international actors and major donors have flirted with supporting civil society but have mainly focused on the elite level.

Even so a small but longstanding section of civil society has quietly mobilised to achieve peaceful coexistence. The so-called bicommunal movements are relatively isolated from the societies they aim to transform, however. They illustrate how a solution of the Cyprus 'Problem' may require a retreat from the hegemonic redefinition of the 'problem' as one of invasion and occupation, ethnic cleansing, international law, justice, minority rights versus self-determination, which has influenced civil society in general. Yet these are international and elite scripts that have hindered a civil peace from emerging, purposefully according to some. Such a retreat may provide space for the relocation of civil peace actors and a re-articulation of identity to transcend the concept of bicommunality in a more pluralist Cyprus. A rhetorical response to the identity issue from internationals was recently to relabel these movements as 'intercommunal' instead of 'bicommunal'. Both labels seem inadequate and are redolent of colonial categories in that they maintain the exclusiveness of Cyprus' communities, separate them from power itself (i.e the elite level), and so maintain the fiction that the peace process actually operates mainly at the elite political level. This reflects the organisation of the high-level structure of peace negotiations under the UN. We refer to peace movements henceforth in recognition of the fact that they have in fact formed their own community and have transcended ethnic identity.

To pursue our argument, three points are made. First, despite massive international intervention of several different types there has not been an agreement because national elites use the conflict to maintain an ethnic territoriality and aspirations towards more power. Secondly, only Cyprus' peace-related civil society has found multiple ways of escape such ethno-nationalism. Yet these movements have long been subject to attempts to institutionalise them by the international community or to co-opt or marginalise them by respective governments, and also have a tendency to 'other' themselves in relation to mainstream civil society. Thirdly, as a consequence peace-related civil society is ensnared in a third space of conflict resolution, literally speaking the UN Buffer Zone in Nicosia. While this is regarded as symbolic and convenient, without relocating such peace movements from the periphery to the centre of society an important piece of the peace process is missing. By doing so it becomes clear where the peace process has actually been taking place.

Talking peace – an unsuccessful endeavour

Despite the seemingly never-ending peace talks, most state actors and international organisations officially believe a solution to the Cyprus issue can only be found at the top level with questions of governance and territory as the main obstacle. Institutions such as the United Nations and European Union have tired of promoting a high level peace agreement but still believe it is the key to, and expect it will result in, a bizonal, bicommunal federal state. To them, the main obstacles to an agreement at the national level are currently issues of how governmental power will be shared between the Greek and Turkish Cypriot sides at a political level, followed by issues of territory, restitution and compensation. Behind closed doors, however, frustration about the stagnation of the process is omnipresent. The 'graveyard' of diplomats has been an undiplomatic description of the 'Cyprus Problem' for generations now.

The issue that the solution that has long been the subject of negotiations, a federation, might be something neither actually wants is hardly acknowledged publicly amongst elites. Yet it is common knowledge in mainstream civil society, while it has long been an inspiration for the peace-related movements' increasingly sophisticated modes of accommodation amongst its members, either Greek or Turkish Cypriots. For them, the differences in general between the two sides appear relatively easily and even comfortably bridged within their own organisations and events. Many participants are influential (if controversial) in their own societies. Why is such dignified accommodation not reflected at the formal political level, where most attention for settlement has long been focused?

Both elite and nationalist governance and the possibility of a solution have become mutually self-sustaining in a longstanding process that Richmond (1998) has described as 'devious objectives': the peace process allows local elites international access and resources such as legitimacy and alliances. It is valued for this rather than for any possible compromise it may lead to. It also retains political agency at the elite levels, which on both sides of the Green Line have long been adept at controlling (or governmentalising) their relationship with citizens, subjects and indeed civil society, often using the fear of the possible disaster of a 'bad peace' (or even a 'good peace') to maintain their grip. This power play between national elites and members of the international community has continued for decades. Even the hope that EU membership would act as a catalyst in solving the Cyprus issue did not materialise, though it has certainly mitigated and improved the social, political and economic situation as far as the two competing sovereignties would allow. In the current situation no change can be expected from Cypriot elites. Even those political actors who have been supportive of a solution over the years have been unable to break the deadlock.

Yet, the *de facto* peace, which is seen as negative at the elite level, is only part of the peace process: a far more positive process at the community level continues. It has slowly strengthened even if small and isolated from mainstream, nationalist civil society and political elites.

Living peace – an intercommunal experiment

Local conflict resolution processes and donor support for civil society have tried persistently to break the deadlock of international and national talks. Despite international support the EU and UNDP claim that both communities have weak civil societies that are neither active in advocating for rights nor participating in the conflict resolution process. Officials assume that the dominance of the 'Cyprus Problem' creates an environment in which other societal topics are subordinated, effectively functioning as an excuse not to engage with social problems for both the governments and civil society. This, they argue, explains why it is not active. Often current governance approaches and their embedded and nationalist political discourse are blamed for disempowering the potential of civil society. It is against this background that the international community has supported NGOs in fostering dialogue between the Greek and Turkish communities. Yet such contacts, frequently subject to ethno-nationalist sanctions, have often been hidden and private rather than public. Even so they have prospered in far more informal and cooperative registers than even external donors – and many local people – expected.

Peace-orientated movements have contributed significantly to keeping communication channels between the Turkish and Greek Cypriots communities on the island open over the long term. Indirectly and subtly they have reached into many corners of Cyprus' polity, economy and societies. Even so, their public face is shaped by their seemingly dependent relationship with the international community, which often regards them as a technical tool within the liberal peace framework and thus a vital part of an internationally envisioned solution to the Cyprus conflict, as well as the island's 'Europeanisation'. Following a global trend, internationals prefer to engage with civil society in an institutionalised form that seems easier to control when executing donor interests. Worldwide, this development has forced many grassroots projects into a donor-driven form in order to survive. In Cyprus this trend has been mirrored. After a turn to civil society in the 1990s in frustration at the failures of the high-level process UNDP and USAID (US Agency for International Development), as the most important donors on the island, have moved away from funding civil society movements in general despite the fact that the high-level process is still deadlocked. As a result UNDP has developed a more strategic approach and now works exclusively with 'selected' partners who have already proved to be reliable and efficient (in their opinion) and run projects fitting the criteria of bicommunalism, public visibility and long-term reconciliation.

Such ambitions are contradictory: calling for intercommunal engagements while reducing civil society support and supporting a public peace process based on ethno-nationalist power struggles is not a viable international strategy. In the longer term, expecting civil society actors to complement an ethno-nationalist peace process was never a viable strategy for any peace movement. This contributed to a distance between mainstream and peace-oriented civil society, easily manipulated by ethno-nationalist elites who could then point to the peace movements as little more than fringe movements intended on disrupting their ethno-nationalist goals. While only few peace activists may now think that the UN model is the sustainable answer to the Cyprus question, they often formally support it. Grassroots resistance against the bicommunal concept is only articulated openly by the Occupy Buffer Zone Movement, which protests against what it describes as a limited view of Cypriot culture by international actors (a point local scholars have also argued). It highlights Cyprus' multicultural society and argues that the bi-solution denies Cyprus' already existing potential for pluralism. The same concern is also raised by other actors but only quietly, as organisations fear for their funding.

Envisioning a solution and based at the focal point of the Buffer Zone, the Home for Cooperation may offer a more public symbol of the doors that the peace movements opened a long time ago. In May 2011 both Cypriot political leaders came to the opening ceremony. It represented a public success for the peace movement that should not be underestimated. Despite its past efforts, peace-related civil society had so far not created a prominent voice in the political process or even become visible to large parts of the island's societies. Now they were beginning to form what has been described elsewhere as a 'local infrastructure for peace', straddling the different communities borders as well as the lines between public and private, both physically and more subtly.

(Re)Locating peace – an opportunity

Donors have often adopted a rather negative view of peace-related civil society's capacity, stereotyping it as ineffective, inefficient and comprised of the 'usual suspects'. Internationals in Cyprus have little understanding of the structural, social, political, professional and cultural constraints and sanctions NGOs and peace activists are subject to, nor of how they have built a community despite these constraints. As a long time observer of Cyprus, on recent visits one of this chapter's authors has been struck by how each generation of international personnel who arrive for their three-year stay repeat the same, often superficial opinions about both the Cyprus Problem and civil society. To some degree this helps perpetuate the limitations of both. He has also been surprised by the local public deference to internationals as well as a much more powerful private critique. Indeed, internationals have little conception of the complex and subtle sanctions peace-related civil society actors face in their political, professional and social establishments and so tend to regard donor manipulation of the involved organisations as cost free. This also serves to disguise their own ineffectiveness in facilitating a civil space for reconciliation and peace work. Further, recent changes in the funding policies of the main international donors have led to a situation in which only a few key 'compliant' players obtain most of the funding. These NGOs then allocate funds to other initiatives that replicate the funding requirements they have to follow. The peacebuilding apparatus is thus more and more institutionalised, suppressing the heterogeneity that peacebuilding requires in such a diverse context.

Perhaps as a result of this, peace-related civil society actors are closely interlinked with each other but tend not connect publicly to large parts of the population on each side. Though their encounters are easier since the Green Line was opened in April 2003, organisations often admit that their outreach remains limited and more people need to become involved in creating the social pressure on local governments that is needed. For the Association for Historical Dialogue and Research and Home for Cooperation these are goals planned for the future. Though this outreach has been gradually increasing, NGOs are still reduced to operating in a small, self-enclosed space: Vogel has named this a third space of conflict resolution.

Peace-related civil society operates in an internationally protected and financed public space, unable to connect to other parts of society. Instead it creates an informal community on its own which eventually becomes an alternative peace process. The public boundaries of this space are set in two ways: from within, by participants who are aware of a range of constraints and possibilities, and from the outside, by elites and mainstream civil society. Participants design the third space in a way that is most suitable for the more sophisticated and contextual peace project they now envisage as a result of their experiences in this third space. From the outside international donors both offer some support because they agree with its ethos of peacebuilding or conflict transformation, but simultaneously create barriers due to their funding requirements and their local insensitivity. Their agendas do not connect to the public politics and related everyday life of mainstream civil society long conditioned to support the all-or-nothing imperatives that ethno-nationalism and competing sovereignties promote. Activists are also threatened by social or professional sanctions by their fellow citizens. Their cooperation with Cypriots 'from the other side' does not conform to the social norms of non-interaction and non-recognition by nationalists. This in turn creates boundaries for the civil societies from the outside. Local governments also play a role in further limiting these attempts at outreach by setting formal boundaries – such as the application processes for permits for advertising intercommunal activities in schools and other public locations.

Despite their isolation, the peace movement is probably Cyprus' best chance to overcome the political deadlock. The 'dead zone' ironically supports the idea of a transcendent Cyprus and its attempts to overcome the struggle over territorial claims and power. The activists themselves know best where to go to challenge their fellow citizens' nationalist opinions – whether coffee shops or other traditional places where politics are discussed, or via far more complex and hidden networks of exchange, or more public spaces of dialogue in state and society when conditions are right. While the third space represents a limited and constrained reach in terms of public capacity, somewhat contradictorily, at a private level the peace-related movements and their participants have long been very widely networked. This private and 'hidden agency' spans international officials and personnel beyond Cyprus and many figures of influence, to presidents, prominent political and economic figures, and all the way down to ordinary citizens in Cyprus' rural villages. Many of them also have experience of other post-conflict environments around the world. This movement has felt its way slowly and haltingly into an important position in the architecture of Cyprus' emerging polity. It will, however, need more external support and recognition – even if only discursive – to transcend the many boundaries around the third space.

Local elites and their supporters are ironically entrenched in their opposition to an elite level peace agreement. Paradoxically, many nationalists claim that peace would be much easier at a social level if only there could be a just solution at the state level first. It is easy to understand why they cannot escape from their self-imposed prison of ethno-nationalism. Yet, it seems to be the case that peace at a social level, though far from easy, is leading the elite level.

Internationals do not need to be trapped by ethno-nationalist rhetoric. They could instead do far more to enable the possibilities the peace movements as follows (this is not an exhaustive list): (i) at a symbolic level by offering legitimating rhetoric to them as a peace exemplar; (ii) at a material level by providing core rather than conditional financial and technical support; (iii) at a normative level in validating their inclusive and cooperative philosophy; (iv) and at a 'project level' in supporting their many projects to facilitate co-existence and cooperation, including those in schools, academia, the variety of professions, politics, economics and trade, tourism, heritage and many more; (v) and very carefully, by ensuring that the third space remains safe and legitimate and available for all to enter and develop and working to reduce the boundaries around it. Donors would do well to see themselves as servants and guardians of this third space and its hidden agency and potential rather than its managers. In this vein, one can only hope that the unrest on the global markets in general, and the European economic crisis that hit Cyprus more specifically, does not serve as an excuse to divert international funds and support from civil society work. With the economic crisis in the South and the growing inner Turkish Cypriot discontent in the North, elite priorities have shifted further away from peace than before, leaving the intercommunal movement as the last active Cypriot pro-reconciliation force.

Conclusion

Cyprus' peace movements offer an insight into how peace might be made after the repeated failures of the elite and international political tracks over the decades. They do not challenge the legitimate rights or long-held identities of any communities on the island. They are subtle about their challenges to power. They have also been open to divergent perspectives and have found ways of coping with the many sanctions their members have been placed under. They have developed a range of internal operating procedures that facilitate debate, cooperation and reconciliation, despite identity differences or competing claims of a various nature. They have managed to do this despite the fact that many individuals involved have suffered the brutalities of war and the sanctions that go with breaking taboos. Their efforts are magnanimous, bottom-up, locally resonant, internationally legitimate and empathetic.

They echo a long history of cooperation and hybridity in Cyprus, which has been kept alive by their participants. Their cultural, social and political patterns offer an insight into how a more formal 'peace process' should be formulated and to what ends. They have found ways of organising projects, meetings and contacts regardless of the obstacles the island's two competing sovereignties have long thrown up, as well as ways of both using and distributing resources. Power has often been used against itself in a subtle, tactical manner, often through the medium of relatively innocuous projects, areas of discussion or action. If this is not a model for peace and governance, government and cooperation in heavily politicised post-conflict environments, then it is hard to imagine what is. It depicts how internationals and elites might proceed if they want to offer a platform for a far better peace process than any that has emerged up to now.

Yet instead, political elites, religious sectors and many social groupings have chosen to ignore these precedents, and indeed have worked to negate them. The location of Cyprus' main centre for peace-related activities in the UN Buffer Zone illustrates the reality of what local ethno-nationalism and conditional international support have meant: the peace movements have retreated in one way but also occupy a third space, which fences off ideas deemed too subversive for society at large, the two states that currently exist and even the internationally-sponsored peace process. Because this third space is mainly networked informally around Cyprus, and indeed around the world, it is more expansive than it looks from a public perspective. However, there will be no solution without this third community's example being heeded on a far larger scale, for the potential peace system they represent: a peace beyond the state as envisaged in the 1960s and 1970s, of sovereignty and nationalism. Their ways of navigating around social and political barriers and issues that capture many in an old-fashioned ethno-nationalist trap is an important lesson on how a solution could be translated both from and into the everyday.

Not to put words into Cypriot civil societies' collective and disparate mouths, their alternative peace process may be far more focused on the everyday conditions of peace in modern Cyprus, and how these would translate into layers of governance for a mutual 'good life'. As with the character of the peace movements and their participants over several decades, this points to a cooperative, inclusive, dignified, contextually sensitive and internationally aware approach, but one that does not seek an end to differences. This represents a level of hybridity in the design of peace, driven locally and internationally by a range of compromises over divergent positions – even in civil society – but is also internationally appropriate in terms of law and norms in their contemporary post-colonial and emancipatory, rather than early to mid-twentieth-century sovereign, registers.

If the 'Cyprus Problem', meaning its elite transcript and its often slavish followers, is to be resolved, the political discourse should be led by those who have long shown the way in the process of political and social accommodation across a range of boundaries. It has to be relocated to where it belongs: to those who have long run their own de facto peace processes. This creates the potential for them to further develop their local infrastructures for peace, which may then offer the possibility of a new polity that transcends old, tired and dysfunctional conflict lines, the states it depends upon and the elite level peace process that has [un]intentionally sustained it.

References and recommended reading

Byrant, Rebecca, *Imagining the Modern: The Cultures of Nationalism in Cyprus* (London: I.B.Taurus, 2004).

Constantinou, Costas, 'Aporias of identity: bicommunalism, hybridity and the "Cyprus Problem"', *Cooperation and Conflict* 42/3 (2007), pp. 247–70.

Hadjipavlou, Maria, 'The Cyprus conflict: root causes and implications for peacebuilding', *Journal of Peace Research* 44/3 (2007), pp. 349–65.

Ker-Lindsay, James, *EU Accession and UN Peacemaking in Cyprus* (Basingstoke: Palgrave Macmillan, 2005).

Loizos, Peter, 'Bicommunal initiatives and their contribution to improved relations between Turkish and Greek Cypriots', *South European Society and Politics* 11/1 (2006), pp. 179–94.

Papadakis, Yiannis, *Echoes from the Dead Zone: Across the Cyprus Divide* (London: I.B.Taurus, 2005).

Richmond, Oliver P., *Mediating in Cyprus* (London: Frank Cass, 1998).

INDEX